T0290483

MARX AND EDUCATION IN LATE CAPITALISM

MARX AND EDUCATION IN LATE CAPITALISM

R. F. PRICE

BARNES & NOBLE BOOKS
Totowa, New Jersey

© 1986 R.F. Price
First published in the USA in 1986 by
Barnes and Noble Books
81 Adams Drive
Totowa, New Jersey, 07512

Library of Congress Cataloging in Publication Data applied for:

ISBN: 0-389-20617-2

Printed and bound in Great Britain

CONTENTS

ACKNOWLEDGEMENTS

Throughout the long period in which this book has been in preparation I have been encouraged by many friends. Some have supplied references or lent materials. Others have read drafts of chapters and made helpful comments. I must specially thank Constance Lever, John Fyfield, Gisela T. Kaplan, Imke Fischer, Nancy Shelley, Erika Price, Marta Rado, Derek Toomey, Mike Berrell, Tom McGlynn and Alan Cubbon. The staff of the Borchardt Library, La Trobe University were also helpful on numerous occasions. For any failings in the final product, however, I must assume responsibility.

INTRODUCTION

One of the roots of this book goes right back to my education by the army in Egypt and what was then Palestine at the end of the Second World War. I read *The Selected Works of Karl Marx* and that justly well-known book by Leo Hubermann, *Man's Worldly Goods*, both part of the 400-volume 'unit library' which set out to provide servicemen and women with something sound to read in the major divisions of knowledge. A more recent root was sent out in Beijing in the mid-sixties when I had a grandstand view of the beginning of the Great Proletarian Cultural Revolution — grandstand because as a foreigner it all happened at a comfortable distance, allowing me to ponder Mao Zedong's version of marxism without the dangers and discomfort suffered by the Chinese. In between and since these two events a lot happened to make me consider it not only worthwhile but in a sense necessary, to take seriously, if to come to different conclusions from other recent writers on the subject, claims that Marx is relevant to education today. In a previous book I tried to argue this for Russia and China, countries which claim to be influenced by Marx's ideas. In part my dissatisfaction with that study forced me to attempt this one.

The Marx I see as offering something to those of us concerned about education in the rich countries of the industrialised world is not the saintly image which used to stare at that of Mao across the Tian Anmen Square in Beijing. Nor is it the maker of quotations to fit all occasions that one encounters in so much Soviet writing. Rather, it is that very human and passionate thinker who, in a life-long dialogue with his friend and co-worker, Engels, tried to see our past and present more clearly in order to enable us to take conscious control of our future. Taking a conscious stand on the side of the exploited against the exploiters, they felt it necessary to understand that exploitative process in order that it could be abolished. Entering into the dreams of working people for a life of freedom and leisure, they argued that this could only come through an understanding of the nature of necessity and the nature of labour. This way of thinking implies a concept of education as *process*, in which *learning* is a central, if unexplored, part of

Marx's enterprise. I hope to show that both his general way of thinking about humankind and some specific ideas of his can be illuminating to educators in their problems today.

While my main purpose will be to relate certain ideas in the writings of Marx and Engels to aspects of the reality of a handful of rich countries I shall, particularly in the section on schools, use a number of recent books as foils to help contain the argument and relate it to an already engaged audience. The first of these books was *Schooling in Capitalist America* (1976) by Bowles and Gintis, a book which was to receive considerable comment in the years that followed, not least by others I refer to here. In 1978 Madan Sarup wrote *Marxism and Education.* Placing education and human self-consciousness as central to 'the possibilities of transforming the repressive social order' (192) Madan explores aspects of 'the new sociology of education' and marxism. Castles and Wuestenberg, in *The Education of the Future: An Introduction to the Theory and Practice of Socialist Education* (1979), take a much narrower focus, Marx's comments on labour and education, and explore this in writings and practice, from Robert Owen through France and Denmark to the Soviet Union and China. Kevin Harris' *Education and Knowledge: The Structured Misrepresentation of Reality* (1979) was followed three years later by *Teachers and Classes: A Marxist Analysis* (1982). Rachel Sharp then added *Knowledge, Ideology and the Politics of Schooling: towards a Marxist Analysis of Education* (1980) to the work she had previously written (with Anthony Green) on an English progressive primary school. Michael Matthews joined the argument with *The Marxist Theory of Schooling: A Study of Epistemology and Education* (1980). Henry Giroux's collection of papers, *Ideology, Culture and the Process of Schooling* (1981) returned us to radical America and an article on 'Dialectics and the Development of Curriculum Theory' to which I shall return. Finally I must mention Sarup's second volume, *Education, State and Crisis: A Marxist Perspective* (1982).

Using these books as a foil has the danger that I shall be concentrating on points of disagreement rather than the many points we have in common. This can leave a more negative impression than is intended which can only be remedied if these books receive the careful attention they deserve. I will close this introduction with my major difference and the major thrust of this present volume. These writers continue to understand education in terms of schooling and the intentional teaching of the young, even when they acknowledge the breadth of social influences which bear upon it. This is not surprising. Many teachers crave for reassurance that what they are doing has social significance. But in so doing they fall into the unhistorical trap from which Marx in other fields tried to rescue us. Institutions, even those with such long and worthy histories as schools, are human constructions and ever changing (as recent cuts and amalgamations have again demonstrated). It is a mistake to allow one's thinking to be conditioned by such institutions. By shifting the emphasis to *learning*, and learning in the widest social-political sense, other aspects of education, including schooling, fall into fresh and, I shall argue, more illuminating places. We need to recognise what aspects of education are tied to specifically capitalist features of our societies and which offer hope for a better alternative. We need to grasp the interrelations of that complex of unintentional and intentional influences which cause us to believe and despair, to dream and hope. Defining education primarily as learning is a first step.

PART ONE: WHAT AND WHY MARX?

1 WHAT AND WHY MARX?

The world of the 1980s is in many ways far removed from that of Marx and Engels. Two world wars, fascism and the Nazi 'holocaust', the long economic boom in the major capitalist countries after the Second World War, the threat of human extinction by nuclear war or slow pollution — these are a few of the events which cause some to so emphasise the new that Marx, Engels and the concerns to which they devoted themselves appear out of date. Of course, in the USSR, China and a number of other countries the writings of Marx and Engels are part of the new gospel from which citations are drawn for every occasion. For many that is yet further proof that Marx and Engels have nothing of value to offer us. But in spite of all that steady interest persists. Whether among scholars who pay increasing attention to our improved sources, or by fresh generations of more practical people, Marx and Engels continue to be read.[1]

The choice of the name Marx in the title, and not Marx and Engels, or Marxism, is in part a matter of brevity and in part to direct attention to Marx's original writings. My debt to marxist writers of various persuasions and my differences and preferences will, I hope, be clear. Engels was both an original and independent thinker and a more readable populariser of positions he and Marx held in common. His *Anti-Duehring* and his letters on historical materialism remain good starting points for further study.[2]

There are two things in the writings of Marx and Engels which I want to explore for their implications for our understanding of education. These are not their relatively few and direct references to the process of schooling, though they will be examined in their place. Rather they are what has often been referred to as Marx's method, and his vision of our human potential. The two are in Marx intimately connected for he saw as his life's work the provision of an understanding, of a theory, which would enable people to organise their lives and fulfil their dreams. But he further argued that not all dreams were possible of realisation. Only through the most open and critical theory could practice result in genuine freedom.[3] But before discussing that let us look at Marx's vision of a possible human future for which he chose the term communism.

3

Communism

The choice of the term communism, a choice which gives fresh problems today, was in part a declaration of a class stand, a stand on the side of the working class, and against many of the upper class, do-gooding ideas known in Marx's day as socialist. Socialism was generally reformist and socialists like Fourier and Saint-Simon did not advocate the abolition of private productive property (the means of production). Finally the choice was for politics as the arena of struggle. Writing in 1843 the young Marx declared:

> [N]othing prevents us from making criticism of politics, partici-
> pation in politics, and therefore *real* struggles, the starting point
> of our criticism, and from identifying our criticism with them. In
> that case we do not confront the world in a doctrinaire way with
> a new principle: Here is the truth, kneel down before it! We
> develop new principles for the world out of the world's own
> principles. (*CW*, 3, 144)

This meant rejecting the elaborating of future utopias and attempting to persuade people to realise them. Marx referred to communism as 'the necessary pattern and the dynamic principle of the
immediate future' (*CW*, 3, 306) and 'the *real* movement which
abolishes the present state of things' (*CW*, 5, 49). In our time Mao
Zedong expressed the same attitude when he cited the peasant saying from Hunan Province: 'straw sandals have no pattern — they
shape themselves in the making' (Schram, 1974, 94). While this
approach was an important step forward at the time there is a
sense in which more careful exploration of possible futures,
proving what is possible, is today a progressive activity.

In his discussion, in the *Economic and Philosophic Manuscripts
of 1844* (The Paris Manuscripts), of three forms of communist
ideas, Marx makes a number of important points. He condemns
two of the forms for remaining 'captive' to private property, one of
them simply generalising envy and greed and being so much under
'the domination of *material* property' that: 'it wants to destroy
everything which is not capable of being possessed by all as *private
property* ... For it the sole purpose of life and existence is direct,
physical *possession*' (*CW*, 3, 294). He goes on to argue that far
from an advance it is a 'regression to the *unnatural* simplicity of
the *poor* and crude man who has few needs and who has not only

failed to go beyond private property, but has not yet even reached it' (*CW*, 3, 295). While Marx condemned capitalism for its brutalising effect on the workers whom he saw suffering terrible poverty he praised it for having established, for the first time in history, a form of production capable of providing a rich life for all. In outlining his view of communism as 'the *positive* transcendence of *private property*' Marx argued it would be a 'complete return of man to himself as a *social* (i.e. human) being — a return accomplished consciously and embracing the entire wealth of previous development' (*CW*, 3, 296). Need one stress that for Marx this meant mental and physical wealth?

In the contradictory world of today, with its rich and employed urged to enjoy the wealth of what is euphemistically and inaccurately called the 'consumer society', with many turning to ideas of conservation, 'green' and 'the alternative society', Marx's discussion of 'Human Requirements and the Division of Labour' (*CW*, 3, 306-22) takes on new significance.[4] With the crippling of workers by capitalist industry being better documented and, with the nuclear energy industry and visual display units (VDUs, computers), taking new forms, Marx's contrast of capitalism with the alternative it opens up is all the more poignant. The thought which points directly at a central issue of education is the much misunderstood passage in *The German Ideology*. Here Marx and Engels write of how in a communist society:

> nobody has one exclusive sphere of activity but each can become accomplished in any branch he wishes, society regulates the general production and thus makes it possible for me to do one thing today and another tomorrow, to hunt in the morning, fish in the afternoon, rear cattle in the evening, criticise after dinner, just as I have a mind, without ever becoming hunter, fisherman, shepherd or critic. (*CW*, 5, 47)

As Thomas has pointed out, this passage is in no way 'advocating a reactionary rustic arcadia'. Its message is the possibilities opened up for the reversal of the division of hand and brain and the narrow specialisation dictated by the capitalist division of labour. Numerous passages in *The German Ideology* speak to this point:

> In a communist organisation of society there are no painters but at most people who engage in painting among other activities. (154)

The all-round development of the individual will only cease to be conceived as an ideal, as vocation, etc. when the impact of the world which stimulates the real development of the abilities of the individual comes under the control of the individuals themselves, as the communists desire. (292; cf. Thomas, 1980, 147-74)

Marx's vision of our potential future has often been mis-understood through isolation of such comments as that on labour in his criticism of the German Workers' Party document, 'The Gotha Programme' (1875). There he writes of labour under communism, becoming, 'from just a means of keeping alive', 'a vital need' (*FI*, 347). In *Capital* he contrasts the 'realm of necessity' in which human beings, under whatever kind of society, have to labour to maintain and reproduce life with that 'realm of freedom' whose fundamental premise is the shortening of the working day (*CAP*, 3, 958). How much nearer we are to that position today with productive capacity restricted and millions unemployed![5]

This vision of the future poses questions for education, whether about the 'knowledge explosion' and problems of all-round development, whether about where and how people come to hear of, and even harder, to accept and act on the vision. It requires certain views about human psychology which even today are contrary to those applied in many schools and held by powerful sections of society. These will be considered in later sections of the book. To end this brief consideration of Marx and communism let us look at an important aspect — Marx's ideas on how it might be brought about. This, too, has educational implications.

An important part of Marx's vision is his conception of democracy, of 'the people acting for itself by itself' as he wrote in the first draft of his statement on the Paris Commune (Draper, 1977, 130). Further on he speaks of:

doing away with the state hierarchy altogether and replacing the haughteous masters of the people into always removable servants, a mock responsibility by a real responsibility, as they act continuously under public supervision. (Draper, 153)

In the final version he sharpens the emphasis on election of delegates who should be responsible and revocable if they use their office to misrepresent those who elected them and he draws attention to proposed measures to encourage public control: pay-ing public servants 'workmen's wages' and having a militia to replace the standing army (Draper, 73-4).

These ideas, which Marx welcomed in their embryonic expression in the shortlived Paris Commune, expand his strong and persisting belief that 'the emancipation of the workers must be the task of the working class itself'. As he and Engels wrote to the German Social-Democratic Party leaders in September, 1879: 'We cannot ally ourselves, therefore, with people who openly declare that the workers are too uneducated to free themselves and must first be liberated from above by philanthropic big bourgeois and petty bourgeois' (Marx, *FI*, 375). All these ideas about democracy must be seen in the light of that statement on revolution which Marx and Engels made in that early work, *The German Ideology*:

> revolution is necessary, therefore, not only because the *ruling* class cannot be overthrown in any other way, but also because the class *overthrowing* it can only in a revolution succeed in ridding itself of all the muck of ages and become fitted to found society anew. (*CW*, 5, 53)

If by revolution is understood the active and ongoing efforts of working people to change their situation and control their lives these words find plenty of echoes today, though yet on a scale and in such fits and starts as to leave the future highly undecided.

Historical Materialism

Marx's theory of social change which became known as historical materialism was first set out in a mature form in *The German Ideology*.[6] Recognising production of the means of subsistence as the way in which men began to distinguish themselves from animals in the course of human evolution (*CW*, 5, 31) Marx went on to recommend that:

> Empirical observation must in each separate instance bring out empirically, and without any mystification and speculation, the connection of the social and political structure with production. The social structure and the state are continually evolving out of the life-process of definite individuals, however, of these individuals,

not as they may appear in their own or other people's imagination, but as they *actually* are, i.e. as they act, produce materially, and hence as they work under definite material limits, presuppositions and conditions independent of their will. (*CW*, 5, 35-6)

Of educational significance is the point Marx made in a letter to Annenkov, the Russian landowner and liberal critic. Marx stressed the *historical* nature of human development: 'men are not free to choose their *productive forces* — which are the basis of all their history — for every productive force, is an acquired force, the product of former activity' (*COR*, 7). *The German Ideology* developed a number of major concepts which were to receive further attention throughout the authors' lives. These were the concept of division of labour, of social class contradiction, of the state as both socially necessary and a class institution, and the proletariat as the special class which can make a revolution to abolish class divisions (Draper, 1977, 1, 1, 189-93 and 1978, 17). As Marx pursued his studies, concentrated on the field of political economy, a conceptual framework evolved around the concept of a *mode of production*. The following diagram sets out the relations of the major categories within a mode of production. Social formation refers to a particular place at a particular time, e.g. Britain in 1860 or France in 1980, a society in which there may be more than one mode of production operating, but in which one is dominant.

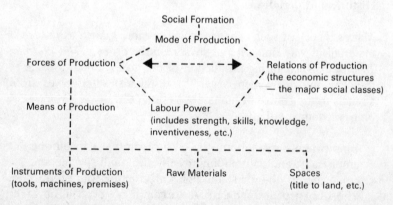

Source: Cohen (1978).

In 1859, in the preface to *A Contribution to the Critique of Political Economy*, Marx set down 'the general result . . . which served as a guiding thread' for his studies (*SW*, 1, 356). 'Briefly formulated', this has remained a quarry for quotations and also, because of its brevity, a source of misunderstandings. Marx speaks of the economic structure of society as 'the real foundation' on which 'rises a legal and political superstructure and to which correspond definite forms of social consciousness'. Then comes the famous sentence: 'It is not the consciousness of men that determines their being, but, on the contrary, their social being that determines their consciousness.' How to interpret that we will see in the discussion of ideology below. As for the metaphor 'super-structure', that has given rise to much discussion and it is only recently that certain marxists have had the courage to treat it as just a convenient form of speech and not a concept (Sayer, 1979, 81p; Cameron, 1980; cf. Cohen, 1978, 231-4). Ink has been wasted discussing whether education, in the sense of schooling, is part of the superstructure or part of the economic base (infra-structure or foundation)! Engels, attempting to clarify the theory in the letters mentioned above, did not help when he produced another sentence which has been much cited and discussed: 'According to the materialist conception of history the determining element in history is *ultimately* the production and reproduction in real life' (to Bloch, 21 Sep 1890). But, significant for education, he stressed the way in which 'political forms of the class struggle', 'forms of law' and other 'reflexes' of 'actual struggles in the brains of the combatants' influence the course of history, especially determining its 'form'. In the preface Marx also listed a number of different modes of production, a list which became dogma for Soviet and later Chinese marxism. Only relatively recently has Marx's open and tentative categorisation been seriously noted. He wrote: 'In *broad outlines* we can designate the Asiatic, the ancient, the feudal, and the modern bourgeois modes of production as so many epochs in the progress of the economic formation of society' (emphasis added). This important passage ends with the vision of capitalist society as the last class-divided society out of which will arise a new and completely different epoch. As Marx put it: 'This social formation constitutes, therefore, the closing chapter of the prehistoric stage of human society.' Today he would, no doubt, wish to qualify that!

Perhaps the nub of this preface is the statement of the relation between the 'relations of production', the social classes, and the 'material forces of production'. Marx wrote:

> At a certain stage of their development, the material forces of production in society come in conflict with existing relations of production, or — what is but a legal expression for the same thing — with the property relations within which they have been at work before. From forms of development of the forces of production these relations turn into their fetters. Then begins an epoch of social revolution.

This is another aspect of that major theme of the *Communist Manifesto*, that the history of post-tribal societies has been 'the history of class struggles'.[7] Another aspect is the relative significance of the social relations, or classes, and the material forces of production. Cohen is one of those who interpret this relationship as a form of technological determinism. This he does in the course of an attempt to improve Marx by applying formal logic to the preface we have been examining. He seeks Marx's support by citing various other passages including the one where Marx says: 'The hand-mill gives you society with the feudal lord; the steam-mill society with the industrial capitalist' (*CW*, 6, 166, cit. Cohen, 143-4). Close examination of these passages in context, however, does not support a simple priority of the technical over the social. Rather, as Sayer has shown in his discussion of Marx's account of the transition from feudalism to capitalism, the fundamental contradiction is between two sets of production relations. The capitalist set, formed within feudal society, embodies productive forces which are 'capable of sustaining a superior technology' (Sayer, 1979, 86). Since the development of the productive forces involves invention and the spread of knowledge this question clearly poses the role of education in the historical process and is, therefore, worth careful consideration.[8]

Of crucial importance for the argument of this book is Marx's conception of capitalism as a mode of commodity production in which the producers are exploited through wage labour, i.e. by economic rather than direct political means. This I will discuss further in the section on late capitalism below. Here I will confine discussion to Marx's concept of exploitation and social class struggle.

Marx's use of the term *exploitation* refers to the appropriation of the surplus in class-divided societies. Related terms are surplus labour, surplus produce and surplus value. In simple terms the surplus is 'the difference between what a society produces and the costs of producing it' (Baran and Sweezy, 1966, 9; cf. Mandel, 1968, 26-8). Surplus value, the form the surplus takes under capitalism, may be thought of as the sum of rent, interest and profit. Marx drew attention to the different ways in which this surplus has been transferred from the class which produced it to another class, a class whose existence was determined by this exploitative relationship. Slaves and slave owners, serfs and feudal lords, working class and capitalist, neither class can exist without the other. Marx himself, in a letter to the US socialist, Wedemeyer, in 1852 (*COR*, 57), pointed out that historians and economists before him had written about classes and class struggle. What he 'did that was new' was:

> to prove: (1) that the *existence of classes* is only bound up with *particular, historic phases in the development of production*; (2) that the class struggle necessarily leads to the *dictatorship of the proletariat*; (3) that this dictatorship itself only constitutes the transition to the *abolition of all classes* and to a *classless society*.

These polar classes are, of course, not the only classes in a social formation, in part because there are other modes of production present besides the dominant one, in part because the surplus is shared out in ways some of which will be explained below. The need for concrete historical examination of each particular case is well made by Draper:

> The way in which a given society divides up into classes is specific to its own social relations. Thus, there are warlord elements in many societies, but a warlord becomes a *feudal* lord or baron only when specific social relations become dominant. There is no rule-of-thumb definition which decides whether the chief of an armed band who resides in a stronghold and lives off the surplus labour of unfree producers, etc. is or is not a member of a *feudal* class. The point can only be settled not by a glossary but only by a concrete examination of the overall social relations of the society. Similarly, merchants become a separate *class* not simply because they buy and sell, but only when buying and selling begins to play a certain role in a given society. (Draper, 1977, pp. 157, 507)

A non-polar class which still plays a significant role in such late capitalist countries as France and Germany is the peasantry. Our understanding of how peasants are exploited, and, therefore, our ability to apply a marxist analysis to pre-capitalist societies in which peasants (free, independent producers) are in the majority has been greatly advanced by a recent book of Geoffrey de Ste Croix.[9] He distinguishes between *direct individual exploitation* (wage labourers, slaves, serfs and debt bondsmen, tenants and ordinary debtors by employers, masters, landowners or money-lenders) and *indirect collective exploitation* (of peasants and other subject classes through taxation, military conscription and forced labour or personal services by the state) (Ste Croix, 1981, 205 and 1984, 105). Ste Croix notes that Marx had himself foreshadowed this distinction in *The Class Struggles in France*:

> exploitation [of the French peasants] differs only in *form* from the exploitation of the industrial proletariat. The exploiter is the same: *capital*. The individual capitalists exploit the individual peasant through *mortgages* and *usury*; the capitalist class exploits the peasant class through the *state taxes*. (Marx, *CW*, 10, 122, cit. Ste Croix, 1981, 206; cf. Engels, *AD*, 382)

Ste Croix also makes a useful point about class consciousness, a question important for education which will be further discussed below. Ste Croix points out that class conflict (or class struggle) 'is essentially the fundamental relationship between classes, involving *exploitation* and resistance to it', but that it may or may not involve either class consciousness or collective activity (1984, 100). Denial of exploitation in this marxian sense is a major feature of bourgeois ideology, both at the popular level of the mass media or at more academic levels in the content of schooling. In spite of this, large numbers of working people seem to acquire understanding, if only at an instinctive level, even when working conditions are relatively good.

Another concept which must be mentioned here is that of the *state*, a topic which will also be dealt with below in the section on late capitalism.[10] Engels traced the origins of the state in the breaking up of tribal society through the division of labour and the division of society into classes. Speaking of the process of primitive accumulation by Spain, Holland, France and England in the seventeenth century Marx said: 'they all employ the power of the state, the concentrated and organized force of society' (*CAP*, 1, 915). In the *Communist Manifesto* the executive of the modern state is referred to as 'but a committee for managing the common affairs of the whole bourgeoisie' (*CW*, 6, 486). The major task of the state was always seen to be ensuring the domination of the ruling class. Other, non-class, tasks were recognised but they were seen to be distorted by the fundamental class bias of the state (Draper, 1977, 1, 258-60). This last is suggestive for state provision of schooling today with its financing of private schools for the rich (England, Australia), the way in which financial cuts have been made, and the state's reaction to unemployment in blaming the schools. Finally on the state, Marx and Engels, especially in their journalistic writings, gave numerous examples of the methods employed by the state to maintain class dominance. Interesting for education are those methods involving ideology and even direct falsification (today, disinformation!) (Draper, 1977, 1, 263-70).

These then are the major concepts and relations of historical materialism. To understand further how Marx used them requires an understanding of his concepts of theory and practice, concepts which will be discussed separately below. But first something must be said about *dialectics*.

Dialectics

What Marx referred to as 'my dialectical method' in 1873, contrasting it with that of Hegel, has a long history in the European, Chinese and Indian traditions. It is, therefore, hardly surprising that people use the term in many senses, and even with little sense. In the USSR much has been written about 'dialectical materialism' separate from historical materialism, and often as a natural science separate from human problems. This was a development from Engels' *Dialectics of Nature*, a work constructed from notes left unpublished by the author. It must be stressed that for Marx and Engels there was never any question of imposing ideas on nature, of forcing reality to fit into any preconceived pattern. If nature is dialectical in any of the senses used this is to be shown in each particular case through, as Marx put it, appropriation of material in detail, analysis of its different forms of development and tracing of their inner connection (*CAP*, 1, 102). Here, only those aspects of dialectics of particular relevance to education can be discussed.[11]

The first aspect of dialectics is as a way of thinking which conceives of *processes* and *relations* rather than as isolated, static things. Engels described this way of thinking in his essay, Ludwig Feuerbach (*SW*, 1, 453-4), contrasting it with the 'still common old metaphysics'. The latter, besides viewing things as rigid and unchanging makes absolute judgements of true and false, good and bad where dialectical thinking 'knows that these antitheses have only a relative validity'. Dialectics in this sense, conceiving things in motion, as transient, ever changing is, as Marx pointed out, 'in its essence critical and revolutionary' (*CAP*, 1, 103).

The second aspect of dialectics is as separate 'laws', conceived in the way Engels set out in *Dialectics of Nature* (1954, 27, 83, 280). These laws he gave as the transformation of quantity into quality and vice versa; the interaction of polar opposites and their transformation into each other when driven to extremes; and the process of negation of the negation, or spiral form of development. Engels saw these as 'nothing but the most general laws' abstracted from 'the history of nature and human society' (1954, 83). That one can make such abstractions to describe human and non-human processes the history of thought amply demonstrates. That an expectation that reality can be so described is a useful one I would defend. To assert them as always occurring aspects of everything, as Lenin, and following him, Mao Zedong did of contradictions — 'all things are contradictory in themselves'[12] — is to go beyond the justified and the useful.

Since I think there is value in judicious employment of these conceptions of the way changes occur, and since writers on Marx and education employ the term dialectic, often injudiciously (cf. Giroux, 1981, 113-25 and Apple, 1979), I will expand on them.

Probably the most used conception is that of contradiction. Mario Bunge, with the natural sciences in mind, defines this as the assertion that:

> every material object, however homogeneous it may look at first sight, is actually inhomogeneous in some respect and to some extent, and is moreover composed of mutually opposed or 'conflicting' (that is, mutually disturbing) parts or features, thus being subject to an inner stress that may develop (eventually enhanced by external forces) to the point of producing a radical (qualitative) change in the object concerned. (115)

He distinguishes between those interactions which involve homogeneous parts or do not result in qualitative change from dialectical ones which involve both. Following Engels, the former should be thought of as mechanical while the latter, dialectical changes, are organic.

Contradiction is sometimes used to refer to changes in which one state changes into another which is in some important way its opposite, or negation. Mao Zedong uses a number of examples in *On Contradiction*: the National Party changing from progressive to reactionary after 1927; or war changing into peace. Before dismissing these conceptions as trivial one should ponder the comment of Marx cited before: dialectics 'is a scandal and an abomination to the bourgeoisie' because 'it includes in its positive understanding of what exists a simultaneous recognition of its negation, its inevitable destruction' (*CAP*, 1, 103).

The conception of change as spiral also involves that of negation as described in the last paragraph, but twice repeated, a negation of the negation as Engels phrased it. This is an alternative way of viewing long-term change from that of the circle, equally common from ancient times in both Europe and Asia. There is a sense in which change repeats itself, that a later state is in one or more ways like that of a previous state. But in the spiral analogy repetition is not exact. On the contrary, it is qualitatively different in important ways. Engels gives the example of early human society and the envisaged future communism. Both are classless, but the future communism would be so in full recognition of the fact and in possession of the cultural heritage of thousands of years.

The expectation that in certain circumstances quantitative changes will give rise to qualitative changes, or vice versa, seems to me to be a useful one, borne out by numerous examples in many fields. Again Mario Bunge supplies us with an interesting example. He takes Engels's example of boiling water in a kettle and shows that the change of state from liquid to gas or from gas to liquid on condensation depends on a 'contradiction'. The thermal agitation of the molecules, depending on the addition or subtraction of heat (quantity) is in interplay with its opposite, the molecular attraction of the molecules (Bunge, 19).

I now turn to a third and neglected aspect of dialectics which I believe could make important contributions to our understanding if it were more widely understood and developed. This is what

Joseph Needham refers to as the recognition of 'integrative levels'. He contrasts mechanical materialism, which he sees as essentially reductionist, with:

> the essence of dialectical materialism, [which] on the contrary, is the acceptance of the existence of diverse levels of complexity and organisation, and the interpretation of them as successive stages of a world-process the nature of which is synthetic or dialectical. Order and organisation are fully allowed for. (Needham, 1944, 122, cf. 1956, 474, 498)

A clear example is that of music. To many mechanical materialists this is reducible to the laws of acoustics. But this is to lose what is essentially musical about these sounds. A dialectical approach is to recognise two levels here. The music depends on the acoustic for no sounds can disobey acoustic laws. At the same time music has its own laws or properties which cannot be reduced to those of physics. Engels, in *Dialectics of Nature,* already pointed out that the objects of physics, chemistry, biology, etc. lie on successive levels of organisation and that while each is in part determined by the level below it, it has its own, irreducible patterns and laws (1946, 319-24, 156-7). In the areas of education which we shall be considering below this concept of levels could be developed to solve the problem of learning at the psychological and social levels. The social is in part determined by the individual but contains things irreducibly new.[13]

Throughout this account I have used 'dialectics' instead of 'the dialectic' preferred by some writers. This was to avoid any suggestion of mystical pattern or cosmic force. Pattern there is, but it is to be discovered, as we shall see shortly, through detailed empirical study and not through preconceptions of an unnecessary kind. Dialectics, rather than *the* dialectic, limits itself to empirically open-ended concepts. Expectation of the likelihood of contradictions, negativity, quality change resulting from quantity change, prepares the mind without forcing it where the evidence points elsewhere.

Theory and Practice

In this section I shall consider on the one hand Marx's conception of theory, his method, and his theory of knowledge,[14] and on the other his conception of practice. I shall include brief mention of the conceptual cluster known as *alienation*.

The early writings of Marx and Engels, especially *The German Ideology*, were concerned to establish their differences with Hegel and his followers over the relation of the ideas and human action. As Sayer argues, they challenge 'the very possibility of distinguishing the material and the ideal as separate spheres in the first place' (1979, 4). Asserting that consciousness has always been and must remain a social product, they argue that as the division of labour finally gave rise to a separation of mental and manual labour so the former was able to detach itself from the real and assume various forms of speculation and '"pure" theory' (*CW*, 5, 44-5). However, 'real, positive science (Wissenschaft)' begins where speculation ends (*CW*, 37). 'Consciousness can never be anything else than conscious being, and the being of men is their actual life-process' (*CW*, 36). In the famous *Theses* Feuerbach is criticised, along with 'all hitherto existing materialism', for conceiving 'the thing, reality, sensuousness . . . only in the form of the object or of contemplation, but not as sensuous human activity, practice, not subjectively' (*CW*, 5, 3). This attack on the material-ideal dichotomy is nicely summed up in Marx's letter to the Russian critic and journalist, P.V. Annenkov commenting on Proudhon's *Philosophie de la misère:*

> What Mr. Proudhon does not understand is that, according to their faculties, men also produce the *social relations* in which they produce worsted and linens. Still less does Mr. Proudhon understand that those who produce social relations in conformity with their material productivity also produce the *ideas, categories,* i.e. the ideal abstract expressions of those same social relations. Indeed the categories are no more eternal than the relations they express. They are historical and transitory products. (*CW*, 38, 102)

With this *dialectical* materialism which embodied the ideal and the ethical in a form of naturalism Marx and Engels offered a remedy for what Needham has described as the 'schizophrenia of Europe' (1956, 2, 303). Applying these principles to the field of education might help to show why it is taking so long for people to effect a cure.

It needs to be added that this naturalism embodies a reflection or correspondence theory of truth. It assumes the existence of a universe prior in time to human existence and independent of human thinking. Or as Ruben puts it: '(a) there can be things which have only natural [physical] properties and (b) if anything has a social or cultural feature, it is *necessarily* a thing with natural or material properties or features too' (1979, 216; cf. Timpanaro, 1975, 34).

Engels, in a letter to Schmidt (12 March 1895), nicely expressed a correspondence theory of truth:

> The reproaches you make against the law of value apply to *all* concepts, regarded from the standpoint of reality. The identity of thought and being, to express myself in Hegelian fashion, everywhere coincides with your example of the circle and the polygon. Or the two of them, the concept of a thing and its reality, run side by side like two asymptotes, always approaching each other yet never meeting. This difference between the two is the very difference which prevents the concepts from being directly and immediately reality and reality from being immediately its own concept. (*COR*, 527; cf. *Anti-Duehring*, 31, 121-2, 127-8)

Here it remains only to say that there would seem to be no non-circular arguments to justify belief in a reality independent of the mind in this way. It remains an assumption. Ruben interprets Marx's eighth thesis on Feuerbach as stating just that, of being a conscious abandonment of 'the need to look for a philosophical solution' (Ruben, 1979, 99, cf. 137).[15]

Marx's Method

This has been discussed often and at length. Marx himself discussed it in the *General Introduction* of 1857 (*GRUND*, 83-111). To begin with, Marx made a distinction which defined his view of theory, not to speak of consciousness and ideology which we will discuss below. This distinction was between phenomenal forms and essential relations, or between *appearance* and *essence*. This distinction is so important as to justify some examples of how Marx made it:

a scientific analysis of competition is possible only if we can grasp the inner nature of capital, just as the apparent motions of the heavenly bodies are intelligible only to someone who is acquainted with their real motions, which are not perceptible to the senses. (*CAP*, 1, 433)

The forms of appearance are reproduced directly and spontaneously, as current and usual modes of thought; the essential relations must first be discovered by science. (*CAP*, 1, 682)

But all science would be superfluous, if the appearance, the form, and the nature of things were wholly identical. (*CAP*, 3, 956; cf. Sayer, 1979, 159, n.14)

Sayer, in his detailed study of *Marx's Method: Ideology, Science and Critique in "Capital"*, shows how Marx, proceeding from the empirical world, the world of sensation, seeks the underlying mechanisms and conditions (Sayer, 1979, 114). In doing this Marx uses a logic which Sayer shows is neither deductive (112, 114) nor inductive (114), but rather what Hanson, following Pierce, calls *abduction* or *retroduction* (115). Sayer describes this as follows:

What he [Marx] in effect does is to postulate mechanisms which should they exist would explain how the phenomena under investigation come to assume the forms in which they are experienced. He then treats the conditions necessary for the functioning of these mechanisms as the material groundwork of the forms themselves. (in Mepham and Ruben, 3, 40; cf. Sayer, 1979, 114-17)[16]

Abduction begins with phenomenal forms and throughout the reasoning process hypothesising is constrained by them. As Marx wrote in *The German Ideology*: 'The premises from which we begin are not arbitrary ones, not dogmas, but real premises from which abstraction can only be made in the imagination' (31; Sayer, 1979, 135).

There is a different account of Marx's method which because of its proponents requires mention here. Alfred Sohn-Rethel, in his interesting book, *Intellectual and Manual Labour* (1978a, 194-6). Sohn-Rethel writes:

> Thus methodologically the subject-matter of Marx's critique is
> not the historical reality of this or that form of social existence
> but, in the first instance, a particular mode of consciousness —
> namely, that of political economy; it is thoughts, not things . . .
> He does not deal directly with realities . . . his approach is
> characteristically different. It is an approach to reality, but by
> way of the 'critique' of the historically given consciousness.
> (195)

The way Marx set about discovering 'the truth about our world',
says Sohn-Rethel, was 'to trace the genetical origin of any current
ideas and concepts, on the very standards of them' (195). This, of
course, is the *immanent criticism* of the Frankfurt School of
marxists, on the fringe of which Sohn-Rethel himself was, which:
'confronts "the existent, in its historical context, with the claim of
its conceptual principles, in order to criticize the relation between
the two and thus transcend them"' (Held, 1980, 183 citing
Horkheimer).

While it is true that Marx developed his theories through a
criticism of those of his predecessors, the classical economists, it is
also true, as Sayer details, that at every step Marx controlled his
theorising by empirical work. Not only did he read 'the whole of
economic literature available in the British Museum' (Sohn-
Rethel, 1978a, 197), a literature which included much empirical
matter in government reports, statistical collections and newspapers like the *Economist*, but he also listened to accounts by both
businessmen and workers.[17] By ignoring this empirical element in
Marx's method the advocates of immanent criticism, however critical, perpetuate a scholastic tradition which the best of them have
tried to escape.

On Practice

Many of the writers on Marx, among them Avineri and
Kolakowski, prefer to use the Greek form for the word practice
which is used in German, *praxis*. Gramsci referred to marxism as
'the philosophy of praxis' both to elude the censor and because it
was 'an accurate description of his point of view' (Kolakowski,
1978, 3, 229; cf. Matthews, 1980, 89). But Timpanaro's warning
of the term's 'vagueness and multiplicity of meanings' is timely and
I shall use the English word practice.[18]

The importance of practice for thinking, Marx's theory of

knowledge, I have already considered. On that side it is only necessary to distinguish Marx's ideas from pragmatism. Kolakowski brings out the contrast when he writes: 'truth is not correspondence between our statements and the way things are, but between our statements and the possible gratifications we may experience' (1972, 190).[19]

With those preliminaries, let us now look at what I believe is absolutely central to education, Marx's practical aim. This he expressed in various ways throughout his life, in words and deeds. The best-known expression is the final thesis on Feuerbach: 'The philosophers have only *interpreted* the world in various ways; the point is to *change* it.' A little earlier Marx had written: 'It is not enough for thought to strive for realisation, reality must itself strive towards thought' (*CW*, 3, 183). Knowledge is needed if change is to be effected, but knowledge without practical efforts to make changes remains ineffectual scholasticism. Since, for reasons which I hope to make clear below, I believe that in the field of education our problem is more a lack of practice than of knowledge — in some cases I consider the requisite knowledge to be unobtainable — I will emphasise the point with three further quotations:

all forms and products of consciousness cannot be dissolved by mental criticism . . . but only by the practical overthrow of the actual social relations which gave rise to this idealistic humbug; that not criticism but revolution is the driving force of history . . . (*CW*, 5, 54)

Ideas can never lead beyond an old world order but only beyond the ideas of the old world order. Ideas *cannot carry out anything* at all. In order to carry out ideas men are needed who can exert practical force. (*CW*, 4, 119)

Clearly the weapon of criticism cannot replace the criticism of weapons, and material force must be overthrown by material force. But theory also becomes a material force once it has gripped the masses. (*CW*, 3, 182)

It is the practice of education which needs both critical study and practice.

Ideology

In Marx's writings there are two important ways in which ideology is defined as different from science — science, that is, in the broader sense of the German word Wissenschaft, which embraces all fields of knowledge. The first, and probably the most important, stems from Marx's distinction between appearance and essence described above. Ideology arises as a reflection of the level of appearance and is verifiable by simple observation and experience. Science demands work to unearth the real relations, the determinants of the phenomenal forms from their concealment at the level of essence (Mepham in Mepham and Ruben, 3, 148; Sayer, 1979, 8). Such an ideology is clearly *false*. It is also equally clearly, being so easily apparently confirmed, powerful. Is not this a major reason why capitalist ideology has such a hold on so many working-class people?[20]

The second concept of ideology is of ideas which represent particular class or sectional interests. In particular Marx referred to the dominant ideology in a society, the ruling ideology, the ideas of the ruling class. He wrote:

> the ideas of the ruling class are in every epoch the ruling ideas: i.e the class which is the ruling *material* force of society is at the same time its ruling *intellectual* force. The class which has the means of material production at its disposal, consequently also controls the means of mental production, so that the ideas of those who lack the means of mental production are on the whole subject to it. The ruling ideas are nothing more than the ideal expression of the dominant material relations, the dominant material relations grasped as ideas; hence of the relations which make the one class the ruling one, therefore, the ideas of its dominance. (*CW*, 5, 59)

An essential feature of the ruling ideology is that these class interested ideas as classless, as universal, as representing the general interest. Marx expressed it thus:

> For each new class which puts itself in the place of one ruling before it is compelled, merely in order to carry through its aim, to present its interest as the common interest of all the members of society, that is, expressed in ideal form; it has to give its ideas

the form of universality, and present them as the only rational, universally valid ones. (*CW*, 5, 60; cf. 245-6)

It is important to recognise that Marx and Engels make a clear distinction between ideology and conscious falsehood. Ideology may be 'false consciousness', but it is purveyed in the belief that it is not false. Otherwise, as Engels long ago noted, it 'would not be an ideological process at all' (*COR*, 511). However, in times of crisis ideology is replaced by conscious falsehood: something which people have been accustomed to, perhaps even inured to since the Nazi propaganda of the 1930s. Today 'respectable' governments, not to mention business firms, dispense 'disinformation' and the mass media openly fashion 'personalities' in order to 'sell'. The line between ideology and falsehood has become often difficult to draw.[21]

Because of its significance for liberation struggles today a few words on Marx and religion are necessary here. In an extended piece in the introduction to his 'Contribution to the Critique of Hegel's Philosophy of Law' Marx spoke of 'the criticism of religion [as] the premise of all criticism' (*CW*, 3, 175). He wrote of 'man, who looked for a superhuman being in the fantastic reality of heaven and found nothing there but the reflection of himself'. Elsewhere he wrote that 'Religion is from the outset *consciousness of the transcendental* arising from *actually existing* forces' (*CW*, 5, 93). He recognised religion was 'a general theory' of our world and 'its moral sanction', its 'source of consolation and justification'. But since our world is 'inverted', or class divided and human beings are exploiters and exploited, religion produced 'an inverted world-consciousness'. It provided an 'illusory happiness', illusions which must be abandoned if humankind's real, this-worldly happiness was to be achieved. It is in this context that the much-cited line about religion being 'the opium of the people' comes (*CW*, 3, 175). The thrust of Marx's argument here and in other places in his writings is the need to focus on changing the real concrete conditions of human existence. 'The criticism of heaven' as he put it, 'turns into the criticism of the earth, the criticism of religion into the criticism of law and the criticism of theology into the criticism of politics' (*CW*, 3, 176). But neither here nor anywhere else did Marx, or Engels, suggest that people should be forced to give up their religion. On the contrary, they specifically spoke against such treatment (e.g. *FI*, 358).[22]

Alienation

To end this review of those concepts in Marx which have special importance for an understanding of education brief mention must be made of alienation. Employing a number of terms rendered in English as fetishism or reification, Marx uses the concept from his early writings through to the end. Its importance for understanding education is as an ideological process whereby something which has a human, social origin is regarded as if it were a natural or physical object (reification) or process (fetishism). One of the best-known examples is Marx's description of the fetishism of commodities in *Capital* (*CAP*, 1, 165). Today many scientists reify science, refusing to consider any social controls on its more dangerous developments on the excuse that 'you can't hold back the progress of science'.[23]

Conclusion

Those, then, are the ideas of Marx which have educational implications. Marx's particular comments on schooling will be reserved for the section on schooling below. To repeat, what we have is a vision of human potential combined with a method for interpreting our world in order to arrive at scientific knowledge necessary to achieve that potential. Emphasising change as the norm and the historically determined nature of human beings and human society, Marx offered a vision of realisable freedom. Emphasising that societies are deeply divided by class and class interest, Marx showed how ideas reflect these divisions, masking them and also revealing them. But he also argued that changing ideas alone changes nothing, that practice is required if practice is to change.

With this rich social framework saturated with ideas, with teaching and learning situations waiting to be more fully theorised, the efforts of writers to elaborate a 'marxist analysis of education' have been meagre and confined to too narrow and focus — schooling. Many teaching-learning situations aimed at practice which these writers have neglected, on the other hand, have lacked the necessary theory. It remains to be seen whether we can do better.

Notes

1. In English there is the splendid Pelican Marx library published in association with New Left Review. This includes a fine new edition of *Capital*, Volume 1 and the important *Grundrisse*. Then there is the planned 50-volume edition published jointly by Lawrence and Wishart Ltd, London, International Publishers Inc., New York and the Institute of Marxism-Leninism, Moscow, which contains much that has not been translated before. The notes and indices to both these collections make the writings easier than many previous editions.

2. In the 1960s it became fashionable to attack Engels for such things as 'positivism' and 'scientism'. Maximilien Rubel, otherwise a valuable critic, was one to do this (1974, pp. 19-24, 424-5). Most useful on these questions are Draper (1977, 1, 1, 24-5) and Gareth Stedman Jones (1977). Engels's letters on historical materialism are those to Conrad Schmidt (5 Aug. and 27 Oct. 1890), to Joseph Bloch (21 Sept. 1890), to Franz Mehring (14 July 1893) and Heinz Starkenburg (25 Jan. 1894). These are included in the various editions of 'Selected Works' and elsewhere.

3. This is well expressed in the letters from the *Deutsch-Franzoesische Jahrbuecher*, *CW*, 3, pp. 133-45. On p. 142 Marx writes: '[It] is precisely the advantage of the new direction: that we do not dogmatically anticipate the world but rather want to find the new world only through criticism of the old' (translation from Draper, 1977, 1, 1, 101). See also *The Communist Manifesto*, section 3, *CW*, 6, pp. 514-17. The distinction between communists and socialists and Marx's choice is explained at some length in Draper, pp. 96-108. For Marx's life at the time he made the choice see McLellan (1973) pp. 99-104.

4. For Marx on conservation see *Capital*, 1, p. 638 and 3, pp. 645-6 and Gandy (1979) p. 73.

5. This passage from *Capital* is so important as to justify citing in full, as is also a related one from the *Grundrisse*:

Just as the savage must wrestle with nature, in order to satisfy his wants, in order to maintain his life and reproduce it, so civilized man has to do it, and he must do it in all forms of society and under all possible modes of production. With his development the realm of natural necessity expands, because his wants increase, but at the same time the forces of production increase by which these wants are satisfied. The freedom in this field cannot consists of anything else but of the fact that socialised man, the associated producers, regulate their interchange with nature rationally, bring it under their common control, instead of being ruled by it as by some blind power; that they accomplish their task with the least expenditure of energy and under conditions most adequate to their human nature and most worthy of it. But it always remains a realm of necessity. Beyond it begins that development of human power, which is its own end, the true realm of freedom, which, however, can flourish only upon that realm of necessity as its base. The shortening of the working day is its fundamental premise. (*CAP*, 3, 959)

As soon as labour in the direct form has ceased to be the great well-spring of wealth, labour time ceases and must cease to be its measure, and hence exchange value [must cease to be the measure] of use value. The surplus labour of the mass has ceased to be the condition for the development of general wealth, just as the non-labour of the few, for the development of the general powers of the human head. With that, production based on exchange value breaks down, and the direct, material production process is stripped of the form

of penury and antithesis. The free development of individualities, and hence not
the reduction of necessary labour time so as to posit surplus labour, but rather
the general reduction of the necessary labour of society to a minimum, which
then corresponds to the artistic, scientific, etc. development of the individuals in
the time set free, and with the means created, for all of them. (*GRUND*,
705-6)

6. Draper calls *The German Ideology* 'the first "marxist" work' (1977, 1, 1,
189) and McLellan recognises the section on Feuerbach, written by Marx alone, to
be 'one of the most central of Marx's works' (McLellan, 1973, 151).

7. The *Communist Manifesto*, as Draper warns, needs to be read remembering
that it was the programmic document of a political party and not a theoretical work
in which all is qualified. Readers interested in the discussion about a social
formation embodying more than one mode of production should consult Anderson
(1980) 67; Althusser (1969); Balibar in Althusser and Balibar (1970), pp. 203-4,
207; and Amin (1974), 138-42.

8. Sayer's discussion of this question is critical. He cites Marx on the primitive
clan, feudal serfdom and the governments of Henry VII and VIII of England to
identify '*conditions* of production' and he argues that Marx 'makes explicit' that
'production relations may *themselves* be productive forces' (83, citing *CW*, 3, 43).
Ellen Meiksins Wood (1981), with her defence of 'political marxism', is relevant
here also. She comments: 'Cohen relies on readings of Marx which are so dubious
that his whole interpretation of historical materialism is put into question' (71. See
Cohen's citations, pp. 99, 146 and Wood's citations, pp. 71-4).

9. This concept of indirect, collective exploitation by the state would seem
also to apply to post-capitalist social formations like the USSR.

10. My account here draws heavily on that of Draper (1977). The reader might
also consult Engels's *The Origin of the Family, Private Property and the State*. No
really satisfactory marxist account of the state as it is today exists, but see Therborn
(1978), and Milliband (1973).

11. Kolakowski (1978) introduces the topic in 'Marx, Engels and their
European Predecessors'. Joseph Needham's second volume (1956) discusses
dialectical ideas in ancient China. Other important references are Timpanaro
(1975, 91, 64), Mario Bunge, a theoretical physicist writing on *Causality*
(1963, 17-19) and, most important, Derek Sayer (1979).

Giroux (1981, 113-26) is the only writer on Marx and education to attempt to
discuss dialectics, or, as he prefers, *the* dialectic. He defines it as 'a critical mode of
reasoning and behaviour' (114), an interpenetration of reasoning and method'; 'a
form of critique [which] functions to bring to awareness underlying contradictions
that support existing forms of alienation' (116); and the notion that relations
between people and not things underlies our 'intersubjective space' (118). All of
this, said defensively, seems to me to be much beyond the useful definition of
dialectics, though it does define aspects of Marx's 'method'. Giroux then gives the
following categories of the dialectic: totally (118); mediation (119); appropriation
(120) and transcendence (121). To these, except the last, the same criticism
applies. How he can say that contradictions, unit of opposites and negation of the
negation are '*often* associated with the dialectic' (121, emphasis added) I find hard
to understand. For me these are precisely categories in need of explication. Thus I
find this chapter both too much and too little.

12. This formulation was Hegel's (1951, 2, 66-7). W.T. Stace, expounding
him, speaks of his speculative audacity (Stace, 1955, 94). Lenin's list of basic
contradictions in nature, in *On the Question of Dialectics*, is copied by Mao Zedong
in *On Contradiction*. See also Sayer's afterword to the 1983 edition of *Marx's
Method.*

13. See also the discussion between Sayer and Bhaskar on the individual and the social in Sayer, 1983 edition *Marx's Method*, afterword to the second edition. Here Bhasker suggests an analogy with unperceivable entities in physics like gravity and magnetic fields, but this is mistaken. A better analogy would be the interrelation of levels that occurs in chemical changes in the dependence of the chemical on the molecular physics level.

14. Discussion of Marx's theory of knowledge has been a fertile if clouded area of Marx study over recent decades. I am endebted to D-H Ruben (1977) and especially Derek Sayer (1979) for helping clarify my thoughts on the topic.

15. Michael Matthews misses this point (85). His account of Marx's correspondence theory is also weaker than Ruben's account. He makes the strange comment that 'the correspondence theory was bound up with a reflective and passive account of human thinking', though he does add that 'Marx rejects this account of human thought' (1979, 82). In addition, he cites Kolakowski's praise of Marx's 1844 *Manuscripts* for their 'epistemological content' (Matthews, 80) without noticing that Kolakowski uses them to give what Ruben describes as a 'consistent, coherent, and thoroughly idealist interpretation of Marx' (Ruben, 86). As Ruben shows, Kolakowski reads into Marx's often difficult discussion of Hegel an interpretive theory of truth (Ruben, 86-92) in which *a priori* beliefs and structures in the mind are imposed on the world (Ruben, 2).

16. According to Hanson this retroductive logic is different from that model of scientific enquiry known as the hypothetico-deductive model, for 'by the time a law gets fixed into an H-D system, the *original* scientific thinking is over' (Sayer, 1979, 115). An example of abduction given by Pierce is that of Kepler's reasoning from the observed longitudes of Mars. These he tried to fit into an orbit and finally 'abduced' that they were such as would be explained if Mars were to be moving in an elliptical orbit (cit. Nidditch, 1960, 317). Marx's abduction of the law of value and theory of surplus value is too complex to be summarised here and must be followed in Sayer (1979, 117-35).

17. See the bibliographies to the three volumes of *Capital*; Ruben (1974, 313); Mandel (1971, 70, 77); and McLellan (1973, 281).

18. Timpanaro also noted the use of praxis allowed writers to avoid speaking about materialism (1975, 56). See Avineri (1970, 132-49) and Fisher (1970, 152-8).

19. Kolakowski writes that pragmatism 'long enjoyed the reputation of being "typically American"' (1972, 182). Statements by William James, one of its founders, suggest a better description would be 'typically capitalist'. James wrote: 'If you follow the pragmatic method . . . you must bring out of each word its practical cash-value, set it to work within the stream of your experience. It appears less as a solution, then, than as a program for more work.' He also said: 'Truth *happens* to an idea. It *becomes* true, is *made* true by events (Cornforth, 1950, 157, 158).

20. Rachel Sharp, in an otherwise rather unsatisfactory account of Marx's concept of ideology, notes: 'the world of appearances, what appears on the surface, *does have a reality* [1980, 93 emphasis added].

Because of the importance of this concept of ideology it is worth noting some examples in Marx's *Capital*:

(i) On the surface of bourgeois society the worker's wage appears as the price of labour, as a certain quantity of labour (*CAP*, 1, 675).
(ii) For the rest, what is true of the form of appearance and their hidden background is also true of the form of appearance 'value and price of labour', or 'wages', as contrasted with the essential relation manifested in it, namely the value and price of labour-power. The form of appearance are reproduced

directly and spontaneously, as current and usual modes of thought; the essential relation must first be discovered by science (*CAP*, 1, 682; cf. translation in Mepham and Ruben, 3, 149).

(iii) Vulgar economy really does nothing else but to interpret, in doctrinaire fashion, the ideas of persons entrapped in capitalist conditions of production and performing the function of agents in such production, to systematise and to defend these ideas. We need not wonder, then, that vulgar economy feels particularly at home in the estranged form of manifestation, in which the economic conditions are absurd and complete contradictions, and that these conditions appear so much more self-explanatory to it, the more their internal connection is concealed. So long as the ordinary brain accepts these conceptions, vulgar economy is satisfied. But all science would be superfluous, if the appearance, the form, and the nature of things were wholly identical (*CAP*, 3, 649).

21. Some on the political left seem to feel that to speak of false consciousness is in some way to demean the working class for believing something. Rachel Sharp appears to be one of these where she writes of the concept of ruling class ideology 'sometimes lead[ing] to a conceptualisation of subordinate classes as passively manipulated victims of propaganda' (1980, 91). But this is a modern example of what Marx and Engels condemned in their early writings, the belief that by changing a name, or here definition, one is changing reality. In the case of ideology as the reflection of appearance this objection should, I would have thought, lose its justification.

22. At this point something should be said about Marx and atheism. The classic reference is in the *Economic and Philosophic Manuscripts* where Marx writes:

Since the real existence of man and nature has become evident in practice, through sense experience, because man has thus become evident for man as the being of nature, and nature for man as the being of man, the question about an alien being, about a being above nature and man — a question which implies the admission of the unreality of nature and of man — has become impossible in practice. *Atheism*, as the denial of this unreality, has no longer any meaning, for atheism is a *negation of God*, and postulates the existence of man through this negation; but socialism as socialism no longer stands in any need of such a mediation. (*CW*, 3, 305-6)

The key point, as Parinetto recently stresses (1983-4, 13) is that as with negative communism, atheism remains dependent on what is negated. Marx had moved on from such a dependency and was, therefore free to take a critical stand on the firm ground of the existence of humankind and nature (*CW*, 3, 305). McLellan does not grasp the significance of this point in his otherwise interesting commentary (1970, 144). Cornel West comes nearer to it (1984, 10-11).

A nice example of the movement still tied to what it is attempting to negate is the women's movement, or rather, those parts of it who assume masculine characteristics in their total rejection of males.

23. Colletti (Marx, *EW*, introduction, 48-56) is a good introduction to the topic of alienation in Marx. Sayer (1979, 31-3) is brief but useful. An interesting book is Meszaros (1970).

2 LATE CAPITALISM

In this section I shall outline those persisting and fundamental features of capitalism which define it in Marx's theory, and the recent trends which appear most significant for education. Education has featured in certain writings on economics from early on, but it is only since about the late 1950s that a definite branch of study, the economics of education, has flourished. M. Blaug, editing the Penguin two-volume collection of readings on the subject, sees this as concerned with two main kinds of questions. On the one hand there are studies of the economic value of education, to individuals or the wider society. On the other are studies of the economic aspects of educational systems (Blaug, 1970, 8). There is concern with job training and manpower forecasting, productivity and efficiency; and with educational planning and 'modernisation' or 'development'. While these studies take into account many of the features of late capitalism to be noted below almost all of them either ignore or deny Marx's fundamental definition of capitalism as a system of labour exploitation.

The education which the economics of education treats is education in the limited sense of schooling. In part this arises because such studies are undertaken within tertiary schools or other institutions closely linked with them. They may be funded by government or business interests and are inspired by an ideology of schooling closely bound up with particular and limited social perspectives.

The questions which Marx's theory would suggest are rather different. They are not primarily how to teach people to fit into the needs of modern capitalist industry and commerce — quite the opposite. One set of questions would be on how capitalist industry and commerce are affecting human beings. What does working in a particular type of firm teach the members of the different social classes concerned? On the level of ideology there are questions about the changing, or persisting, ideologies associated with change, or persistence, in different forms of business: small (petty bourgeois) business; big business, especially the multinationals and conglomerates which dominate today's world economy. There are questions about how these ideologies are propagated and about why they are attractive, and for whom. Then there are a number of questions concerned with the work ethic, especially now that the long boom is over and the capitalist countries have large-scale and chronic unemployment. What are people learning from work, and from the denial of work? There is overwhelming evidence that while most workers find work meaningless and boring they are equally, if not more, unhappy with unemployment. At the same time there is little evidence of widespread acceptance of marxist explanations for present conditions or visions for an alternative. A broader definition of education opens up better possibilities of understanding this state of affairs.

With these questions in mind, let us begin by looking at Marx's analysis of capitalism as a system of commodity production whose 'direct object and decisive motive' is the production of surplus value (*CAP*, 3, 1020). Marx granted the positive role capitalism has played in history in its restless pursuit of wealth: the development of the productivity of labour through the ever-increasing employment of science and technology; the enormous expansion of human needs beyond the level of 'mere subsistence'; and the potentially humanising effect of replacing human labour by that of machines (*GRUND*, 325; cf. 422). At the same time he saw its negative aspects teaching the workers the need to overthrow it. In today's terms those negative features would be the chronic problems of unemployment and stagflation, and the subordination of social needs to the pursuit of profit defined in the most abstract, exchange value terms.[1]

Marx's analysis of commodities, goods produced in order to be sold, concentrates on *exchange value* rather than *use value*. The latter is 'a relation between the consumer and the object consumed' which does not distinguish different types of society or historical periods (Sweezy, 1956, 26). Exchange value, a relation between people, is a key to understanding capital and capitalism. One of the characteristics of late capitalism is the increasing penetration of exchange value relations into areas of life previously dominated by considerations of use value.[2] Posed in terms of humanism versus commercialism these aspects of commodity production enter, if ill understood, into much of contemporary protest.

Marx made the distinction between different modes of production the *form in which surplus labour is extorted from the immediate producer* (*CAP*, 1, 325). This point is so important it demands lengthy citation:

> Although one part only of the workman's daily labour is *paid*, while the other part is *unpaid* . . . it seems as if the aggregate labour was paid labour. This false appearance distinguishes *wage labour* from other *historical* forms of labour . . . With the *slave*, on the contrary, even that part of his labour which is paid appears to be unpaid . . . Take, on the other hand, the peasant serf . . . this peasant worked, for example, three days for himself on his own field or the field allotted to him, and the three subsequent days he performed compulsory and gratuitous labour on the estate of his lord. Here, then, the paid and the unpaid parts of labour were visibly separated, separated in time and space; and our Liberals overflowed with moral indignation at the preposterous notion of making a man work for nothing. (*SW*, 1, 317-18)

> The Roman slave was held by chains; the wage-labourer is bound to his owner by invisible threads. The appearance of independence is maintained by a constant change in the person of the individual employer, and by the legal fiction of a contract. (*CAP*, 1, 719)

The threads are indeed invisible and union negotiation over 'a fair day's wage for a fair day's work' does little to make them visible. Gut feelings about exploitation remain too often at the phenomenal level, though under the right conditions they prepare understanding.

Marx's analysis of capitalism pre-dated the great expansion of the British and other empires after 1880,[3] a fresh division of the world which has had educational as well as political-economic consequences. Not least of the effects has been the pattern of migrant labour today and the rise of ideologies as different as racism and multi-culturalism. Marxist thinking on this new stage of capitalism was set for decades by the pamphlet Lenin wrote in Zuerich in 1916; *Imperialism, the Highest Stage of Capitalism.* He defined imperialism as a stage dominated by monopolies and finance capitalism. Export of capital because particularly important and the division of the world between the political powers was paralleled by a division between big economic trusts (Varga and Mendelsohn, 1940, 194).

A major and increasing feature of capitalism in this century has been the importance of the big firm. Whether called monopoly, oligopoly or multinational, it has increasingly determined our lives and impinged on our consciousness (Mandel, 1968, 406-19). In the more recent past the trend has been to so diversify the product as to almost replace use value considerations by financial, exchange value ones, and multinationals have become conglomerates (Bluestone and Harrison, 1982, 124-6). This has been accompanied by the shift of industry to areas of lower cost, either wage or tax (Adam in Radice, 1975, 89-103; Crouch and Wheelwright, 1982, 102-8; Levinson, 1978, Part 1, Chapters 3 and 4). This whole process has been accompanied by shifts between sectors of the economy which also require educational evaluation. Manufacture has declined as a percentage of the economically active population from perhaps 35 per cent to 25 per cent and less while commerce and services have grown from 10 per cent and 12 per cent respectively to 16 per cent and 35 per cent. Agriculture has shrunk the most, from 25 per cent to 6 per cent (McHale, 1972, 45). Yet sections of the political left continue to talk as if the majority of the population was still the industrial working class!

While the manufacturing sector of late capitalist economies has declined there has been a spectacular growth in what has come to be known as the military-industrial complex. The links between industry and war have been strong from the beginning but the development of nuclear weapons and research and development of chemical and biological warfare has taken things to a new stage. The complex involves a heterogeneous network of institutions. In addition to the obvious army, naval and airforce establishments, there are units like the Army Medical Research Institute of Infectious Diseases at Fort Detrick, USA, (Harris and Paxman, 1982, 222) and the chemical and biological research units at Porton Down, UK (Harris and Paxman, various). The industrial arm of this complex includes both government-owned munitions factories, like the famous Woolwich Arsenal in London, and private companies with such well-known names as Vickers-Armstrong, Douglas Aircraft Co., General Electric, Dow Chemicals (Hersh, 1968, 250, 254) or the Mitsubishi group in Japan (Halliday and McCormack, 1973, 109-18). Employed by both of these arms are many of the world's famous, and other less famous, educational institutions. In 1966, for example, the Pentagon listed no less than 57 US universities and their affiliated non-profit research units among the top 500 defence research contractors. The temptation such contracts offer is clear when one reads how Johns Hopkins University received more than $50 million and the University of Pennsylvania, fourteenth on the list, $5.9 million (Hersh, 219). The other countries of late capitalism could tell a similar story.

The educational implications of this vast military-industrial complex are manifold. On the moral-political level there is the awesome threat of a blunting of human feeling. Numerous witnesses testify that this occurs. Henry Nash describes how the bureaucratic sub-division of labour in the Department of Defense where he once worked as an intelligence analyst splintered the work and hence the feeling of responsibility. He and his colleagues, he recalls, 'never experienced guilt or self-criticism' and remained steadfastly insensitive to their work's 'homicidal implications' (Thompson and Smith, 1980, 63; cf. Hersh, 262). On the other hand, there are heartening signs that human variety can withstand such influences and even react against them. Prominent scientists who had worked on the first atomic bombs later campaigned strongly against nuclear weapons: Szilard, Bohr, Einstein and Rotblat (Cox, 1981, 26-7, 196-7). Even army generals, better known for retiring to join defence-related industries as advisors (Halliday and McCormack, 108) are today speaking up on peace platforms around the world.

On the level of knowledge creation the military-industrial complex should be considered as a significant factor in biasing the process of research and discovery. Research that could be devoted to health goes into ways of propagating ill-health: bacteriological and chemical warfare. Energy, the basis of life, becomes nuclear fission and fusion, the development of which threatens to gradually destroy all life when nuclear war does not accomplish the task more quickly. Research which could improve our food supply goes instead into defoliants, pesticides and other means of destruction whose disastrous consequences are hardly considered by those influenced by an armaments' ideology. Transport and communications, the latter the archetype of contemporary capitalism, are heavily geared to war.[4] A feature of this question is the proportion of trained human power which is involved, a difficult matter to estimate. One estimate, in a UNESCO-Pugwash symposium publication, suggested that worldwide 'something like 40% of all research and development is undertaken for military ends' (Robin Clarke in *New Scientist*, 27.1.83).

This last has a significant effect on job training and selection, particularly in the fields of the natural sciences. The ambitious learn early that military related research is the area where jobs are to be had, and, moreover, jobs where money for equipment is no object. To those interested in the use and development of complex technology this must be a great temptation. At the same time one should not ignore the side effect which this state of affairs has on the development of a critical mind. It is hardly hidden that an interest in certain kinds of literature, contact with certain ideas, is regarded by the employers of the military-industrial complex as suspect and that a security clearance is necessary for these desirable jobs. The effect this has on the development of knowledge cannot be without significance.

Finally on this point, what of the effect on the wider public? There is certainly evidence in recent years of considerable awareness of these questions and activities to change the situation (to be discussed in Chapter 11 under the heading The Peace Movement). But it seems more likely that still a majority of people learn a feeling of helplessness and distrust. Rather than participating in public affairs people turn inwards and cultivate their private affairs.

A different aspect of late capitalism is the growth of agri-businesses. Centred in the major capitalist countries they spread out through the Third World, creating a world market in agricultural products, and with it malnutrition and unemployment in many countries. Leaving aside the moral-political education questions of a neo-imperialist nature, and looking for a mainly metropolitan direction for the moment, what are the educational issues? Considered in connection with the fast food and related industries these are numerous. Some involve the creation of knowledge, especially of nutrition, but also of the long-term effects of various additives. Others are questions of the distribution of knowledge, from the dangers of interfering with the world's stock of genes in the efforts of agribusinesses to standardise and control ownership over human resources, to the destruction of the flavours of fruits and vegetables in the process of standardisation for convenience of packaging. Health *is* an educational matter!

One educational aspect of capitalism about which a number of writers have written is that of *deskilling*. Marx himself drew attention in *Capital* to the way in which the worker in manufacture is mutilated and turned into 'a fragment of himself', while in large-scale industry he or she is converted into 'a living appendage of the machine' (*CAP*, 1, 482, 614). Harry Braverman addressed the question again in his *Labour and Monopoly Capital: The Degradation of Work in the Twentieth Century* (1974). In the course of examining the relations between labour and management, the recent scientific-technological revolution and changes in the labour market, he paid particular attention to the movement begun by F.W. Taylor (1856-1915). Chief engineer of a large steel company and eventually president of the American Society of Mechanical Engineers, Taylor published his influential *Principles of Scientific Management* in 1911. These can be summarised as follows (Taylor's own words are cited from Braverman; summary in Clegg and Dunkerley, 1980, 91):

1. The principle of dissociation of the labour process from the skills of the workers. 'The managers assume ... the burden of gathering together all the traditional knowledge which in the past has been possessed by the workmen and then of classifying, tabulating, and reducing this knowledge to rules, laws, and formulae ...' (Braverman, 112).
2. The principle of the separation of conception from execution. 'All possible brain work should be removed from the shop and centered in the planning or lay-out department' (Braverman, 113).
3. The principle of the use of monopoly over knowledge to control each step of the labour process and its mode of execution. 'Perhaps the most prominent single element in modern scientific management is the task idea ... This task specifies not only what is done, but how it is to be done and the exact time allowed for doing it ... Scientific management consists very largely in preparing for the carrying out these tasks' (Braverman, 118).

Widespread application by industry of these principles has resulted in what has come to be called deskilling. It is important to note that this concept is not a static one, but, as Zimbalist stresses, 'historical and dynamic' (1979, XV). It is 'a long-run tendency' for a loss of craft skills and traditional abilities to occur through job 'fragmentation, rationalisation and mechanization'. As Clawson notes, this process is often strongly resisted by the workers (1980, 204; Zimbalist, 294-7), to such an extent that there have been attempts by some managements to adopt schemes of 'job enrichment' (see job satisfaction in Jones, 1976). The whole question requires much further study.

Accompanying the practice of 'scientific management' is an ideology of efficiency which affects education in various deleterious ways. This we must return to in more detail below. Here it is only necessary to note its presence and that it is intimately bound up with the trend from emphasis on production to finance, to extreme abstraction, where human needs and social considerations are left behind in the concentration on pure profit.

To end this section on late capitalism something must be said about that much-used concept *bureaucracy*. Marx himself drew attention to the main features of bureaucracy in 1843 in his *Contribution to the Critique of Hegel's Philosophy of Law* (*CW*, 3, 44-54). But modern theory derives rather from Max Weber (Gerth and Wright Mills, 1970, 196-244). Whatever one may decide about the efficacy of the concept as a theory of technical rationality for our understanding of the workings of organisations, and here the work by Clegg and Dunkerley should be consulted (1980), as a description of their structure it is important. It certainly serves as a contrast both with models of autocratic power and of grassroots democracy to which many aspire today, but perhaps more at the level of rhetoric rather than science (cf. Clegg and Dunkerley, 1980, 137-70). We will return to these questions below. To end here let us look at Max Weber's propositions reformulated by Albrow. According to him bureaucracy has the following characteristics:

1. The staff members are personally free, observing only the impersonal duties of their offices.
2. There is a hierarchy of offices.
3. The functions of the offices are clearly specified.
4. Officials are appointed on the basis of a contract.
5. They are selected on the basis of a professional qualification, ideally substantiated by a diploma gained through examination.
6. They have a money salary, and usually pension right. The salary is graded according to position in the hierarchy. The

official can always leave the post, and, under certain circumstances, it may also be terminated.

7. The official's post is his sole or major occupation.

8. There is a career structure and promotion is possible either
by seniority or merit, and according to the judgement of
superiors.

9. The official may appropriate neither the post nor the
resources which go with it.

10. He is subject to a unified control and disciplinary system.
(Albrow, 1970, cit. Clegg and Dunkerley, 1980, 79-80)

These then are the characteristics of late capitalism which must
be recognised if education is to be understood in today's world. As
in Marx's day, a system of hidden exploitation, it is both richer and
more thoroughly permeated by the values and practice of the
pursuit of profit. Sectors which previously had moved according
to older values have been drawn into the sphere of commodities
and exchange value and while accreditation, certification and
schooling have enormously increased, whether education in the
sense of the pursuit of enlightenment has is an open question.

Notes

1. The editorials of _Monthly Review_ are a ready source for a marxist analysis
of current economic problems.

2. Book publishing is a case in point. Before the Second World War many
firms were content with a modest profit and would make a loss on such things as
poetry if it could be covered by profits on other books. Increasingly every book is
expected to make the standard profit and 'frills' are cut. In the contemporary,
increasingly business-modelled university cost-accounting takes precedence over
study (use value). A teacher wishing to help a higher degree student in a different
department must be financially compensated for by transfer between departments.
Increasingly the viability of teaching classes is judged in terms of numbers and
finance rather than on educational need.

3. For an account of this colonial expansion see Barratt Brown (1970, 86-95),
Mandel (1968, Chapter 13) and Stavrianos (1981, Chapter 13). For a
contemporary discussion of imperialism see Owen and Sutcliffe (1972).

4. McNeill, commenting on the US National Aeronautics and Space
Administration (NASA), remarked: 'new technologies allowing men and machines
to move about in space always had military implications and application. This made
the separation of military from civilian research and development of space
technology almost meaningless' (1982, 369).

PART TWO: EDUCATION AS CONTENT

3 EDUCATION AS CONTENT

In this part I shall focus on education as that which is or can be learnt, as the content of the educational process. Most of what I shall say will be about *knowledge*, the cognitive aspect of content. A more thorough study than can be attempted here would have to give more attention to the emotive, feeling side of what is learnt. It is clear that attitudes and interests, in the sense of engaged attention and curiosity, play a major role in human learning. Themselves learnt, in the form of motivations they condition the learning of other things. However, since attitudes and interests cannot be separated from the things towards which they are directed, whether these be exercising a skill or considering some area of knowledge, little more than noting their importance can be said under 'content'. Approach must rather be through a study of the learning-teaching process.

Beginning with the discussion of how knowledge has been classified and organised I shall go on to consider its creation and distribution. Marx's distinction between true knowledge or science and ideology will be evaluated against other ways of conceptualising knowledge. The touchstone will again be the kind of knowledge necessary for emancipation and that conscious choice which for Marx would be human freedom.

Classifying Knowledge

Consideration of the way in which knowledge is classified can serve to illuminate the problems of specialisation and the fragmentation of knowledge which, certainly among the highly schooled, divide, isolate and weaken. Understanding of the relationships between the different areas of knowledge could help to give a sense of the totality and a control which seems to be sadly lacking today.[1] These questions have not gone unrecognised. C.P. Snow added a new term to our cocktail-party jargon with the publication of *The Two Cultures and the Scientific Revolution* in 1959. It became popular to characterise the natural scientists as illiterate and those who had studied the humanities as innumerate.

41

That argument can be followed back through A.N. Whitehead, Matthew Arnold and T.H. Huxley. On another plane of argument there has been the dispute about the social versus the natural sciences, and between history and the social sciences.[2] On another level again there was the revolt of students in the late sixties and through the early seventies which has challenged the nature of the content of their schooling. In 1968 the students at Nanterre, France, questioned the nature of social psychology (Cohn-Bendit, 1969, 30-1). In other cases the criticisms came from established academics.[3] In these last the criticism moved from the level of the totality to internal criticisms of the content of particular disciplines.[4]

The major sociologists have in various ways all been concerned with the way knowledge is organised. Karl Mannheim made a classification of types of knowledge, that based on scientific criteria being true knowledge. Religions, philosophy and certain other forms of knowledge he saw as relatives to classes. He divided sets of ideas according to whether they served the interests of the privileged or under-privileged groups in society. The former he termed *ideologies*, the latter, with their future orientation, *utopias* (Mitchell, 1973, 113). Durkheim, Levy-Bruhl and Max Scheler in their different ways related types of knowledge to their particular view of the social framework (Gurvitch, 1971, 4-7). Combined in these writings are questions relating to the distribution of knowledge and to a value hierarchy of types of knowledge. Scheler, for example, while recognising a 'plurality of types of knowledge' ended up supporting a traditional European value hierarchy 'crowned by theological knowledge, followed closely by philosophical knowledge' (Gurvitch, 6). Alfred Schuetz, by contrast, placed emphasis on the individuals' learnings in the 'everyday life-world', that 'province of reality which the wide-awake and normal adult simply takes for granted in the attitude of common-sense' (Schuetz and Luckmann, 1973, 3). Knowledge is divided into such areas as skills, useful knowledge and knowledge of recipes (107). In addition to such 'knowledge relevant for "everyone"' the social stock of knowledge contains knowledge which is differentiated and role-specific (299-301). Thus the field of discussion is broadened and the basis is laid for a more adequate discussion of the distribution and functions of knowledge.

Georges Gurvitch asks some interesting questions and sets out a framework for studying the sociology of knowledge. While he is right to believe that this cannot serve 'to invalidate false knowledge, "demystify" it, or "disalienate" it, as Marx wanted to do' (1971, 12), he does provide a comprehensive approach which could assist towards that process, especially where 'false knowledge' means knowledge reflecting class interests. Gurvitch sees the main task of such a sociology of knowledge as establishing the functional correlations between different types of knowledge and different social categories ('global societies, social classes, particular groupings'[16]). In addition he sees it as having other tasks. It should study: (a) the relationship between the hierarchy of types of knowledge and the hierarchy of other cultural products; (b) the role of knowledge and its agents in the various types of societies; (c) the different modes of expression, communication and diffusion of knowledge, and how these are related to various social subjects; (d) the tendency of various types of knowledge to become either differentiated or combined; and (e) cases where there is a disjunction between the social frameworks and the different types of knowledge (17).

Gurvitch sees philosophical and scientific knowledge as 'relatively most detached from social frameworks' (13), a view which Marx would lead us to qualify, perhaps, depending on how one interpreted 'most'. His other five categories of knowledge he sees as 'most deeply involved in social reality and the network of its structures' and therefore the major object of a sociology of knowledge. He distinguishes *types* of knowledge from *forms* of knowledge. The former are:

1. Perceptual knowledge of the external world;
2. Knowledge of the Other, the We, groups, classes and societies;
3. Common sense knowledge, often called 'knowledge of everyday life';
4. Technical knowledge — not the same as 'political science', etc.;
5. Scientific knowledge;
6. Philosophical knowledge (23-36).

The forms of knowledge can be conceived as cross-cutting the above types in a three-dimensional grid;

1. Mystical knowledge and rational knowledge;

2. Empirical knowledge and conceptual knowledge;
3. Positive knowledge and speculative knowledge;
4. Symbolic knowledge and concrete knowledge;
5. Collective knowledge and individual knowledge (37).

We will return to Gurvitch's work in the section below on distribution of knowledge. Here let us turn to another writer who sets out to cover 'anything that is known by somebody and . . . any activity by which someone learns of something he or she has not known before, even if others have' (Machlup, 1980,7). Machlup's purpose is to provide 'statistical estimates of the costs incurred by society in the production and distribution' of knowledge (1980, 74). For us his classification is a reminder of areas of knowledge neglected by the more academically restricted scholars, e.g. 'small-talk and pastime knowledge'.[5] It may be that it is in this area of knowledge we should search for aspects of ideology potent in supporting capitalism. Certainly it is here one should look for the education of the feelings, e.g. by games and sports.

In introducing his classification of knowledge Machlup says he believes in a subjective classification, one based on '*who* knows and *why* and *what for*' rather than one based on '*what* is known' (1962, 21). He gives as example a knowledge of economics which 'is instrumental knowledge for me as economic consultant, but purely intellectual knowledge for the physicist'. I have doubts about a classification, but none at all about the need to ask just such questions. Machlup is also right to draw attention to the distinction between 'living knowledge', the knowledge which is actually 'stored in the head of an individual' compared with that which is stored 'on the shelves of their national libraries' (1980, 167). He asks the interesting question whether:

> if knowledge of the multiplication table is successfully transmitted to an additional five million people, does this represent more or less growth in the stock of knowledge in society than if knowledge of gene-splitting and recombinant DNA is transferred to an additional five hundred people? (1980, 169)

He contrasts the spending of money on space research, 'generating knowledge accessible to very few', with money for remedial teaching, but can offer little more than 'raising questions and pondering the difficulties' (1980, 169-70). Perhaps his problem is that his aim is to measure in quantitative terms what are really qualitative matters requiring other criteria for judgement. But that he raises these questions in such a context is surely significant.

One might have hoped, with the promising title *Knowledge and Human Interests*. Habermas, conscious heir to the Frankfurt School, would have contributed something useful to these discussions. His division of knowledge at first looks promising. He sees empirical-analytic knowledge linked with work or instrumental action grounded in technical interest (advantage). By contrast, historical-hermeneutic knowledge, linked with interaction, is grounded in practical interest. Only critical knowledge, linked with power, with the asymmetrical relations of constraint and dependency, is grounded in the emancipatory interest. Unfortunately this neat division cannot be sustained. As Held has argued, Habermas's distinction between work and interaction is not a clear one and therefore the 'distinctions between types of "action and interest structure" become equally questionable' (Held, 1980, 392). Mary Hesse has noted that 'many theories enlarge our pragmatic knowledge (for example, about fossils or quasars) without necessarily forming the basis of technology' (Held, 393). In addition, the distinction between the empirical-analytic and the historico-hermeneutic sciences, between the 'verification of lawlike hypotheses' and 'the interpretation of texts' (Habermas, 1972, 309) is questionable, as Held, following Giddens, shows (Held, 392). Giddens comments:

> it is a clear implication of writings such as those of Kuhn, which claim that scientific development involves a discontinuous series of paradigms, that hermeneutic problems are as basic to science as to more sedimented 'traditions'. Science is certainly as much about 'interpretations' as 'nomological [lawful] explanations'. (Giddens, 1977, 149)

While having reservations on Kuhn as an authority (cf. Gaukroger, 1978, 4-7) there is no question about Giddens's final sentence. Moreover, separation of the technical and the practical is precisely what needs to be overcome in our present situation when high technology threatens us so direly. While there is no doubt that interests and knowledge are linked, one can only conclude that Habermas's approach is too abstract to be helpful.

What is helpful in the approaches of Schuetz, Gurvitch and

Machlup is their broadening of the scope of knowledge considered, the insertion into our discussions of the 'everyday life-
world', common sense knowledge, and the knowledge embodied in
'small-talk and pastimes'. If we are to change our world in the
democratic direction envisaged by Marx the content of this knowledge must be understood and changed. Recognising that this is
essentially a practical question, what then of theory? Surely a
sound classification of knowledge would help to distinguish
between ideology and true knowledge (science). Would it not also
help if we could develop the conception of knowledge stratified
according to levels of organisation of matter, that concept
mentioned above in the discussion of dialectics?[6]

The Problem of Abstraction

In the first section of *The German Ideology* Marx and Engels
hailed the division of 'material and mental labour' for enabling
thought to '*really* represent something without representing something real' and to 'proceed to the formation of "pure" theory'
(*CW*, 5, 44-5). At the same time they were aware that this
advance was limited by its occurrence in a class divided society.
Writing much later, in *Theories of Surplus Value*, on the French
economist and politician, Necker, Marx commented that knowledge and labour had become separated. Knowledge 'confronts the
latter as capital, or as a luxury article for the rich'. He goes on to
cite Necker himself, a sentence penned in 1784! 'Lastly, is it not
certain that this inequality of knowledge has become necessary for
the maintenance of all the social inequalities *which gave rise to it*?'
(*TSV*, 1, 307; cf. Draper, 1978, 2, 488).

The problem is more than simply wanting to abolish the division
of hand and brain, as it is often called. That wish Marx and Engels
shared with the utopians before them, Fourier and Owen. The
problem is also one of the degree of abstraction and its applica-
bility to particular types of problems. This was most clearly raised
in the writings of Alfred Sohn-Rethel.

Sohn-Rethel writes about those peculiarly pure abstractions
characteristic of mathematics, concepts like point and line. These,
he argues, arose, not from some special quality of mind, but rather
from the peculiar nature of commodity exchange and its tangible
form, money.

[The] constituent elements of the exchange abstraction unmistakably resemble the conceptual elements of the cognitive faculty emerging with the growth of commodity production. As conceptual elements these forms are principles of thought basic to Greek philosophy as well as to modern natural science. (Sohn-Rethel, 1978a, 6-7)

Following Marx's analysis of money and commodity exchange Sohn-Rethel comments that this concrete object is at the same time abstract, universally exchangeable against all other commodities (1978b, 125). Though its concrete form may change its value remains, unchanging and guaranteed. 'Anybody who carries coins in his pocket and understands their functions bears in his mind, whether or not he is aware of it, ideas which, no matter how hazily, reflect the postulates of the exchange abstraction' (Sohn-Rethel, 1978a, 591). Money also possesses the qualities of durability, divisibility, mobility and immutability, thus perhaps contributing to the mathematical nature of the scientific abstractions (1978a, 58). The proof that 'the real abstraction operating in exchange engenders the ideal abstraction basic to Greek philosophy and to modern science' (1978a, 28) lies in the coincidence of these two phenomena in Greece at the turn of the seventh century BC (1978a, 67). George Thomson draws similar conclusions:

In early Greek philosophy we see this 'false consciousness' gradually emerging and imposing on the world categories of thought derived from commodity production, as though these categories belonged, not to society, but to nature. The Parmenidean One, together with the later idea of 'substance', may therefore be described as a reflex or projection of the substance of exchange value. (Thomson, 1955, 301; cf. note by Tomberg in Ullrich, 1979, 90)

Whatever the case of historical origin is, and here the case of China needs consideration, there is no doubt about the similarity of the real-abstract, money, and the high abstractions of mathematics. Nor can there be doubt about the need to consider carefully the function of such high abstractions, compared with lower-level ones, in our explanations of the world. On this let us look at the ideas of some other writers.

The French physicist, Pierre Duhem (1861-1916), writing on *The Aim and Structure of Physical Theory* (1962), and building on the ideas of Ernst Mach (39) and Macquorn Rankine (52), distinguishes between two kinds of thinking: *abstraction* and *imagination*. These he links with the French and the English respectively and he is at pains to stress the superiority of the former (64)! Abstractions, he emphasises, are representations serving 'to classify laws' (32) and are *not* designed as explanations (32, 39). He writes:

> It is not to this explanatory part that theory owes its power and fertility; far from it. Everything good in the theory, by virtue of which it appears as a natural classification and confers on it the power to anticipate experience, is found in the representative part ... (32)

As examples of abstraction he gives 'the notions of number, line, surface, angle, mass, force, and pressure (62), precisely those high abstractions about which Sohn-Rethel writes. He joins these with the powers of reason, especially deduction, and cites Euclid's *Elements* and Archimedes' writings on the lever and floating bodies (63).

The imaginative or hypothetical way of thinking operates by way of models and analogies with 'some other class of objects or phenomena whose laws are already known' (53). The examples Duhem chooses (70) are out of date, but the comments he makes on the inferiority of the use by imaginative thinkers of 'numbers furnished by measurement' and their manipulation 'according to the fixed rules of algebra' (63) is interesting. The objection here is not to classical algebra, but to what Duhem calls symbolic algebra (76). He applauds the expression of laws in different physical fields by indistinguishable 'groups of equations' as a means of making fresh discoveries (96-7). But what is suggestive here is the relation between geometry and algebra, discussed by Joseph Needham in connection with the difference between Greek and Chinese mathematics and the rise of modern science in Europe. Needham writes: 'Greek geometry deals with pure and abstract figures, the size of which was quite immaterial once the axioms and postulates had been accepted ... But the Chinese preferred to think only of concrete numbers (though, as in algebra, they might not be any particular number)' (Needham, 1954, 2, 156). Discussing the birth of the experimental-mathematical method, 'which appeared in almost perfect form in Galileo', Needham notes the quintessential 'application of algebraic methods to the geometric field', but he adds: 'this geometry was not just geometry as such, but the logical deductive geometry of Greece. The Chinese had always considered geometrical problems algebraically, but that was not the same thing' (Needham, 1954, 3, 156). The focus here is on the historical, whereas what I am looking for is discussion in terms of epistemology and education. While this has so far not been attempted, further stimulus is provided by another distinction discussed by several writers, that between 'artisan' and 'scientific' thinking. Sohn-Rethel describes the way of thinking of the former as limited to 'practical "know-how"' and 'the expertise of his hands' unaided by 'abstract knowledge', i.e. of the pure-type abstractions I have been discussing. It is, he says, 'knowledge of how one *does*, not of how one *explains* things'. He goes on: 'This practical knowledge can be conveyed by demonstration, repetition of words, depending on practical understanding of the task involved. Cookery books are a clear example' (Sohn-Rethel, 1978a, 112). Such was the pre-Greek mathematics, the 'art of the rope', tied to the moment of use and the particular location (101). By contrast Greek geometry: 'became something quite different from the measurement itself. The manual operation became subordinated to an act of pure thought which was directed solely towards grasping quantitative laws of numbers or of abstract space' (102).

The abstract concept to which Sohn-Rethel devotes most space is that of *inertia.* As he comments:

> Inertial motion such as Galileo applies in his research is in empty space and strictly rectilinear, which makes it unmistakably non-empirical. Space, empty of air, is no object of perception in the terrestrial sphere, and in outer space, where we may claim to see it, none of the observable phenomena moves in rectilinear but all in orbital fashion. (125-6)

He goes on to stress the parallel with the 'absolutely abstract' yet real movements of money and capital in the market, and to make the significant point that by the time of Galileo exchange processes were beginning to move from the sphere of commodities into that of production (128-9). With the growth of modern capitalism so too grew modern science. The division of head and hand was increased by 'the inroad of mathematics' into more and more human activities (113). Knowledge became dominated by 'this socialised mind of man' which was: 'money without its material attachment, therefore immaterial and no longer recognisable as money, and indeed, no longer being money but the "pure intellect"' (130).

The question of the relation of artisan thinking and modern science is often posed in terms of theory and practice. Needham and Bernal have both put it in these terms. The former commented that: 'Perhaps the Galilean innovation may best be described as the marriage of craft practice with scholarly theory' (Needham, 1954, 3, 159). Bernal, discussing Galileo, notes that his experiments were, in contrast to those of thirteenth-century scholars, 'exploratory rather than illustrative' and that Galileo questioned his own theories when experiments gave unexpected results (Bernal, 1965, 2, 433). Bernal stresses the complex interrelations of the social and technical:

> The same period — 1450-1690 — that saw the development of capitalism as the leading method of production also witnessed that of experiment and calculation as the new method of natural science. The transformation was a complex one; changes in techniques led to science, and science in turn was to lead to new and more rapid changes in technique.

> Up to the end of the seventeenth-century science had far more to *gain* from its renewed contacts with practical work than it had to *give* in the way of radical improvements in technique. (Bernal, 2, 373, 375)

Both writers give numerous examples of this fruitful interplay. To note only one example: the mechanical clock and the trade of the clockmaker. Needham writes: 'The clock is the earliest and the most important of complex scientific machines. Its influence upon the world-outlook of developing modern science was incalculable' (Needham, 1954, 4(2), 435, 545-6).

Bernal agrees: 'the rare trade of clockmaker . . . was in the Renaissance to become for science what the millwright was to be for industry' (Bernal, 1, 317).

It might be noted that the knowledge of the artisans, ancient and modern, is of intractable materials (wood, clay and metal ores) and the design of ships or carts whose complexity until recently defied scientific analysis (Needham, 1954, 4(2), 47-50).

Natural Science and the Marxian Vision

Science, in the English, limited sense of the natural sciences, has changed for many people in the course of the past 30 years from a means of enlightenment and hope to the expression of all that threatens us and is wrong with the world. In 1947 a group of young British scientists could write:

> Science offers means to use unprecedented powers with which a finer, more beautiful and happier world than ever before can be built. With mankind using a vigorously developing science for social ends, the future can be bright and inspiring. (*Science and the Nation*, 249)

J.D. Bernal, himself a major contributor to both the theory and practice of science, writing in a 'quickly-written' book in 1958: 'felt it was necessary to bring together the dark and the bright side of the new power that science has given to mankind' (Bernal, 1958, ix). In what is now an interestingly dated book he wrestled with the political and scientific-technical problems of a *World without War*. But his view of science remained that it was fundamentally a neutral tool distorted more in the use to which it was put than in its 'general theories' (Bernal, 1965, 1, 50).[7] His own solution was the better organisation and use of science rather than exploring its intrinsic nature. Among the first to lift discussion on to its present level was Herbert Marcuse. Already in 1964, in the section of *One-dimensional Man* subtitled 'technological rationality and the logic of domination', he raises the problems of the emphasis in science on quantification and over-abstraction; a rationality for the domination of nature by man being turned towards the domination of man by man (130-5); and the possibilities for the development of an essentially different science (136). But for a long time his was a lone voice. Sohn-Rethel was not published.[8] Followers of the hippy and counter-culture movements, while accepting Marcuse's opposition to capitalism, were not listening to his deeper message and rejected the skills which would have allowed them to follow his argument. Roszak, author of *The Making of a Counter-culture* (1968) and *Where the Waste-land Ends* (1973), rejecting the forms of capitalist society, swept science aside in favour of 'liberating consciousness' through espousing 'the dream, the myth, the visionary rapture, the sacramental sense of reality, the transcendent symbol' (Roszak, 1973, 379, cit. in Irvine *et al.*, 1979, 341).[9] Clouds of cannabis floated through university student unions. Renouncing thought in favour of feeling, 'intellectuals' rejected the intellect!

The fear of the mathematical, of course, goes back much further than the counter-culture and hippy movements. Ullrich notes a history from Hegel to Bloch. Commonly the fear was that 'the "abstract", quantitative mathematics forces the processes of Nature into laws external to it' (Ullrich, 1979, 410). While criticisms have come from the highly numerate, such as Lancelot Hogben,[10] a majority of critics could be classed as innumerates. On Mao Zedong's criterion of 'no investigation, no right to speak' they should stay silent (Mao, *SW*, 3, 13, 23). Hogben, in 1956, writing of the: 'feverish concern of biologists, sociologists and civil servants to exploit the newest and most sophisticated statistical devices with little concern for their mathematical credentials or for the formal assumptions inherent therein', went on to say:

> This state of affairs would be more alarming as indicative of the capitulation of the scientific spirit to the authoritarian temper of our times, if it were easy to assemble in one room three theoretical statisticians who agree about the fundamentals of their speciality at the most elementary level. (Hogben, 1963, 94)[11]

Problems abound on different levels of abstraction. They have been nicely put by Robert Young:

> The status of scientific abstraction and quantification has been gained largely at the expense of open debate about the competing values and value systems which underlie alternative forms of social relations. Once again, quantification is not the same as reductionism. In principle, it leaves as rich a list of phenomena as you like and makes no claim to explain the more complex in terms of the simpler, the more mechanical or material. But it can be impoverishing, even when not in tandem with reductionism, though the impoverishment is of a different

sort: closure of *qualitative debate.* In effect, it depoliticises whenever qualitative and evaluative aspects are made less prominent than the numerical representation. (Irvine *et al.*, 71, emphasis added)

Returning for a moment to Sohn-Rethel, he opens up new ground but is unable to sustain it. Instead he speaks vaguely, agreeing with Ernest Bloch that we must 'aim to establish "an alliance of society with nature"'. He states emphatically that this cannot be done 'by dispensing with science', but demands a science backed by 'the unity of mental and manual work' (Sohn-Rethel, 1978a, 181). He adds that such a science 'is methodologically the same as the science in capitalism' (183), a view contradicted, among others, by Ullrich (462). However, at the same time certain properties which today characterise science as 'bourgeois' must be 'counteracted'. But Sohn-Rethel does not go further than to say these are associated with the connection of the 'basic categories of science' with 'the second nature', i.e. the realm of the exchange abstraction, and are thus 'totally alienated from the qualitative realities of the first nature' or realm of use values (183, cf. 28). He sees socialism as able to counteract the bourgeois properties of science in that its essential feature is 'that the people as direct procedures must be the controlling masters of both the material and intellectual means of production, and that they act in concert to establish their prosperity within nature in its global unity' (194). But this is little more than an expression of faith. As Ullrich, who makes a sympathetic criticism of Sohn-Rethel's ideas points out (91-7), it is necessary to specify quite exactly the mechanisms of domination within scientific theory (95). He also warns against reducing all the problems to the sphere of commodity circulation and neglecting that of production (92, 93). He formulates a number of questions bearing on his own problematic of technology as domination which are connected with the approach of Sohn-Rethel. Since the problematic is so important and still so poorly explored I shall cite them in full here:

1. How can the genesis of concepts of 'pure reason' and thus the elements of science (wissenschaft) be explained materialistically: (a) Historically-materialistically, through what social formation? (b) What role then does commodity circulation play? (c) Which other factors, e.g. phylogenetic, come in?

2. Assuming the historical analysis proves science does not arise in material production: (a) What significance has this for material production? (b) Is this science necessarily anti-production? When yes, in what measure and in what aspects? (c) What characteristics make this production-remote science into a medium of domination (Herrschaftsmedium)? (d) Does the class character of science only express itself in the fact that it arose in connection with appropriation and thus made possible the essential separation of the work of head and hand? (e) Or does it then have additional structural features which enter into science itself, which through their application strengthen the separation of head and hand now, as it were, 'factually justified' (sachgerecht)?
3. How does capitalism integrate the anti-production science in its means of production?
4. Which features of capitalist-scientific production stem from science and which from the logic of capitalism?
5. It is transcendence of the separation of the work of head and hand possible with the retention of scientific technology? (a) Or is — alongside a change in the relations of production — also a 'new technology', an 'other logic' necessary? (b) When no, does technology change through an 'other use' of 'its' logic? (Ullrich, 95-6)

Leaving aside the problem of a future science in which mathematics may be better and more widely understood, brought down from its throne to serve as a fellow worker, it remains to be asked in quite concrete terms what are the kinds of abstractions which ordinary people will need to make if they are to govern themselves. Rudolf Bahro, struggling, unsuccessfully, to handle such questions in a critique of the 'real existing socialism' of East Germany, speaks of decisions about the proportion to be devoted to accumulation and consumption, between building homes and building monuments, or between expenditure on education and expenditure on the propagandist self-portrayal of the power structure (Bahro, 1978, 151-2). In making choices like these it is questionable to what extent high-level abstraction is involved. Clearly these decisions begin and end in the qualitative world in which low-level abstraction is required. Bahro, and to date few others, see it in those terms, and that is part of the problem. Clarity on the nature of abstraction and its role in the scientific process is one requirement for solving the educational problems involved in Marx's vision of a human future.

The Concept of Culture

A concept which could help, not to explain the links between ideas and action, but to make clearer the complexities, is one not present in the writings of Marx and Engels themselves. This is the modern use of the word *culture*. Originally used, as Raymond Williams points out, as 'a noun of process' denoting the culture or culti-vation of crops, animals or the human mind (Williams, 1977, 13), in the eighteenth and nineteenth centuries culture was linked with the term *civilisation*, implying an Enlightenment sense of 'histori-cal process and progress' and an 'achieved condition of refinement and order' (Williams, 13, cf. Merquior, 1979, 42). It is in this sense that Marx uses it in his criticism of an early form of communism in the 1844 Manuscripts:

> How little this annulment of private property is really an appro-priation is in fact proved by the abstract negation of the entire world of culture and civilisation, the regression to the *unnatural* simplicity of the *poor* and crude man who has few needs and who has not only failed to go beyond private property, but has not yet even reached it. (*CW*, 3, 295)

Engels, a year later, was using formulations in need of the term in its modern form when referring to the working class. In his book, *The Condition of the Working-class in England* he spoke of it as 'a race wholly apart from the English bourgeoisie' and went on to say: 'The workers speak other dialects, have other thoughts and ideals, other customs and moral principles, a different religion and other politics . . .' (*CW*, 4, 419-20) But before the label *culture* could be firmly attached to such a concept cluster it had to break, and that break is not yet complete, with the concept of 'refine-ment' and 'the arts' (Williams, 19). For our purpose culture should be seen as a complex of ideas and actions, of beliefs and values, true knowledge and ideology, of symbols and rituals.[12] It assumes that groups make their own cultures rather than have them thrust upon them, which is not to say that this is a conscious process. In other words, culture is 'a constitutive social process' (Williams, 19). It also assumes with Paul Willis that:

> there are likely to be distinctions and contradictions between these forms, so that for instance, actions may belie words, or logics embedded within cultural practices and rituals may be quite different from particular expressed meanings at the level of immediate consciousness. (Willis, 1977, 172-3)

Such a concept of culture helps us to reflect on the interplay of individual and group and one group and another. It assumes a 'common sense' mixture of ideology and real knowledge (cf. the penetrations of Willis, 119-44) and enables us to enquire into it.[13] But a final note of warning: subcultures are historical like other social forms and one must be careful not to reify them, not to see them as fixed and stable.

Notes

1. It has been one of the positive features of the self-study of marxism in past decades, whether in the various communist parties or other socialist groups, that many have acquired a view of the totality of knowledge.
2. Useful entries into the literature are Krimerman (1969) and Therborn (1976). The Tuebingen Conference of the German Sociological Association in 1961 is represented by the collection of papers, Adorno, *et al.* (1976).
3. Examples are Gouldner (1971) and Robin Blackburn (1978).
4. Discipline here is used for the broad field as practised by a specialist; subject is used for that part of a discipline taught to students who may or may not aspire to become practitioners of the discipline itself.
5. Fritz Machlup wrote *The Production and Distribution of Knowledge in the United States* in 1962. By 1980 his project had expanded to envisage eight volumes and occupy 60 research assistants! Machlup's classification of knowledge is as follows:

1. Practical knowledge: useful in the knower's work, his decisions and actions; can be subdivided, according to his activities, into (a) professional knowledge; (b) business knowledge; (c) workman's knowledge; (d) political knowledge; (e) household knowledge; (f) other practical knowledge.
2. Intellectual knowledge: satisfying his intellectual curiosity, regarded as part of liberal education, humanistic and scientific learning, general culture; acquired, as a rule, in active concentration with an appreciation of the existence of open problems and cultural values.
3. Small-talk and pastime knowledge: satisfying the non-intellectual curiosity or his desire for light entertainment and emotional stimulation, including local gossip, news of crimes and accidents, light novels, stories, jokes, games, etc., acquired, as a rule, in passive relaxation from 'serious' pursuits; apt to dull his sensitiveness.

4. Spiritual knowledge: related to his religious knowledge of God and of the ways to the salvation of the soul.

5. Unwanted knowledge: outside his interests, usually accidentally acquired, aimlessly retained. (1980, 108; cf. 1962, 21-2)

It is interesting to notice the class and male sexist, if not ethnocentric bias of this scheme. That should not, however, prejudice its consideration.

6. A tentative scheme for such a hierarchy of levels is:

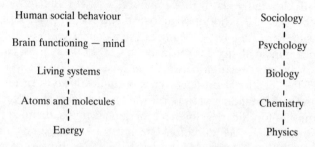

Human social behaviour	Sociology
Brain functioning — mind	Psychology
Living systems	Biology
Atoms and molecules	Chemistry
Energy	Physics

Clearly there is much to be developed at the upper end of this schema.

7. In this edition Bernal corrects his former acceptance of Soviet distinctions and distortions about 'bourgeois' and 'socialist' science; cf. the 1954 edition. At the same time he clearly states that science and class have been and are connected and that research on this 'needs to be continued and refined and will lead in the end to a far deeper understanding of science and society' (1965, 50-1). He also notes here the suspicion which ordinary working people have always had of science because of its 'identification ... with the governing and exploiting classes' (49).

8. Sohn-Rethel's manuscript was ready in 1951, he writes in the preface to *Intellectual and Manual Labour*, but 'despite strenuous efforts by [George] Thomson and Bernal, was turned down by the publishers Lawrence and Wishart as being too unorthodox for them, and by bourgeois publishers as being too militantly Marxist!' (xiv).

9. Griffiths, Irvine and Miles, in Irvine *et al.*, *Demystifying Social Statistics* (340-2) give a thoughtful summary of the anti-science movement and go on to sketch various alternative science movements.

10. Hogben is author of 'popular' works, *Mathematics for the Million* (1936), and *Chance and Choice by Cardpack and Chessboard* (1950).

11. The reader can obtain some help from a not easy book: Roy Weatherford, *Philosophical Foundations of Probability Theory*, and on another level, Irvine *et al.*, *Demystifying Social Statistics*.

12. This is both wider than the definition of Daniel Bell (1979, 12) and narrower than that of either Malinowski or Parsons (Merquior, 49).

13. There is a great need for someone to analyse the current use of the term 'multicultural' in places like Australia and Canada from the conceptual standpoint given here. In the academic industry which has grown up, not to mention the politicians, there would seem to be much that is ideological in the sense of partial interest. Which is not to dismiss the real problems and genuine interests which exist and need elucidation.

4 THE PRODUCTION OF KNOWLEDGE

Recent years have seen increasing numbers of studies of the production of knowledge, both in the natural sciences and the arts. Approaches have been both psychological and sociological, with a growing number of the latter. Many of them conceive of creativity as a special human ability. Surprisingly, in view of the marxist conception of the close relation between the social conditions and the nature of the ideational product, marxist studies have been few.[1] Yet greater understanding of how knowledge is produced is clearly a prerequisite for the development of any genuine democratic society. Inspired by Marx's vision one must ask what limits and what encourages, in what directions, the creative process. One must ask how to develop the creative powers already displayed by so many — in a society which seems so often to encourage passivity and consumption rather than production. And one is challenged to question the social value of much of the knowledge produced. In the following short survey I shall attempt to set out a framework for further studies.

The Scope of Knowledge

In the broadest consideration of education the definition of Machlup, with its inclusion of the most mundane 'small-talk and pastime knowledge', is helpful. He writes: 'by production of knowledge we understand any human (or human-induced) activity effectively designed to create, alter or confirm in a human mind — one's own or anyone else's — a meaningful apperception, awareness, cognizance, or consciousness of whatever it may be' (Machlup, 1962, 30). But production as I shall use it here refers to an initial production, not a reproduction process. Machlup appears to use 'production' in a double sense here which includes activities which belong to the dissemination or distribution of knowledge rather than the process of creation. These teaching processes I prefer to treat separately below.

The production of knowledge must result in some socially recognised product, whether in the form of words, a text, however short, or in the form of some more tangible object. Whitley noted that research which is unpublished is, generally speaking, 'research that has not been done with respect to the public system of science and hence cannot form part of the corpus of public knowledge' (in Knorr *et al.*, 316). In the arts, knowledge may take the form of a painting, sculpture, a piece of music or a film. It will embody some *idea* and in some meaning of that much-advertised word, something 'new'. In the sciences it will more typically be a contribution to theory, often accompanied by the accumulation of some experimental data. It may be a knowledge of *how* or a knowledge *that* something occurs. The production process may be an extended one involving conscious and unconscious processes, flashes of inspiration.[2]

The Production Process

While this process takes place in countries dominated by the capitalist mode of production it is part of trying to understand to distinguish where a production of knowledge fits firmly within the capitalist mode and where it remains outside it. Just as it is possible for economic activities typical of other modes of production to exist alongside the capitalist mode within a social formation, so is it possible for knowledge to be produced in ways typical of other previous modes. Much, especially artistic, creation continues to resemble that of the independent artisan. There are also continuities with the feudal guilds. But few if any can escape some influence from the dominant mode and a great part of the production of knowledge is directly involved in it.

One of the problems of education here is the same one which keeps recurring. The processes of creation and discovery are human activities performed within a social structure. They must be understood on both the individual and social level, in terms of psychology and sociology (cf. Wolff, 1981, 22). In the present context the emphasis is on the latter.

It must be emphasised that the production of knowledge is a historical process, strongly influenced by the existing stock of knowledge. Engels made this point nicely in a letter to Conrad Schmidt in October 1890. Speaking about the law, he wrote:

As soon as the new division of labour which creates professional lawyers becomes necessary, another new and independent sphere is opened up which, for all its general dependence on production and trade, still has its own capacity for reacting upon those spheres as well. In a modern state, law must not only correspond to the general economic position and be its expression, but must also be an expression which is *consistent in itself*, and which does not, owing to inner contradictions, look glaringly inconsistent. (*SW*, 1, 385)

One can put any of the disciplines in the place of law in this citation. Whatever the influences of 'production and trade' the state of existing theory in the various disciplines imposes certain demands which are difficult to ignore, and which must be taken into account in any description of the production of knowledge. At the same time the countries of late capitalism are saturated with ideologies celebrating individualism and competition. Commodity production has extended into almost every aspect of society, However independent of the institutions of capitalism a producer of knowledge may be the pressure to produce in the commodity form is intense.

Let us look next, in outline, at the institutions within which the production of knowledge may take place. Private capitalist firms employ large numbers of people in research and development, both directly and on a consultancy basis. Others are employed by the state. They may be employed directly in research institutions, in the universities and other colleges in the tertiary education sector, or they may work for national broadcasting organisations, or government 'think tanks'. The judiciary must not be forgotten in its role of knowledge creation, even if that is only a small part of its duties. In certain times and places royal commissions or their equivalents may make a significant contribution. In addition to these two sectors of society there are a number of other important producers of knowledge. These include political parties, trade unions and such groups as peace groups and ecology groups. The question here is the relation between the type of knowledge produced and the institution within which it is produced. One might expect it would support the ideological position of the institution, with the qualification that such institutions as universities allow a very wide range of research and ideological position. In any case, this is an empirical question requiring study. For the present only some of the more obvious conditions within some of these institutional types which affect research can be noted.

Looking back at the diagram of a mode of production, in the Marx section above, we see knowledge as one of the qualities possessed by the workers in the category 'labour power'. But knowledge is, of course, embodied in the instruments of production, the machines and technical processes used in material production. It is here that production of knowledge in the form of technological research and development fits into the capitalist mode of production as one of the productive forces. In this form its value is embodied in the value determination of the costs of production. But saying this is only to locate education at a high level of abstraction. If we are usefully to understand the nature and contribution of scientific research analysis must be undertaken in much more concrete terms. Let us begin, however, with another high abstraction, the distinction between applied research, like that embodied in the production forces above, and 'pure' science, usually linked in our minds with institutions like universities.

In 1972 a group from the Department of Liberal Studies in Science of Manchester University in England reported a detailed study into the process of innovation in British industry (Langrish *et al.*, 1972). They chose as their sample firms which had won the Queen's Awards for technological innovation in 1966 and 1967. They pointed out that words like 'pure', 'fundamental', 'basic', 'non-mission-oriented' and 'curiosity-oriented' are used by different people in many different senses (33). Their research challenged widely the held belief, expressed by the UK Council for Scientific Policy, that 'basic research provides most of the original discoveries from which all other progress flows' (34). Their cautious conclusion was that 'the transition from pure knowledge to wealth is less simple and direct than is commonly supposed' (39) and 'most technological advances derive immediately from those that precede them' (40). They see the major importance of what Byatt and Cohen call 'curiosity-oriented' research, ('research justified by curiosity in fields where no application is apparent'[36]), in providing techniques of investigation, in training people to use these techniques and generally training people to think scientifically (40).

At a different, still high level of abstraction are discussions of the relative degree of investment in knowledge, or 'information', in different sectors of the national economy or between the economies of different nations. Bernal (1958) gave figures for the UK, USA and USSR in the middle fifties. He compared civilian research and development (R&D) expenditure with military R&D and with total expenditure on the military. At that time Britain spent 61 per cent of its scientific budget on military R&D, a figure higher than any other country at that time (163). In the same book Bernal hazarded the guess that a future optimum research effort might involve some 20 per cent of the population of a country being 'directly or indirectly involved in scientific tasks' (88, cf. 184). Charles Levinson discusses the expansion of R&D expenditure during the sixties and its distribution between different sectors of the economy. He draws attention to chemicals, plastics, electronics, computers and space, noting that in the principal industrial countries between half and three-quarters of all R&D expenditure goes into aircraft, electricity and chemicals (Levinson, 1978, 44-6). The connection here with the military, and therefore safe government funding, is obvious, even when there are non-military spin-offs. Such a level of abstraction reveals certain relations and trends but we need a more concrete analysis still if we are to become clear about those exchange value-use value distinctions which so crucially separate capitalism from the humane society of Marx's vision. As an example let us look at a study of the drug industry.

The information on research which Brian Inglis used in his book, *Drugs, Doctors and Disease* (1965) was in large part taken from the USA Senate Sub-Committee investigating trusts and monopolies under Senator Kefauver. In both the USA and the UK there was government concern about the high cost of drugs. The industry's defence was the high cost of research. What emerged is of great interest for an understanding of the wider questions of social versus financial interests and the nature of knowledge encouraged by a capitalist economy. First of all it is useful to note the classification of types of research suggested to the Kefauver Committee by David Novick, chief of the cost analysis department of the Rand Corporation. Based on US experience he proposed a fourfold division: (1) basic research; (2) applied research on new discoveries; (3) application of new knowledge; and (4) improvements of application of new knowledge. Novick estimated that in US industry 70 per cent of expenditure on R&D was on the fourth type, improvements to applications already discovered, with only 1 per cent of expenditure going to basic research. The Kefauver Committee went further for the pharmaceutical industry, declaring that, particularly for antibiotics, 'virtually all of the research and development work' was of type 4 (Inglis, 62). The meaning of this statement becomes even clearer when one reads the evidence on the actual working of drugs. Dr Haskell J. Weinstein, a medical man and former employee of one of the big firms concerned, explained that much of what passed for research was concerned with making varieties of drugs which would get around the patents of other companies, or, by combining drugs with 'inconsequential additives' would enable the marketing of a 'new' brand. Dr Frederick Meyers of the University of California supported this, saying he thought much research went on modifying 'the original drugs, the drugs based on the real research . . . just enough to get a patentable derivative but not to change it enough to lose the original effect' (Inglis, 60-1). These findings need to be seen against the nature of drugs being manufactured. Dr A. Console, former medical director of a big firm, divided drugs into four types: (1) effective drugs, prescribed only for patients who need them; (2) drugs prescribed for patients who did not need them; (3) drugs from which patients derived no benefit; and (4) drugs which had a greater potential for harm than good. He thought that less money was being spent on promotion and development of the first category than of the other three (62). Finally, on the question of research costs the Kefauver Committee found that for 22 of the major US pharmaceutical companies 'the sums spent on research "were in marked contrast to the amounts lavished on promotion"' (59). In 1958 eleven companies spent between 5 to 11 times as much on advertising, promotion and selling as they did on research (60).

This is an early and well-documented study which can now be matched by disturbing information on a number of industries and research lines, the nuclear energy industry being only the most spectacular example. We shall return to these questions later from the point of view of teaching and learning.

Another aspect of the production of knowledge relates to the extension of bureaucracy in late capitalism. Here it is interesting to contrast the approach of J.D. Bernal with that of *Fortune* assistant managing editor and author of *The Organization Man*, William H. Whyte. The former, already in 1938, welcomed the trend towards co-operative research projects taking as their goal some socially desirable end. He spoke of a future in which research would be conducted 'ideally, by teams of people consciously interested in the aims of the enterprise and able and willing to work together creatively to further it, without personal animosities and jealousies'

(Bernal, 1958, 204). Whyte, surveying the present realities of US capitalism, deplores the shift from what he calls 'the entrepreneurial to the administrative' (202). He argues that consideration of roles (an anthropologist, a chemist) rather than the qualities of a particular individual, and attempts to pre-plan research by committee inhibit, rather than promote, the inspiration on which genuine discovery depends. He gives as example the successful research done at General Electric and Bell Laboratories where bureaucracy had been minimised (192-5). An aspect of the bureaucratisation process which Whyte singles out for comment is the effort which has to go into grant applications before any research can be embarked on. He cites Curt Richter of Johns Hopkins University on the subject:

> We pick out the one tangible part of the application — the experimental design — how the man (or woman!) plans to work out his project. We are asking more and more questions. Aware of this, applicants elaborate their designs in more and more detail. A vicious cycle has set in. In making application for a grant before WW2, a few lines or at most a paragraph or two sufficed for the experimental design; now it may extend over six to eight single-spaced typewritten pages. (208-9)

More recently a Swedish colleague has estimated that he spends about one-quarter of his time preparing his submission for a renewal of his research grant, hardly a socially useful division of labour!

Producers and their Products

In the previous section the focus was on the production process. Here we shall shift the focus to the producers and their products and look particularly for aspects of late capitalism which shape them. At the same time one might ask to what extent the experience of producers of knowledge encourages them either to accept or reject capitalist values. Or, to put it another way, to what extent does their experience make them critical, especially in a marxian way.

To repeat what was said above, the individual producer may be a person of independent means. This has certainly been true of many literary figures and occasionally of natural scientists. Numbers of writers, artists, craftsmen, and increasingly with possibilities for obtaining tax concessions, technical consultants have the class position of petty commodity producers, selling their knowledge product on the open market. But the great majority of producers must labour as wage workers in either state or private capitalist institutions. The production of knowledge may be what they are paid to do, or it may be more or less a by-product of their employment. Research for many in the less prestigious universities and colleges, and especially academics of junior rank given high teaching and marking loads, find that while research may be expected of them conditions of their employment relegates it to the category of 'more' and only the heroic manage to produce. Their superiors, freed by their labours, are able to make research a main line occupation rather than just a by-product.

The resources required for successful knowledge creation vary widely according to the nature of the knowledge area. To advance our knowledge of mathematical theory little is required beyond imagination, some study of previous knowledge, and access in some form to the scholarly community. How different are things for the modern musician, requiring access to electronic instruments and computers, or the particle physicist. Here apparatus may cost millions of dollars and access to the scholarly community a long and competitive climb.

One should, perhaps, begin one's list of required resources with a consideration of skills. This immediately takes us into the area of social inequalities. Being born into the right family and going to the right school provides possibilities for learning the right skills — right here, of course, being right for the final production process in the particular case considered. Being born in the right country or city may be important, giving one ready access to skills not available elsewhere. The academic success of many Central European refugees in the Americas and Australasia owes something to their skills in various languages compared with native speakers of English under no such environmental pressure to learn a foreign tongue. While much of this is accident the class structure and unequal distribution of wealth which allows some to have easy and others no access to learning is very much part of the capitalist system. Equally, one important criterion of success for much knowledge production which is typically capitalist is *access to the labour of other people*. The forewords of most academic productions acknowledge this, whether thanking research assistants, secretaries, or the authors' wives whose domestic labour has provided them with the time and quiet to produce.[3] Without the use of other people's labour it is very hard or impossible to produce high quality work in most areas.

Continuing to think of material resources, access to a good library is essential for most knowledge production, while possession of one's own gives one even greater advantages. Here the economics of capitalist production and reproduction of materials plays a significant role. Only the long-established and wealthy institutions can afford to provide adequately for studies of both breadth and depth. The contrast between what current technology permits in the way of easy reproduction and what financial stringency and commercial interests allow is enormous and growing with the development of computers.[4] Copyright is also a factor hindering the wider provision of materials.

Knowledge production is very dependent on the mutual stimulation of sympathetic minds. This may be possible through direct interaction, but the competitive nature of contemporary capitalism often inhibits this. It may be easier for scholars in different countries, not in such direct competition, to share ideas than those whose promotion and job chances could be threatened.[5] In some institutions it is possible to bring together a group of like-minded scholars who form a 'school', but this is rare. In other cases the stimulus of a particular journal or learned society may be important. The ability to travel in order to maintain contacts depends on such things as one's personal wealth and willingness to use it for 'business' purposes,[6] the policy of one's workplace on giving time off to travel, and the availability of funds for such activities, not to mention the general state of the economy and government funding policies. In universities the institution of sabbatical (study) leave has, where it has operated, been of considerable help in bringing scholars together and exchanging experience.[7]

Hagstrom lists a number of different ways in which scholars keep in touch with each other's work: (1) various forms of publication, together with papers read at meetings and not published; (2) informal contacts through formal meetings; (3) contact by correspondence and visits; (4) informal contacts within departments; (5) contacts with former students and current graduate students; and (6) contacts outside the discipline or specialism of the particular producer (1965, 41). Point number (2) is interesting. Earlier Hagstrom draws attention to the importance of special invitation meetings.

> Because these smaller and more informal conferences are usually open solely by invitation, only the more eminent men attend. Some of the large society meetings, on the other hand, are attended by less eminent men, men from low-status organisations, and especially persons from industry. Since this is so, eminent men often disparage them ... (Hagstrom, 29)

Apart from the sexist use of men there is the question of what eminent means in the context of knowledge production. The 'exalted in rank or office' (*Chamber's Dictionary*) are precisely those with greatest access to the labour of others when it comes to production. Would the quality of knowledge production be different, perhaps, were less eminent men *and women* more often able to command the resources for such informal meetings? There are good reasons for believing that it would be.

One clear way in which the bureaucratic organisation of late capitalist universities and other tertiary level institutions hampers the production of useful knowledge is what is usually referred to as the 'publish or perish' syndrome. This relates to the need for criteria for promotion and job seeking, and the need for 'objective' evidence of merit. Eric Ashby, writing in the English *Listener* (1 June 1961) put the point sharply:

> [The] young man who is inspired to devote his career to the real purpose of a university, which is teaching at the frontiers of knowledge, finds himself obliged to enter a different career: the rat-race to publish. And to publish what? It must be 'original': miniscule analyses ... (cited in Hagstrom, 55)

The result is an expanding flow of papers whose quality is often in inverse ratio to the pressure to produce them and whose claim to be a contribution to knowledge in any socially meaningful sense is doubtful. Fear of stepping outside conventional thinking joins with pressure of unmanageable quantity to produce endless summaries of the literature and discussion of someone's comments on another's comments, rather than trying to tackle some real-life problem. In addition to this weight of paper detracting from the time to think and produce is the increasing numbers of reports which scholars are expected to turn in on the excuse of account-ability and the need for institutions to appear to be active.

Something which affects the production of knowledge, but about which little seems to be understood, is what might be called *fashion in knowledge.* Educators have noticed the swing from radical ideas in the late sixties and early seventies, ideas which were in fashion during the early decades of this century, and away from them in the late seventies and early eighties. Such fashions may comprise a broader or narrower field of ideas and be true of wider or narrower groups of people. It may only be that a par-ticular method is popular in a particular branch of learning for a period of time. Or it may be that a particular person's work attains the status of *authority.* Understanding these questions requires critical consideration of the role of institutions (why particular institutions achieve and maintain a reputation), the relation of fashions to ideology as interest, such things as the way in which the mass media and advertising can consciously create 'authorities' in our contemporary '(mis)information society'.

While fashion might seem more applicable to the arts and social sciences the natural sciences are equally prone. Something of this emerges in recent work on the sociology of the natural sciences, the efforts of scholars to penetrate the mystique of 'science' and show how it is 'really done'.[8] Richard Whitley, writing about 'making sense of [natural] scientists' activities', points to the need to understand:

> how the intellectual components of [a] field are structured and mutually ordered such that it seems reasonable for a particular topic to be pursued in a particular way and the outcomes to be understood in certain ways ... (Knorr *et al.*, 1981, 303)

Elsewhere he speaks of cognitive institutionalisation. By this he means: 'the degree of consensus and clarity of formulation, criteria of problem relevance, definition and acceptability of solutions as well as the appropriate techniques used and instrumentation' (Whitley, 1974, 72). All of these are to some extent determined by fashion, implied in the use of the term 'consensus'. In some measure these 'intellectual components' are ordered by the teaching establishments, usually the departments of the universities, where the scientists were trained. In some cases important agents of institutionalisation are the learned societies and institutions to which a majority of scientists and academics belong. These range from bodies like the Royal Institution of Civil Engineers, established in England in 1818, through to latecomers like the Institute of Biology, only established after the Second World War. They exert influence through training and certification programmes and through their journals and meetings, establishing the intellectual norms for their members. In the sixties and seventies counter-organisations were established in many fields with names like Concerned This or Radical That. These helped to legitimate a different set of norms.

To end this section a set of institutions will be briefly considered which many believe to have played a major role in shaping the production of knowledge. These are the *foundations*, especially the 'big' foundations, i.e. those 315 throughout the world (in 1979) with assets of over $10m. each. Ninety-five per cent of these are based in the USA (Whitaker, 1979, 14). They include household names like Ford ($2,354m.) and Rockefeller ($747m.), the Nuffield Foundation in England, the Volkswagenwerk Stiftung in Germany and a host of less well-known ones. Founded by the rich for many reasons, among them being the avoidance of tax and the establishment of a reputation for philanthropy, their declared purposes have been and continue to be highly varied. In judging their educational effect attention must be focused on what they do, on what they finance.[9]

Of 30,242 foundations listed in the USA only 140 issued regular public reports (Goulden, 1971, 74). It is, therefore, hard to get a detailed picture of how they spend their money. Whitaker gives a table of grants over $10,000 by US foundations between 1962 and 1971. This gives the following breakdown of total expenditure between various fields: education, 33 per cent; health, 14 per cent; international, 14 per cent; welfare, 13 per cent; sciences, 12 per cent; humanities, 9 per cent; and religion, 5 per cent; (1979, 183, cf. Heimann, 1973, 166). But these figures do not take us much further. Money given to build and/or equip medical laboratories in a university or hospital is also an aspect of education requiring consideration (e.g. Rockefeller) (Goulden, 30, 145-6).

The attitude of the tax authorities has been made clear on a number of occasions. In the USA a foundation may not attempt to influence legislation by propaganda or take part in political campaigns. The Sierra Club lost its tax-exempt state by supporting legislation on behalf of conserving redwood forests. In Britain Shelter and Political and Economic Planning (PEP) have received warnings for going beyond 'charitable' functions. In 1971 both the Humanist Trust and the Rationalist Press Association lost charitable status, though as Whitaker notes, it is hard to see how their actions differ from those of many religious bodies which continue to enjoy it (158-66). Interestingly, Cadbury and Rowntree, both Quaker trusts, prefer to pay taxes and therefore work unhampered by such regulations (164).

Much of the public argument which has gone on about the foundations has been about their support for programmes of a right or left political colour. They have been accused from both ends of the political spectrum. Many of the smaller foundations in the USA are of obvious right-wing persuasion, often publicly dedicated to the overthrow of communism or the defence of the free enterprise system. The Chance Foundation, founded by a member of the John Birch Society's national council, has supported the Schwarz Christian Anti-Communism Crusade, the Intercollegiate Society of Individualists and America's Future Inc. The Ada Hearne Foundation, founded by another John Birch council member, supported the American Economic Foundation and the Christian Freedom Foundation (Whitaker, 168). Then there is the J. Edgar Hoover Foundation. In the Federal Republic of Germany each of the main political parties has its own foundation which besides supporting the work of the party at home has also played an important role overseas (170-1). Accusations of left-wing bias depend on a relatively small number of cases in which such foundations as Ford supported decentralisation proposals in the New York school system (Goulden, 246-57) and the Congress of Racial Equality (CORE) (Goulden, 257-67). Whitaker evaluates such accusations with understatement: 'To allege that the generality of foundations tends to be pink would be an unfair libel', and he goes on, 'far-left foundations do not exist' (167).

How then should we assess the effect of these bodies on the production of knowledge? Goulden draws attention to the shaping of the research and publication emphasis of American universities in preference to classroom teaching, and to the emphasis in American medicine on 'research and experimentation rather than on basic patient care' (120-1). Whitaker, noting the close relations between foundations, government and academics, questions whether such a system gives the country the 'impartial, original or disinterested commentary or advice' that is required. Rather, 'alternative thought has been effectively muffled' (Whitaker, 179). He ends his long and careful survey with the thought that 'elite subsidiz(es) elites' (235) and foundations' grants 'buttress hier-archies in universities' (236).

Notes

1. Neither Sharp, Harris nor Matthews in their books about knowledge choose to consider the production of knowledge in the sense used here. A study I have found particularly helpful is Janet Wolff's *The Social Production of Art*.
2. There is numerous testimony to intuition, to unconscious thinking, in both the arts and natural sciences.
3. I don't speak here of that gross exploitation where work is produced unacknowledged. This is far more common than academics like to admit. Sometimes it is simply that research assistance becomes the production itself, or more than the term 'assistance' would warrant. In rarer cases work of students or colleagues is simply stolen. Then there are those cases where knowledge appears to have been deliberately falsified, perhaps as a joke (The Piltdown Man skull?), the dating of Knossos by Evans, or evidence on IQs (Kamin, 1974). Competitive pressures make such things inevitable.
4. An interesting minor effect of capitalism is the uneven development of instruments used by business executives and those only used by more menial workers. One example of this would seem to be the microfilm photocopier which is currently greatly inferior to 'ordinary' photocopiers. Or are current improved models still confined to military intelligence establishments?
5. I have recently had personal comments from scholars on this point from places as far apart as Australia, Germany, Sweden and Canada.
6. The expense account philosophy has bitten deep into the academic world.
7. Australia, which has a generous and far-sighted policy, is one of those places where study leave has recently come under strong attack.
8. As is becoming better known, the way in which science is written up in scientific journals and described in school textbooks is largely of a 'fictional character' (Latour in Knorr *et al.*, 1981, 68).
9. It would be interesting also to know what they do *not* finance, but even where that information is available it would not be the whole story. For one must also consider those projects which someone might have proposed if they had thought it worth the effort to apply! This last is yet another example of 'self-censorship' which I would argue plays a significant role in education — and my argument appears to be supported by the tactics of political security organisations in various countries.

5

THE DISTRIBUTION OF KNOWLEDGE

The distribution of knowledge will be discussed here in two senses: what do different categories of people know, and by what processes and through what institutional structures is that knowledge conveyed to them. As before, knowledge will be extended to include skills, attitudes and other things which human beings learn in the course of their lives. A thorough discussion of the first of these meanings of distribution would involve a detailed account of cultures and subcultures, something which cannot be attempted here. Discussion of the second meaning will be divided between this and the last section of the book where the process and structures of teaching will be considered.

While consideration of the distribution of knowledge is clearly pertinent to the question of a genuinely democratic society, to anything like Marx's vision of self-determining communities, one must be careful not to follow uncritically the prejudices of the schooled. Consideration of the present conduct of public affairs by the more highly schooled should not give complacency about special fitness.[1] Further consideration suggests that what is at fault is a system which denies a majority of people access to the necessary information required for rational decision and then uses that as an excuse for perpetuating undemocratic practices. Secrecy and censorship are firmly entrenched structures which continue to resist attempts to abolish them. 'Freedom of information' and 'open government' are fundamental educational questions. This is recognised in that now less often heard expression: not giving people 'ideas above their station'.

What I have just said assumes that knowledge is intrinsically useful, that the information and skills are to be used directly in performing some social function. That is to ignore another function which knowledge serves which for certain classes of people may be more important, and which must militate strongly against the first function of intrinsic use. That is, knowledge for many people serves as an ornament, a symbol of status to be displayed, often in a highly ritualised manner. DiMaggio and Useem draw attention to this function of knowledge in their discussion of government support for the arts in the USA. They suggest that for the upper-middle class, which they see in status terms as marginally within 'the elite', attending art exhibitions, the opera, classical concerts and the like provides 'symbolic identification with the upper class' (1978, 365). This use of knowledge for display is difficult to distinguish from using knowledge for pleasure or entertainment. Much of the quotation-capping and literary citation-allusion indulged in, e.g. in French schooled circles, probably serves both functions. Andre Gorz drew attention to an aspect of knowledge as a cultural status symbol when he showed that for certain technicians the calculus was required to pass their technical school course but never required by their work situation (1972, 34-5).

This said, there are serious practical problems requiring facing in making available to those who need it the information they need. There are also theoretical questions ranging from the identification of those interests and structures which prevent or hinder the free flow of information; questions about distinctions between ideology and science; through to how to handle the 'knowledge explosion' about which so much is said. Greater understanding is required of just what knowledge is needed, by whom and when. The last, then, takes us to a consideration of school knowledge compared with knowledge required, and perhaps best learnt, on the job. This leads on to questions about preparation versus learning as and when required, about retraining, and about the knowledge requirements for each of these strategies. Experience has been acquired in all these areas separately but few mechanisms or motivations currently exist for the kind of overall consideration necessary in the context of fundamental social change.

Clearly, from Marx's long-term perspective, the essential knowledge in the distribution of which we should be particularly interested is that which furthers people's understanding of their immediate lives and empowers them to consciously control their future. Such knowledge ranges from things like nuclear energy, on which the future of any human life at all may hang, to questions about genetic engineering. Identification of essential knowledge will require further consideration of teaching-learning methods, at present clearly failing to make certain types of knowledge easily available. Some, like Luckmann, seem pessimistic about the prospects. He remarked: 'Not only is "everyone" not motivated to learn certain role-specific knowledge . . . in addition, more and more tedious and complicated processes of learning are requisite for assimilating the knowledge ...' (Schuetz and Luckmann, 301).

J.D. Bernal, on the other hand, was optimistic, noting how with increasing systematisation knowledge has become easier to handle. He instanced his own subject, chemistry, where a knowledge of 'some two hundred laws gave one command over millions of substances'.[2] Whatever one thinks of that argument there is no doubt of the importance of motivation. Here experience suggests that when people are given the motivation of being able to make use of knowledge to their benefit they do their best to acquire it. It would thus seem to be very much a practical question.

With these general considerations in mind, then, let us look briefly at our two meanings of distribution.

What Different People Know

The first and most fundamental question here is how to significantly define 'different'. The differences in what Luckmann calls 'role-specific' knowledge possessed by a carpenter and a plumber may be essential in limited circumstances. But they are of quite a different order from the difference between knowledge held by the capitalist class and denied, where possible, to the (broadly defined) working class. This again is different from the distinction between knowledge of the 'fine arts' and what the British Arts Council once referred to as 'facile, slack and ultimately debasing forms of sub-artistic under-civilised entertainment' (Pearson, 1982, 82). In all these cases possession of certain types of knowledge serves to differentiate people. Detailed, concrete analysis is required to reveal the significance of such differentiation. If long-term democratic control over human society is the aim then the capitalist class-working class distinction is the most fundamental.

Gurvitch is one of those who has recognised this and attempted to explore it further. He writes about 'social classes and their cognitive systems' but then analyses knowledge in social situational and group rather than class terms. He speaks of 'the managerial society of organised capitalism' and the 'quasi-class of techno-bureaucrats' and of 'the proletarian class' and 'factories and workshops' as 'social frameworks of knowledge'. The techno-bureaucrats include: (1) the expert technicians; (2) the planners; (3) the "organisers" or managers of the vast economic enterprises, trusts, and cartels, as well as the political parties and occupational associations; (4) the bureaucrats — top civil servants of the public services; and (5) military technicians' (Gurvitch, 1971, 112). Within each of these groups Gurvitch ranks the types of knowledge they possess:

Techno-bureaucrats (111-14)	Managerial society (199-206)
1. Technical knowledge.	1. Technical knowledge.
2. Scientific knowledge.	2. Political knowledge.
3. Political knowledge.	3. Perceptual knowledge of the external world.
	4. Common knowledge.
	5. Knowledge of the Other and the We.

The proletarian class (101-9)	Factories (71-2).
1. Political knowledge.	1. Technical knowledge.
2. Technical knowledge.	2. Political knowledge.
3. Perceptual knowledge of the external world.	3. Commonsense.
4. Knowledge of Others and the We.	4. Perceptual knowledge of the external world.
5. Philosophical knowledge.	5. Knowledge of the Other and the We.

Gurvitch comments that in the managerial society science is incorporated into technical knowledge and that political knowledge, philosophical knowledge and common sense are all highly technicised. He also comments that: 'the techno-bureaucratic class holds the major technical secrets which permit the manipulation of nature, and, through its mediation, of other men, groups and societies' (111). But his conclusion, 'There is no doubt that this knowledge gives to its possessors . . . the desire and possibility to abuse their power' (111), misses the point. Knowledge *is* power and is an essential factor in the class struggle between capital and labour (Braverman, 1974; Zimbalist, 1979). Apart from problems which this particular categorisation of knowledge presents, the level of abstraction is also too high. What is immediately at issue is the workers' power to control their work and to make informed and rational choices about the risks they are prepared to take. More concrete studies, like those collected in Zimbalist, are more helpful in pointing to the kinds of knowledge required by workers. They also make problematic Gurvitch's complaint, that the proletariat has 'never yet woken from its philosophical sleep and torpor' (Gurvitch, 108).

In thinking about the relation between the division of labour and the distribution of knowledge a more useful concept is that of *deskilling* which I introduced earlier. Zimbalist defines this in the course of answering misinterpretations of Braverman's *Labour and Monopoly Capital*, which was subtitled: *The Degradation of Work in the Twentieth Century*. He writes:

> Braverman's analysis, however, is historical and dynamic. Briefly, its central thesis regarding skill might be put as follows: There is a long-run tendency through fragmentation, rational-ization, and mechanization for workers and their jobs to become deskilled, both in an absolute sense (they lose craft and tra-ditional abilities) and in a relative one (scientific knowledge progressively accumulates in the production process). (Zimbalist, xv)

What this last point means is that skills are built directly into the machine and may not be understood by the worker who uses it. But as Zimbalist and other contributors point out, this thesis refers to a tendency and does not mean that particular workers are unskilled or necessarily less skilled than previous workers. Here again, too abstract an analysis loses the reality of the process. Since the matter is important I will look at a few examples.

Zimbalist himself describes 'technology and the labor process in the printing industry', that 'last craft holdout' (103-26). He cites the reaction of one of the make-up men in 1978: 'To me it's no challenge anymore. Editors used to come up and work with you. "Does this fit? Can we make this work?" You had a sense of artistry. You were a craftsman. Now you paste it on the board. There's nothing to it' (Zimbalist, 111). As Sol Fishko regretted: 'Each new development makes the presses simpler to operate and our people easier to replace' (Zimbalist, 116). Phillip Kraft, describing 'the industrialization of computer programming', notices a similar trend. Already by the end of the nineteen sixties 'pro-gramming had been fragmented into three major sub-divisions — systems analysis, programming, and coding' (Zimbalist, 7). By the mid-seventies Kraft could conclude:

> Programming is still very much an occupation in process, and generalisations must therefore be both tentative and subject to careful examination. It is clear, however, that programming has

experienced a steady process of fragmentation and routinization while programmers as a group have experienced a rapid deskilling. (Zimbalist, 17)

David Noble, on the other hand, in a fascinating article on the politics of introducing numerical control machines in the machine tool industry, notes that 'the deskilling of machine operators has also, on the whole, not taken place' (Zimbalist, 41). This has in part been because of resistance by unions and in part because of the unreliability of the machines. This section of industry, at least under strong union leadership in a state-owned weapons factory in Kongsberg, Norway, is one where the workers have counter-attacked and established trained union personnel, 'data shop stewards', to monitor all new technology (47-9).

It is important to be clear on the argument in all this. Management, which for the past nearly one hundred years has been attempting to remove all control from the workers, is interested in 'job enrichment' for the workers in order to enrich the firm. But from the other side it may look rather different. A British chemical company packer described it thus: 'you move from one boring, dirty, monotonous job to another boring, dirty, monotonous job. And then to another boring, dirty, monotonous job. And somehow you're supposed to come out of it all "enriched". But I never feel enriched — I just feel knackered' (Zimbalist, xviii). 'Enrichment' which produced a contented workforce could still leave workers without the knowledge of 'how the system works', and this is surely the most serious deskilling of all. The technological aspect of this is the polarisation of knowledge in the high technology industry of which Ullrich warns (Ullrich, 1979, 442). The other aspect is political knowledge. Arguments about workers' control, even when they rise to the level achieved in the Lucas firm, and the generation of knowledge on product diversification, export possibilities and job saving remain limited to a narrow section of today's workforce. Lucas shop stewards (Wainwright and Elliott, 1982) made an important contribution, but they have not given us the knowledge required for a political economic programme for the whole British labour movement. Others must do that.

Knowledge and Youth

The distribution of knowledge between different sections of youth both within and between schools has become an increasing subject

of controversy since mass schooling became the rule in the centres
of late capitalism. Study after study has shattered the dreams of the
liberal reformers. The long-term study of a sample of British
children born in 1958 reported in 1972 that:

> there is clearly a strong association between social class and
> reading and arithmetic attainment at seven years of age. The
> chances of an unskilled manual worker's child (Social Class V)
> being a poor reader are six times greater than those of a pro-
> fessional worker's child (Social Class I). If the criterion of poor
> reading is made more stringent the disparity is much larger.
> (Cited by Halsey in Cosin *et al.*, 227)

Social class here is, of course, not the marxian distinction, but that
of social stratification theory. On such a basis studies of access to
tertiary schooling and especially to universities in England and
Wales show a similar picture. In spite of the overall expansion in
places one careful survey summed it up:

> So the expansion of educational provision has not involved a
> major redistribution of opportunities between children of dif-
> ferent classes. The benefits went to children of all social levels.
> As in the case of material standards of living, the average rose
> fairly steadily, but disparities between the classes remained
> sharp. (Westergaard and Resler, 1976, 324)

They go on to report a very slight narrowing of the differences,
with greater access to academic secondary schooling than to the
university at the time of the studies.[3] Bordieu, reporting for
France, gives essentially the same picture:

> It is striking that the higher the level of the institution of learn-
> ing, the more aristocratic its intake. The sons of members of
> managerial grades and of the liberal professions account for
> 57% of students at the Polytechnique, 54% of those at the
> Ecole Normale Superieure (noted for its 'democratic' intake),
> 47% of those at the Ecole Normale and 44% of those at the
> Institut d'Etudes Politiques. (Dale *et al.*, 1976, 110)[4]

Attempts were made to explain these findings in terms of both
inherent psychological differences and differences in upbringing.

Statistical computation revealed correlations and concepts of cultural deprivation, linguistic deprivation and social disadvantage were formulated. Particularly in the USA 'compensatory education' programmes were tried out. But, unsurprisingly in a society in which adult life is so unequal and social conflict is structural, the differences — with short-term and individual exceptions — persisted.

Reactions on the left to this situation have varied. One is to blame poverty of provision, particularly in the school. Another is to criticise the means of testing. These seem to be the main lines of Maurice Levitas's argument (1974, 134-52). He comments that 'any reluctance to label the working class or its attributes as inferior is certainly to be applauded (146). But it does not get one very far. Another stance is cultural relativism where it is argued that all cultures should be regarded as equally valid. This would seem to imply accepting the facism and sexism of those working-class 'lads' whom Willis so sympathetically and penetratingly describes, which I hasten to add is *not* the stand Willis himself takes (Willis, 1977). Recognition that working class youth are *active*, that their cultures are *constructed* and not simply taken off the hook in the capitalist cultural supermarket (Willis, 1977; Corrigan, 1979; Hall and Jefferson, 1976) may be a factor in winning them respect. But that is only a small part of helping them to win real freedom.

Some Significant Groups

One of the significant features of late capitalism has been the growth of that section of the population which earns its living by selling its expertise. The traditional professions of medical doctor, lawyer and architect, backed by legally supported associations to control entry and conduct of business, have been more recently joined by numbers of others having lesser status. Their special knowledge is their claim to expert status and most of these groups take pains to guard it. The medical profession, with its hostility to any other group pretending to similar expertise, or to sharing its knowledge even with patients, is a well-documented but not too extreme example. This state of affairs is being challenged from within and without. From within there have long been minority groups like the Socialist Medical Association which have challenged some of the expert assumptions and stressed broader social service aspects of their work. More recently the challenge has come from the outside, from groups wishing to break down the distinctions between expert and laity altogether. Women have challenged the medical profession over problems of female medicine and hygiene. With reference to the law, house purchasers, armed with special kits, have taken upon themselves the work normally performed by solicitors and estate agents. But these are small beginnings and the gulf remains. The experts, by their claim to special status at the same time devalue the rest of us. We are robbed of our confidence and often denied a hearing.

In *The German Ideology* Marx spoke about those 'who make the formation of the illusions of the class about itself their chief source of livelihood' (*CW*, 5, 60). There he spoke about them as a division of the ruling class, the 'mental' as against 'material' labour. But later, in *The Eighteenth Brumaire,* he referred to 'the literary representatives' of a class and pointed out that, like its political representatives, they did not have to belong to the class. All that was required was that 'their minds are restricted by the same barriers' and that they are 'driven in theory to the same problems and solutions' as the class (*SFE*, 176-7). Here it is not so much possession of particular knowledge as its production and dissemination which is in question. Nevertheless, since the distinction is a fine one and they are important mention here is justified. Identification is bound up with the problem of identifying 'the illusions of the class'. One immediately thinks of spokespersons for various political parties or business organisations. But these people may only be the transmitters of ideas fabricated elsewhere. Here there is a problem of who is agent and what form the agency takes. A research group or 'think tank', like the US Council on Foreign Relations or the Club of Rome, may be composed of individuals with diverse ideological functions, while collectively the agency acts as producer and depository of 'illusion'. While the empirical spadework remains largely in the future to have the concept is to direct the digging.

A number of groups have been thought of as in various ways 'deprived', including often those not being in possession of sufficient or the right kinds of knowledge to maintain or improve their material position. The groups I have in mind are the chronically sick, the old and the unemployed. People in these categories are poor. The rich sick and old are in quite other categories. In the face of dominant ideologies — the work ethic and attitudes to 'dole bludgers', for example — which they may or may not fully internalise themselves, members of these groups are often lacking in self-confidence. This may be made worse by a lack of vital information, as when information about social services is withheld from them (Schragg, cit. Brake and Bailey, 1980, 22). On the other hand, especially among the younger unemployed there may develop special informal information networks. Recently radical social workers have developed new approaches with special importance for political education.

A number of 'protest' groups specialise in particular areas of knowledge. They include women's groups; peace groups; ecology groups; homosexuals. Much of this knowledge is central to the issue of humankind's future, to survival and to a really human 'quality of life'. Membership between these groups, e.g. the peace and ecology groups, may overlap but, contrary to certain re-actionary ideologists, there is as yet no theoretically meaningful *internal* relationship.[5] The interesting questions are the relations between these groups and other more mainstream groups, and the extent to which their special knowledge becomes more widely accepted and integrated into practice leading to fundamental change. I will return to considering these groups below.

The Distribution Process

The distribution process can be looked upon as a teaching process, a way in which knowledge is offered or thrust upon the potential learner. It is with that in mind that I shall examine some of the 'teaching agents' in the final section of this book. At this point I want to examine a few more general issues, paralleling the general approach to 'what different people know' above.

To repeat a point made before, the capitalist search for maximum profit has meant the extension of the exchange value relationship ever more deeply into the knowledge production and distribution processes. Consequently, knowledge has become very big business. Looking through Machlup's (1962) list of 'media of communication' and 'information machines' gives us both a 'world map' and a chronology, reminding us what needs to be theorised: printed matter; photography and phonography; stage and cinema (where he also discusses the visual arts, painting and sculpture); broadcasting (radio and television); advertising and public relations; telephone, telegraph and postal services; and finally — the electronic computer. While the state leaps out at us when we read radio (BBC/ABC) or postal services, a majority of items remind us immediately of private capitalism. Names like Hollywood, Bell Telephones or IBM come to mind. But the contemporary form of this capitalism and its significance is less well known and less obvious. Fortunately the media and 'culture' have generated a large academic industry, some of whose products can assist us in overcoming this lack of information.

In the area of the commercial distribution of knowledge the power of advertising makes itself obvious whether on television or in the field of sport. The exact effect of this must be examined in particular cases. Richard Hoggart is correct to point out, in his foreword to *Bad News*, that while owners and controllers sometimes use direct interference and sometimes use indirect influence, this is far from the whole picture.[6] Reduction to conspiracy theory leaves out much that needs understanding if we seriously want to change things. Some of these other matters we will now address.

Differentiation of Content

By this I mean the differentiation of content for different publics. Examples are the 'popular' press compared with what is insultingly distinguished as 'the quality' papers. On the BBC there was the Third Programme. Television in some countries divides on popular and serious channels. Sometimes the terms used are high and low culture; others speak of art and entertainment. One of the better guides here is Raymond Williams. In *Communications* he pointed out that 'the great tradition' is 'a mixed inheritance, from many societies and many times as well as from many kinds of men [and women]'. He warns that it is taken up and 'used by a particular social minority' which, often adding 'certain works and habits of its own', 'identifies itself with' it (1967, 108, 102, 103). At the same time he argues that aesthetic evaluations of good and bad do not easily distribute themselves between neat groupings of forms. 'Variety, the circus, sport and processions', clearly popular forms, should not be seen as absolutely different from 'the minor decorative arts, the passing comedies, [or] the fashionable artistic performers' (105). Some forms, like opera, have passed from the popular to the elite.[7] William's most telling point is his definition of the really good.

The challenge of work that is really in the great tradition is that in many different ways it can get through with an intensity, a closeness, a concentration that in fact move us to respond. It can be the reporter breaking through our prejudice to the facts; the dramatist reaching so deeply into our experience that we find it difficult, in the first shock, even to breathe; the painter suddenly showing us the shape of a street so clearly that we ask how we could ever have walked down it indifferently. It is sometimes a disturbing challenge to what we have always believed and done, and sometimes a way to new experience, new ways of seeing and feeling. Or again, in unexpected ways, it can confirm and strengthen us, giving new energy to what we already know is important, or what we knew but couldn't express. (1967, 106)

This is essentially the position of those two figures from the Frankfurt School, Horkheimer and Adorno, but they go further. In their essay on 'The Culture Industry: Enlightenment as Mass Deception' they complain that the 'mass-media' stunts the 'consumer's powers of imagination' (1973, 126). This they see, in the case of the cinema, in the technical nature of the means. Sound films: 'are so designed that quickness, powers of observation, and experience are undeniably needed to apprehend them at all; yet sustained thought is out of the question if the spectator is not to miss that relentless rush of facts' (1973, 126-7). They go on to argue that 'amusement under late capitalism is the prolongation of work' (137). While it is sought as an escape from 'the mechanized work place' it is the 'automatic succession of standardised operations', rather than the 'ostensible content' which quickly fades, which makes its impression. Pleasure is therefore just another form of the same process.

Pleasure hardens into boredom because, if it is to remain pleasure, it must not demand any effort and therefore moves rigorously in the worn grooves of association. No independent thinking must be expected from the audience: the product prescribes every reaction ... (137)

While these eloquent cries of pain at the dehumanising of man warn us of the threat of passivity and mindless consumerism they do less than justice to the complexity of the situation. This is in part a result of the ambivalent relation to empirical research which

Horkheimer and Adorno had (Curran *et al.*, 19; Negt in Woodward, 81, 83) and perhaps also a reflection of their class and European origin, reacting as exiles in the USA. A more sympathetic look at the consumers reveals that besides obvious passivity there are also counter-tendencies and what Willis in another connection called 'penetrations' (Willis, 1977).

Mass Media for Communication?

Oskar Negt discusses how the counter-cultural movements in Germany and France in the sixties failed to make use of the powerful modern means of communication. They preferred to use leaflets, posters and pamphlets, 'a mode of production based on craftsmanship' which once again proves its effectiveness in 'the politicization of direct experience', in strikes, demonstrations and other 'grass roots movements' (in Woodward, 1980, 73-4). Like the Frankfurt School which he is criticising, Negt seems pessimistic of the possibilities which the 'technologically highly developed mass media' with their 'abstract audience, i.e. listeners, watchers, or readers' allow. Yet he cites Brecht on how radio could be transformed:

> The radio must be transformed from a mechanism of distribution into one of communication. The radio would be the most fantastic mechanism of communication imaginable in public life, a tremendous channel system. That is, it would be that if it realized the capacity not only to broadcast, but also to receive; not only to make the listeners hear, but also to make them speak; not to isolate them, but to put them into contact with each other. The radio would thus have to abandon its status as supplier and see to it that the hearer assume that status. (in Woodward, 77)

An analysis of 'community radio' and listener talkbacks and phone-ins in such places as Australia, using Brecht's perspective, would be illuminating. I suspect they are rather far from it. They remain within the familiar forms and lack that active organisation of people around their own interests of which Jack Zipes writes in the same volume (Woodward, 109).

Analysing the News

Studies by the Glasgow University Media Group of news programmes on television in Britain are a model of what should be more widely attempted. They throw light on the process by which, working with an ethos of 'impartiality, balance and objectivity' and trading on 'the unspoken and dominant ideology of our society — the liberal notion that there is a fundamental consensus', television news ended up a clear expression of the interests of capital (1980, 402). The Media Group make clear that this is not through being 'simply ruling-class propaganda' (124). On the contrary:

> a news talk is usually open to a plurality of interpretations but there normally emerges a preferred reading of actions and events which, as we will show, is often inimical to the interests of labour . . . there is an attempt to reduce the plurality of meanings inherent in any social conflict to a set of simple formulae or frames of reference which are at base an ideological defence of the legitimacy of the *status quo.* (124)

John Westergaard adds to the picture of how the interests of capital are served, not through 'subjection to active pressure', but rather from 'everyday acceptance of the inertia of "things as they are"' (Curran *et al.*, 101). '[In] the world which broadcasters see it as their task to reflect . . . political dispute is described and interpreted in the terms which those actively engaged — politicians, party and pressure-group spokesmen — themselves implicitly set to their disputes' (106). This 'world of things as they are' is one in which the real alternatives are seldom mentioned, and if so only as utopia, idealism or worse.

Studies like those of the Glasgow University Media Group are rare, unfortunately, and they are concerned with only a very limited part of the knowledge distribution process. In order to understand the mixture of science and ideology presented, and the mechanisms of transmission at work more needs to be done over a more representative area. Comparative studies of presentation in different countries, using the same methodology, would be specially helpful. The Group itself points to the type of studies it would like to see: 'Ideally participant observational studies of the production offices should be matched to content analysis and audience research relating to the same period' (1980, 409). It is good that we have such a promising start.

While speaking of further study it might be apposite to mention here that in addition to the nature of the knowledge distributed, scientific or ideological, there is the more difficult problem of reception, of what people actually learn. There is a vast amount of data on who watches what, attends what kinds of performances, how many families have television and the like. Those who sell advertising space like to assume seeing is not only believing, but also behaving. Fortunately for human survival we have reason to believe they are wrong. I shall return to this in the section on learning below. To end this section I want to examine some important barriers to the distribution of knowledge.

Barriers to Knowledge Distribution

Three major barriers to the free circulation of information are secrecy, censorship and copyright. The first two long pre-date capitalism and are notorious features of those mis-described 'communist' countries which have replaced it. But they are clearly in the interest of capitalism and detrimental to that free flow of information and knowledge which a genuinely different kind of society would require.

It was Marx who, in a very early work,[8] wrote: 'the general spirit of the bureaucracy is the *secret*, the mystery, preserved within itself by the hierarchy and against the outside world' (*CW*, 3, 47). Max Weber was to develop this theme. He wrote:

> Every bureaucracy seeks to increase the superiority of the professionally informed by keeping their knowledge and intentions secret . . . in so far as it can, it hides its knowledge and action from criticism . . .

> The concept of the 'official secret' is the specific invention of bureaucracy, and nothing is so fanatically defended by the bureaucracy as this attitude, which cannot be substantially justified beyond these specifically qualified areas. (Gerth and Mills, 1970, 233)

> Whenever increasing stress is placed upon 'official secrecy' we take it as a symptom of either an intention of the rulers to tighten the reins of their rule or of a feeling on their part that their rule is being threatened. (cit. Thompson, 1970, 3)

A year before Marx wrote the above words he had been defending the freedom of the press in his first contribution to the *Rheinische Zeitung*. He used an argument which still needs to be made today:

> In order to fight against freedom of the press, one must defend the standpoint that the human race is incapable of reaching maturity . . . If man's immaturity is the mystic reason which speaks against freedom of the press, then censorship is in any event a most highly reasonable measure to assure that men never mature. (cit. Rubel and Manale, 1975, 25; differently translated, *CW*, 1, 153)

This last is the educational point, already made a number of times but worth repeating. We need full information if we are to be democratic beings, free and fully human. Of course there are distinctions to be made between the private and the public, distinctions which are violated every day in late capitalism by both the state, with its vast systems of prying and spying on its own citizens, and by journalists in their endless quest to titillate jaded audiences with a 'human' story. And of course there are times when, as in war, certain information must be withheld. The important educational principle, is that these exceptions should be demanded from below and not imposed from above, that they should come out of a community-in-the-making. In late capitalism's deeply divided society freedom is only going to be maintained through constant vigilance, and recent decades have had advances and retreats.

Britain, a country where so many struggles for freedom and democracy have occurred,[9] has recently seen much public discussion of secrecy. The Fulton Committee reported in 1968 that the proceedings of the Civil Service were 'surrounded by too much secrecy' (Bunyan, 1977, 22). Following election pledges by the Conservative Party to eliminate unnecessary secrecy a committee was set up under Lord Franks, but their recommendations have been ignored. Bunyan notes that:

> The Franks Committee detailed seven limitations on the disclosure of information. Paramount among these are the sanctions exercised within the Civil Service where a civil servant 'who tends to overstep the mark, to talk too freely, will not enjoy such a satisfactory career as colleagues with better judge-

ment and greater discretion'. The other limitations are: formal
Civil Service disciplinary procedures; recruitment and vetting;
security classifications and privacy markings; the D-Notice
system; the Public Records Act (which keeps closed public
records for thirty, forty or one hundred years at the discretion of
the government); and finally, the three Acts themselves.
(Bunyan, 23)

The three Acts Bunyan refers to are the formidable Official Secrets
Acts of 1911, 1920 and 1939. In addition there are the Incitement
to Mutiny Act, originally passed in 1797; the Incitement to Disaffection Act of 1934; and various Emergency Powers Acts which
can be brought into temporary action. If all that were not enough
— and Bunyan gives examples of their use — there is always a high
court injunction, as was used to prevent the publication of
materials of public interest in the student occupation affair at
Warwick University in February 1970 (Thompson, 1970, Chapter
51).

Interesting moves in the opposite direction have been the
various Freedom of Information Acts. The first came into effect in
July 1967 in the USA, a country which as well as being the most
powerful and fully capitalist of the countries of late capitalism is
also regarded as being one of the most open where information is
concerned (Rourke, cit. Lees, 1979, 334). In 1982 Australia
passed a similar, but weaker Act.[10] In both cases certain documents remain inaccessible. Section 33 (1) of the Australian Act
speak of 'exempt documents' where 'disclosure of the document
under this Act would be contrary to the public interest' and goes
on to list security, defence, international relations and relations
between the Commonwealth and the states. While such Acts are to
be welcomed one must remember that it will be a small and
already well-informed number of people who will make use of
them. Nevertheless, it is interesting to see the fear which they
engender among wide sections of what for brevity one may call the
ruling class (Lees, 1979; Coxon, 1981).

Censorship, the other face of secrecy, will be used here to cover
a variety of means by which the distribution of knowledge is prevented. At one extreme it overlaps with secrecy, and many of the
same instruments are used for both purposes, e.g. the British
Official Secrets Acts. If distinction is necessary it should be made
according to whether information which originates with govern-

ment or property is being prevented from wider circulation (secrecy), or whether the action is taken to prevent discussion of topics, information on which is or has been more or less widely dispersed. It is surprising, considering the importance which such action has when applied to the young, that it is not mentioned as a concept by writers on curriculum or the history of schooling, even where they speak about particular instances of it. Yet it is readily recognised by writers on Soviet schools! In the English-speaking countries of late capitalism discussion has rather been on the related concept of *indoctrination*. Other related, and *under*-examined, concepts are *maturity*, and *innocence*, concepts which if not always described under these labels lurk behind many defences of censorship in the school. Open discussion and greater clarity, while not removing problems of material interest, such as power and authority — the nub of so many questions of secrecy and censorship — might help to dispel some of the prejudices and confusion and make clearer what is possible and desirable.

Censorship is exercised over discussion of moral, mainly sexual, matters and political-economic and religious questions. It is exercised by organs of the state, by religious authorities, in the past acting for the state in these matters, and by various other agents in society like the vigilante groups in the USA and elsewhere which have initiated witch-hunting of teachers and book-burnings. Threats to censor often encourage that most insidious form of censorship, self-censorship, and must often be intended to do so. In the academic world, with its competition for promotion and, more recently, for jobs, self-censorship takes the form of choosing 'safe' subjects for research and not pressing conclusions beyond certain limits. Space is often the excuse for avoiding relevant but dangerous digressions. With the growth of 'academic marxism' over the past two decades there has been a preference for elaborate terminology and obscure, highly abstract writing styles which in part reflect the pressure to conform. It reminds one of what Wickham Steed, famous British journalist and one-time editor of the London *Times* wrote about 'the press and the law' in 1938:

> What the law of libel really does is to put a premium upon oblique writing, upon emphasis by under-statement, and upon the use of all the arts and dodges which fertile minds can devise to circumvent an omnipresent though invisible legal censorship of which the fairness cannot be relied upon. (Steed, 189)

Steed presupposed writers who wanted to 'circumvent'. Leaving that aside, his addition, 'This is definitely not to the public interest', in the much wider context is even more true today.

The ways in which censorship is performed vary from country to country, from one institution to another within a country, and from one time to another. They may be open and obvious, or subtle and difficult to detect or prove. Censorship is applied to both the items of knowledge, whether in writing or in some other form of recording, and to the means of dissemination. There are laws, such as those relating to safety, which at times can act as censors, if often unintentionally.[11] Regulations about the holding of meetings may often act as a censor, more wealthy or well-connected groups having easier access to meeting places than others. Writing of Australia in 1968, Geoffrey Sawer, Professor of Law at the Australian National University, commented:

> although there is a general liberty of association and of meeting, it is a good deal more restricted than corresponding liberties in the USA; one can speak meaningfully of a *right* of meetings only in relation to meetings held on private premises with the consent of the occupier, and then only if the meeting is for a lawful purpose and peaceably conducted. What an American liberal would regard as the *right of protest* is severely circumscribed by the emphasis which both the Common Law and Australian statutes place on *preventing a breach of the peace*. (Sawer, 1968, 233)[12]

Adding that 'Australia is also a much-censored country', Sawer went on to describe the complicated situation that being a system of federated states produces (233-8). One can draw little comfort from Sawer's remark that: 'one of the minor paradoxes of Australian politics is the readiness of federal politicians to enact these terrifying statutes and their unwillingness to put them into effect' (233-4). Nor, when one is concerned with the education of independent, rational and self-determining human beings, is there any comfort in the fact that censorship of printed material is for obscenity rather than political content. With the difficulties of definition and the atmosphere in which proceedings are often conducted the worst of possible worlds often seems to result.[13]

An important means of censoring the distribution of knowledge is by control over persons. This may be by preventing them having access to use of the media, e.g. the radio or television, or through either excluding them from certain jobs by sacking or not appointing in the first place. The Berufsverbot in Germany has its counterpart in England, working, as E.P. Thompson points out, by processes the details of which neither the public nor the House of Commons can be told (Thompson, 1980, 158). The list of victims is a long one. Peter Brueckner, psychology teacher at the University of Hanover is suspended on suspicion.[14] Bertell Ollman was offered a Chair and then the offer was not confirmed.[15] But the major victims in all this are not the obvious ones, but the people who are prevented from hearing the victimised speaker or being taught by the victimised teacher. These people are thereby less well informed than they need be.

A history of censorship in the schools would be much fuller if it were not for the control which authorities have exercised on the syllabuses and a generally observed consensus as to the limits not to be overstepped. In the period after the Second World War there have been examples, especially in the USA during the McCarthy period, when teachers and librarians have been harrassed and books removed from school and other libraries on the grounds of being 'communist'. The USA is also the country where the teaching of biological evolution was banned for long periods in various states, and teachers victimised for trying to teach it. With changes in the general political climate things change, and the sixties and seventies saw more liberalisation in the schools of late capitalist countries. While there have been moves towards more censorship again in some quarters, on balance there is probably more openness today to social issues and the realities of today's world.

Consideration of censorship raises a fundamental difficulty which seems incapable of other than practical solution. There are certain ideas, like racism or the sadism associated with certain pornography, which marxists, along with many others, find intolerable. How to handle such problems without using methods which themselves are intolerable and encourage wider, socially harmful repression remains unsolved. In today's world the marxist answer of relying on the actions of the working class ignores the question of manipulation and that sections of the working class can hold intolerable ideas. The alternative of relying on the 'enlightened' few has led in the past to widespread censorship and intolerance.

The third barrier to the distribution of knowledge, copyright, is of a quite different nature from secrecy and censorship. While one could conceive of capitalism without, or with minimal application of the latter two, copyright is a natural application of capitalist principle to the products of the mind. Ideas are commodities. In their book entitled *Copyright: Intellectual Property in the Information Age* Ploman and Hamilton note that the concept developed during the seventeenth and eighteenth centuries and that, fittingly, 'the first country to adopt a "modern" copyright statute was England' (1980, 11). Defined 'basically' as 'the individual right of an author to dispose of his work in return for remuneration' (30) Ploman and Hamilton add that 'in fact copyright has become one of the most complicated and esoteric branches of law'. National and international law cover different aspects. The Berne Convention, originally concluded in 1886, in addition to writings, includes lectures, addresses and sermons (32). The US Copyright Act of 1976 lists seven categories to include music, graphics and film and sound recordings. It is a paradox that the same industry which sells recordings and, therefore, supports copyright also produces tape and tape recorders whose use would benefit from its abolition! It is a more fundamental criticism of capitalism that when technology for the first time makes possible the easy, cheap and accurate copying of all kinds of knowledge needed if people are to become really well educated, there has been an international movement to tighten copyright laws. The issue has been clouded by talk of *authors'* rights, when it is clearly the big companies, like the music recorders, which stand to gain most. It is a sad reflection on teacher unions that they have not been heard in defence of a *freer* access to information. While the problem can hardly be solved within capitalism, some concessions have been made for educational purposes and these could be improved rather than worsened.[16] Distinction could be made between those for whom the creation of an idea-commodity is a major source of livelihood and others, like academics, for whom any return through copyright would be marginal to an adequate salary. In the meantime developments in technology daily demonstrate the absurdity of the present situation and the possibilities of an even richer potential future.

School Knowledge

Any consideration of the distribution of knowledge must pay

attention to that portion of our total knowledge which is selected for teaching in the schools. Bernstein is right to see the process of selection and handling of school knowledge as reflecting 'both the distribution of power and the principles of social control'. But it is questionable to what extent he is also right to say 'educational knowledge is a major regulator of the structure of experience' (Young, 1971, 47). To be clear on that requires that we ask 'for whom?' If we are thinking about research workers in the universities, constrained by the particular fragmentation of today's knowledge, Bernstein is probably right, though we have seen how such workers, influenced by the world of industry, or the upsurge of social protest, can break through such limitations. If we are thinking of the 'Smash Street kids' I would have thought, on the contrary, that their experience of other knowledge was the 'major regulator' of their attitudes to 'educational knowledge' and the school generally. To probe the question 'for whom?' leads one to that most pertinent question: the relation between the knowledge presented in the schools and the knowledge learnt by students. Until recently it was assumed that what was taught was, at least in large part, learnt. Somehow a more realistic understanding of learning must be added to questions about the content of teaching, about school knowledge.

Discussion of school knowledge has been largely theoretical, in terms of what *should* be taught and the criteria of choice. Those who would study the content of what is taught face considerable difficulties. The content of schooling exists on a number of different levels with different degrees of accessibility:

official syllabi and outlines;

in textbooks and various teaching materials (including recordings, films and still pictures);

in classroom practice, the daily teaching-learning exchange in which these various materials are realised;

in what is examinable through various forms of tests and assessment;

and in learnings which, though highly important, are not available for observation.

In order to understand the relation of learning to teaching one would need to know what occurs in classroom practice. But this is among the least accessible levels. More useful studies appear to have been done on children's literature and comics than on school and teaching materials.[17] Harris suggests a framework for study: the examination of inter-ideological support; content as ideology; benign content and exclusion (1979, 158). The last, what is excluded from the schools, is perhaps the most important. It might be summed up as: serious consideration that society might be fundamentally different.[18] In concrete terms it might be sex education; religion or religions other than that of the local society; or political questions about exploitation and repression which are excluded. However, a major difficulty is that even when items appear in a syllabus or textbook they may or may not be taught in the classroom, or may be given quite different interpretations by teachers, and students.

School knowledge is often handled under the title of 'curriculum studies'. This broadens the topic to include those affective questions, motivations, attitudes and feelings, which so often got pushed aside in traditional approaches to school knowledge. Even Bernstein at one point says: 'I mean by curriculum the principles governing the selection of, and relation between subjects' (3.70). In another place he defines it 'in terms of the principle by which certain periods of time and their contents are brought into a special relationship with each other' (3.79). He goes on to say that by relationship he means such things as the length of time devoted to a particular content: whether the content is compulsory or optional; and whether the boundaries between one piece of content and another are 'clear-cut or blurred'. All this refers to what we should now probably call the 'open curriculum' to distinguish it from what has come to be known as the 'hidden curriculum'.[19] This is the curriculum which shapes much of the affective. It is the norms and values which are implicit in the way schools are, in the pattern of behaviour exhibited and expected and the routines and rituals. Apple refers to Jackson's treatment of the effect of 'crowds, praise, and power', of long periods of waiting, 'with the teacher as the child's first "boss"', and 'how children learn to falsify certain aspects of their behaviour to conform to the reward system extant in most classrooms' (Apple, 1979, 84). These are certainly important teachings-learnings, but I shall confine remarks here to the open curriculum.

One of the influential English writers on school knowledge in the period after the Second World War was Paul Hirst. A colleague of R.S. Peters and co-developer of the analytic philosophy of education,[20] he concentrated on what *should* be taught, advocating a liberal education conceived in cognitive terms. Hirst believes that knowledge consists of meaningful and true propositions and that it can be divided into seven classes according to certain criteria:[21] mathematics; the physical sciences; the human sciences; history; religion; literature; and the fine arts (Matthews, 168; Lawton, 1975, 80). Speaking about a liberal education as 'the comprehensive development of the mind in acquiring knowledge' Hirst wants curricula which will:

> introduce pupils as far as possible into the interrelated aspects of each of the basic forms of knowledge, each of the several disciplines [the 7 above]. And they must be constructed to cover at least in some measure the range of knowledge as a whole. (in Archambault, 1965, 132)

In addition to the doubtful nature of Hirst's criteria for distinguishing classes of knowledge (Matthews, 168-9), there is also an unacceptable view of a uniform 'public', exhibited in the following extract: 'The logic of a form of knowledge shows the meaningful and valid ways in which its terms and criteria are used. It constitutes the publicly accepted framework of knowledge' (Hirst, 1965, 135). There is no single 'publicly accepted framework of knowledge', nor in a class-divided society can there be.

An influential American writer on curriculum, Philip H. Phenix, speaks about human beings as 'essentially creatures who have the power to experience *meanings* (1964, 5). He groups knowledge in to what he calls *Realms of Meaning* (1964, 28; cf. Lawton, 1975, 80 and Stenhouse, 1975, 18). He believes that 'general education is the process of engendering essential meanings' (1964, 5). He speaks about 'the finest treasures of civilization' which 'can be so mediated as to become a common inheritance of persons who are seeking to realize their essential humanness' (1964, 14). But it would seem he believes that all who seek may not find, for he says: 'The fruits of inquiry by professional scholars are largely beyond the comprehension of the layman, even though he may be intelligent and formally well educated' (1964, 14). The problems with this elitist position will be discussed below when we consider learning in some detail.

Much of more recent discussion on curricula has been dominated by the work of what has come to be called 'the new sociology of education'. This established itself with the influential work: *Knowledge and Control: New Directions for the Sociology of Education*, edited by Michael Young in 1971. In it Young deplored 'the almost total neglect by sociologists of how knowledge is selected, organized and assessed' (19). He claimed to raise questions 'about what might be meant by the notion of knowledge being socially organized or constructed' and this phrase has been repeated frequently in the genre I am examining, alas without much consequence. It is hard to see how a classification of knowledge areas according to whether they are open or closed, narrow or broad, of high status or low (Young, 1971, 32-3) can be expected to answer 'how curricula . . . arise, persist, and change, and what the social interests and values involved might be' (24). To answer these interesting and important questions one must look at who controls the curriculum, the answer to which ranges from the highest levels of the state in some countries to the classroom teacher in others, and the many influences which bear on these agents. To look, as Young does, at 'the last twenty years' in England, with some reference to the USA, is quite insufficient. Is it different in France or Germany, to name only two perhaps rather different, but also capitalist countries? Then there are the discussions of curricula recurring through this century to which Apple and others refer (Apple, 1979, Chapter 4).[22]

Young offers as a 'revolutionary alternative' a curriculum which is 'based on knowledge which is differentiated but not stratified' (1971, 36). To guide us he tries to understand 'the dominant characteristics of high-status knowledge'. These he identifies as:

> literacy, or an emphasis on written as opposed to oral presentation; individualism (or avoidance of group work or co-operativeness) . . . [and] unrelatedness . . . which refers to the extent to which [academic curricula] are 'at odds' with daily life and common experience. (1971, 38)

However, Young himself goes on to show the limitations of this approach: the tentative and formal nature of the characteristics and their lack of the 'operational rules' necessary for 'analysing questions of substantive content' (39). Sarup sees Young as posing the question of whether we could change the criteria of high-class knowledge to make it concrete, oral, related (to ordinary working life) and communal (co-operative) (1978, 16). These, Young tells us, are the criteria of social actions, and he goes on to speak of the devaluing of these and the valuing of '"knowledge for its own sake"' (39).

In another volume Michael Young turns his attention to the details of teaching science. The abstractions of *Knowledge and Control* are abandoned for more concrete analysis. His theme is relatedness and science as social practice. He rehearses important points which have been made regularly in such discussions without reality being thereby changed. At one point he comes near to what seems to me to be an unsolved difficulty. He supposes a lesson which 'starts with a concrete example of pupils' life experience — the way camping gas cookers work' (Whitty and Young, 1976, 56). He suggests that 'the *real* problem is learning Boyle's Law and how volumes of gases change under pressure' and that stress will be on 'deriving and doing calculations from Boyle's Law', activities which are 'for many, boring and difficult and pointless'. The point is not that this is not all too often how it is. The point is the really difficult problems associated with such an example. These include the nature of theories essential for particular social understandings; the degree to which problems require mathematics to solve them; and the interrelation of parts of a syllabus to wider wholes. Perhaps this example indicates the dangers of taking examples out of context in order, as Young said of Perry Anderson elsewhere (1971, 28), 'to suit his thesis'! Young's observations on biology teaching are hardly more fortunate. Making the valid comment — though it needs careful analysis — that 'school biology is increasingly characterised by a reductionism to molecular levels of explanation' (Whitty and Young, 57), Young at the same time asks for 'the physics, chemistry and biology of ourselves'. It is also untrue that 'molecular levels of explanation' *necessarily* lead to a 'passive view of man increasingly subject to control by genetic and other experts'. That is another problem requiring careful and informed exploration.

Summing up his excursion into 'the schooling of science' Young identifies three products: 'pure scientists'; 'applied scientist[s]'; and 'the anti-science anti-technologists who can see science *only* as domination' (59). Their interrelations, Young claims, have up to now negated attempts through science (education) to 'undermin[e] dogma and lead [...] to social emancipation' as Richard Carlile and others in the nineteenth century had expected. This leaves out at least one important group mentioned in the essay itself: those pure scientists (or were they applied) belonging to the British Society for Social Responsibility in Science whose assistance in the case of the plastics' factory Young acknowledges. Perhaps there are others? More importantly, the categorisations are too stereotypic to be useful in answering the question why various groups might be against teaching in the interest of working people and human survival. Nor do they help answer what Sarup saw as important questions raised by 'the "new" sociolog[ists]' ('how school knowledge is selected, by whom, and for what purpose?') (Sarup, 1978, 187). Finally, there is nothing in Young's article to prove his 'three kinds of people' *are* the result of 'the schooling of science' rather than the 'wider process of economic and political domination' to which he refers in the same paragraph (59).

Young's discussion of 'relatedness' takes us to the radical educators of the late sixties and early seventies for whom 'relevance' and 'relating the school to life' were watchwords. However, they so concentrated on the human relations of the classroom as to lose connection with any wider culture, if not consciously rejecting it. This tendency has been analysed in its Australian manifestation by John Hinkson (1977). He concentrates on experiments with social studies curricula, community schools and parental involvement. While recognising the positive achievements of many of the radicals, he criticises the movement generally for reducing education to therapy and he draws attention to the 'increasing popularity' of counselling. He writes:

> therapy is linked to a question about the quality of knowledge for social practice. For counselling of the puzzle-solving variety, the subject has apparent autonomy, but it is autonomy *without the knowledge that might give it substance.* The counselled are expected to generate ideals and choices without an opportunity to reflect on *possibilities* via a culture that conceives of more than what is given in immediate social reality. (Hinkson, 52)

Further on he gives a useful definition of therapeutic social relations. These are:

> (1) where the particular content of the social relations — public knowledge, beliefs and values — tends to become, in practice, unimportant. This indifference can take two forms: (a) a will-

ingness to constantly change beliefs or an 'addiction' to novelty;
(b) where the beliefs are superficial and don't inform the action
of the person in any comprehensive way.
(2) where content is reduced largely to concrete immediacy —
the 'here and now' of social structures. (Hinkson, 79-80)

Moving from the pedagogically valuable idea of relevance and a
justified feeling that traditional subject curricula are not necessarily
the best, many radicals failed to go beyond 'local and personal
issues' (Hinkson, 59). They failed to make the marxist distinction
between appearance and essence, or as Hinkson puts it:

> if we look at the radical project of re-making theory and
> practice by the creation of a more concrete knowledge, a pro-
> duct of concrete, face-to-face relations within the community, it
> is not sustained . . . Concrete experiences of anyone in these
> communities are simply not understandable in their concrete
> manifestation because of the abstract nature of our society.
> Marx made it clear that concrete economic events can only be
> understood via abstract theory in a market society . . . This is
> also the case in most areas of life in modern society. Concrete
> relationships with bureaucrats, social workers, the local branch
> of the large corporation, schools, become a nonsensical
> common-sense outside of an abstract process of understanding.
> (Hinkson, 69)

One must add a caveat: the level of abstraction must be right!
Denis Lawton, a persistent supporter of a common culture
curriculum and critic of both radical and Black Paper positions,
questions relevance from a different slant. Recognising the importance of 'subcultural or regional differences' he asserts that: '*if* an
environment is an extremely limiting one, then to base the whole
curriculum on "relevance" to it may be to "sell the children short"
in a dangerous way' (1975, 28). He sees as the schools' first task,
as it were as a 'charter of pupils' rights' (1978, 51), the transmission of 'public forms of knowledge which comprise our
national, and to some extent, our international culture' (1975, 81).
This, he claims, is 'much more substantial than the kind of basic
skills which Rhodes Boyson and others (Black Papers) have been
talking about (1978, 52).
One recurring point made by radical educators should be

mentioned as it is sure to arise again. That is the question of what
are referred to as 'middle-class values' and 'culture'. Lawton comments in a chapter on 'social class and culture' that 'in some ways
many schools could be said to be middle-class institutions' (1975,
49). But he goes on to say that: 'to accept that most teachers are
middle-class is very different from accepting that *everything* that
the school offers is middle-class culture and, therefore, of no value
to working-class children'. Lawton also objects to suggestions that
'high-culture' is middle class. He says: 'it is very misleading to see
art, music and literature as middle-class, and that it is even more
ridiculous to see science, mathematics and history as middle class'
(1975, 51; cf. Taylor in Richards, 1978, 10). One must agree that
middle class is not a useful concept in this or most other contexts.
It is certainly not one used by Marx for analysis of the social
classes as relations of production. But to recognise class differences, using class in the weak sense of a social stratum, between
pupils and teachers, as Lawton allows, is important. Nor should
one rule out class influences on our knowledge simply because
wholesale labelling is inappropriate. Examples of how precisely in
the natural sciences developments have been shaped by the
capitalist class division recur in this volume.

It is time now to say something about those few remarks which
Marx made about the content of schooling. I have discussed them
at greater length elsewhere (Price, 1973, 1974, 1977). The two
paragraphs most often cited are from the 1866 'Instructions for the
delegates of the Provisional General Council' of the (First) International Working Men's Association, and from the first volume of
Capital. The first reads:

By education we understand three things:
Firstly: *mental education.*
Secondly: *bodily education,* such as is given in schools of gym-
nastics, and by military exercises.
Thirdly: *technological training,* which imparts the general principles of all processes of production, and, simultaneously
initiates the child and young person in the practical use and
handling of the elementary instruments of all trades. (Marx,
GCFI, 345)

The second reads:

> As Robert Owen has shown us in detail, the germ of the edu-
> cation of the future is present in the factory system; this edu-
> cation will, in the case of every child over a given age, combine
> productive labour with instruction and gymnastics, not only as
> one of the methods of adding to the efficiency of production,
> but as the only method of producing fully developed human
> beings. (*CAP*, 1, 614)

The context of these statements is important. They both embody
Marx's acceptance of what was: e.g. mental education, or
(uncritically!) that part-work schooling was proving successful.
The first statement was in a document proposing a programme for
working-class organisations and was aimed at improving what was
provided for working-class children, ignoring others. In neither
case were the statements part of an argued case about knowledge,
school knowledge or other aspects of education. Nevertheless, the
point about combining education and productive labour recurs
elsewhere and was an enduring belief of Marx's.

The technological training, or polytechnical education as it is
usually called, which Marx describes in the first passage is a cognitive process largely concerned with the interaction of human
beings and non-human nature. While the first part of Marx's
injunction has been largely ignored in the schools of capitalist
countries that on using various kinds of tools has been widely
adopted from kindergartens to senior secondary schools, though
usually in ways little connected with industrial production and certainly without drawing inspiration from Marx. The *Capital*
passages on combining education with productive labour, in part a
result of misunderstanding the situation reported by factory
inspectors, I believe contain an important element of truth. Young
people need to be involved in the socially useful, adult world and
not isolated from it, fobbed off with simulation games and
preparation for the future. The nature and extent of this participation must be determined in the light of particular, local circumstances, even individual circumstances. That Marx was concerned
with the social aspects of learning is shown by another passage in
Capital which I think should be read together with the first.

> It is also obvious that the fact that the collective working group
> is composed of individuals of both sexes and all ages must under
> the appropriate conditions turn into a source of humane

development, although in its spontaneously developed, brutal, capitalist form, the system works in the opposite direction, and becomes a pestiferous source of corruption and slavery, since here the worker exists for the process of production, and not the process of production for the worker. (*CAP*, 1, 621)

Combining labour and education has, of course, been advocated by all positions on the political spectrum (Pinkevitch, 1929, 158-201) and in the form of job training is a popular theme with business leaders and governments. The literature is vast and much of it is illuminating. That an essential part of a general education is understanding how the political economy of the world, in broad terms, works probably few would deny today. But translating that into a school curriculum is only part of what those inspired by Marx's vision need to think about.[23]

To conclude, Marx directs attention to the interests, especially class interests, which lie behind the selection and provision of school knowledge today and the problem of providing suitable curricula if schools are to help in the process of social change. In the former task Marx's concept of ideology is central, requiring application in a much more thorough way than has been attempted so far.[24] Analyses using the definition of ideology as both appearance rather than essence and the class interest bias should yield fresh insights. Studies must include questions of abstractness, especially questions of (appropriate) levels of abstraction, both in systematic and traditional subject studies and looser structured, topic-organised curricula. There will, of course, be considerable difficulties in any attempts to move from analysing ideology versus science in syllabi and teaching materials to studying the process of teaching itself. But to clarify what is being presented to both teachers and, through them, learners, is already a step forward in an area up to now vague and full of untheorised assumptions.

As for what one would offer in place of what is taught today, the guiding question is surely: at this historical moment what is it we should teach which is in the interest of the great majority of working people, and in the interest of human survival? As a corollary to this I would also ask what is possible (for pedagogical, psychological, etc. reasons); and why various groups or persons might be for or against such teaching and what to do about that. This would involve *systematically* exploring the ideas, actions and interrelations of the various institutions, organisations, societies and groups which influence the selection and presentation of curricula. These include organs of the state at both central and local level, political parties, trade unions, capitalist business organisations, religious organisations and organisations of academics and teachers. The importance of examination bodies has already been confirmed by research. What, if any, difference does it make when this is part of the state apparatus, a semi-independent academic body or a commercial enterprise? What does this tell us about the nature of education in contemporary capitalism? What role do school subject associations, education authority advisory services (curriculum and research departments, inspectorate advisory services, resource centres, or in-service education provision), or teacher education institutions (departments and colleges) play? A neglected question on which I will say something further below is that of censorship and copyright. At present our knowledge of each of these areas separately is insufficient.[25] Of their interrelations and how we might theorise about them there is nothing.

Notes

1. The letter of Engels to Baron von Boenigk is still relevant to this question. (See Draper, 1978, 2, 534 and the Marx-Engels *Werke*, 37, 447-8).

2. In a private communication during a visit to the Philosophical Society of the University College of the South West, Exeter, in 1950.

3. Halsey reports similarly, using a 1910-29 and 1930-49 comparison (Cosin *et al.*, 228).

4. Very detailed information for France is given in Baudelot and Establet (1972), pp. 72-83.

5. Willis reports Asian shopkeepers and students as being seen as 'cissy' by 'the lads', some of whom engage equally in 'queer-bashing' and 'Paki-bashing' (Willis, 153).

6. Hoggart speaks of 'low conspiracy theory' and 'high conspiracy theory', meaning direct interference and indirect influence respectively (*Bad News*, 1, xi).

7. I was reminded of this by Constance Lever in a personal communication.

8. *A Contribution to the Critique of Hegel's Philosophy of Law*, written in 1843.

9. See, for example, Christopher Hill's *The World Turned Upside Down*, and E.P. Thompson's The Making of the English Working Class.

10. The Freedom of Information Act, 1982.

11. In Britain prior to the 1952 Cinematograph Act regulations about the use of inflammable and non-inflammable film often served unintentionally to censor what small, informal audiences could see.

12. See also the publications of both the British National Council for Civil Liberties and the US National Emergency Civil Liberties Committee for problems of meeting and assembly.

104 *The Distribution of Knowledge*

13. Sawer draws attention to the difficulties of definition. Obscenity in common law means the 'objective tendency to deprave or corrupt', a difficult phrase to interpret surely? In statute law it means 'works which "unduly emphasize matters of sex, horror, violence or crime or are likely to encourage depravity"' (235).

14. Author of *Zur Sozialpsychologie des Kapitalismus* (1972), his case is discussed in the impressively supported Festschrift, *Zum Beispiel Peter Brueckner*, edited by Alfred Krovoza and Klaus Ottomeyer.

15. Ollman took the courageous step of filing a civil suit against the President and Board of Regents of the University of Maryland: see *Critique*, 14, 109-20. For other accounts of censorship see: Krishan Kuman in Curran *et al.*, 231-48 on the BBC; also Michael Tracey's articles, 'Yesterday's Men', 249-69 for a system in which the intent to censor is only one of many factors.

16. These are noted for Australia in James Lahore (1980).

17. For example, Dorfman and Mattelart, *How to Read Donald Duck: Imperialist Ideology in the Disney Comic*, or Dixon, *Catching them Young*.

18. Harris gives it as 'anything that would seriously work against the vested interests of those providing education', i.e. 'the state and the ruling groups in society' (161). While I sympathise with the sentiment I find the formulation too sweeping and conspiratorial.

19. According to Apple (1979, 84, 180 n. 2) this term was first used by Philip Jackson in *Life in the Classroom* (Holt, Rinehart and Winston, New York, 1968), pp. 3-37.

20. Michael Matthews attempts a marxist critique of this school, naughtily referring to it as APE (1980, 156-76).

21. Hirst's criteria are: (1) distinctive concepts; (2) logical interrelations or conceptual structure; (3) distinctive truth tests; and (4) distinctive methodologies for formulating the truth claims.

22. In the early seventies a young teacher spoke to a group of La Trobe University diploma of education students on work he was doing with a community class in a local high school. Many of the phrases he used could have been quotations from Russian educators of the 1920s, whose works he neither knew nor had access to.

23. Stephen Castles and Wiebke Wustenberg (1979) write about polytechnical education in various countries and in theory, while Harold Entwistle (1979) comments (with useful references) on the background of Marx's comments on schooling.

24. Apple (1979); Giroux (1981); Harris (1979); Sarup (1978 and 1982); Sharp (1980) all discuss ideology, but only Apple and Harris deal specifically, and then briefly, with the content of school knowledge.

25. The volume by Geoff Whitty and Michael Young, *Explorations in the Politics of School Knowledge* has some good contributions on individual topics and Section 4 moves towards putting some of the pieces together. It is suggestive of what could be done.

PART THREE: EDUCATION AS PROCESS AND STRUCTURE

6

EDUCATION AS PROCESS AND STRUCTURE

Marx's conception of the process of human history as 'revolutionary practice', a 'coincidence of the changing of circumstances and of human activity', embodies a concept of education as a learning-teaching process. The essential questions about human beings, their human nature, their thoughts, feelings and actions, must be pursued in the 'ensemble of social relations', in 'associated humanity'.[1] This is grasped, if darkly, in current talk of 'lifelong learning', in the realisation of the limited role of the schooling of the young. But the conceptualising required by social scientists, educators and even more by the wider human group whose understanding is needed to 'change the world' has hardly begun. Education continues to be equated with schooling and the functions of schools to be misunderstood.

Conceiving education as above all a learning process need not imply intentionality or linking with a teaching process. The degree to which such linkage does occur is a historical, social question and also a question of personal history. It is one of the features of late capitalism that we have become accustomed to thinking such a link necessary and to expect intentional learning in a teaching situation before practice is seen to be legitimate. Yet in earlier social systems and among the less schooled much of what people know and can do is the result of everyday living, common observation and common sense.

In order to clarify the process of learning the unintentional and the intentional need to be grasped separately and in their interaction. If for intentional we substitute voluntary we immediately confront that important element, the will, or motivation. It is more commonly admitted to be important than that other concept, the unconscious — which tends to throw 'materialists', even dialectical ones, into 'a state'. Both require treatment in any definitive examination of the learning process.

Teaching is usually thought of as an intentional process. But it makes sense to ask what it was which brought about some or other learning where no intentional teaching agent was involved. The 'hidden curriculum' is of this latter nature. It is important to recognise that learning occurs both in the absence of, and often contrary to, intentions. This needs to be said since all too often assumptions are of the simplistic 'learning equals teaching' variety, whether the topic is the effect of certain schooling or the gross learnings in a social system.[2]

Of course, many people, especially professional teachers, like to reserve terms such as education, learning and teaching for what they regard as the more lofty and positive aspects of these processes. Education is enlightenment to be distinguished from indoctrination, training, or instruction. While such distinctions have an impressive genealogy such specialised usage can cause us to overlook other aspects of education which signally affect the enlightenment which is desired.

Others will ask whether, if education is a lifelong process of learning which occurs in all or any situations, we have not expanded its definition to a point where it is uselessly vague and all-embracing.[3] There certainly is such a danger and we must return to the question later in the discussion. Here I want to pose a different problem which intrudes into discussions of education, whether these arise in political-social or pedagogical contexts. That is the problem of the subject of education: is it the individual or some group? Both in theory and practice we seem to slide about between these two levels, often unaware we are doing so.

On this question the dialectical principle of integrative levels would seem to offer clarification, if only of a preliminary, stage-setting nature. The group, or social level, the level of sociological theory, stands above, yet depends upon the individual, psychological level in such a way that nothing which occurs at the group level can contradict the processes (laws?) of individual psychology. At the same time the social processes are not the sum of the individual and there are new, sociological processes which cannot be reduced to the psychological. That is easy to say, even easy to conceive, but much more difficult to exemplify, to elaborate as 'a rich totality of many determinations and relations' (Marx, *GRUND*, 100).

While I would argue that it is characteristic of Marx's thinking to stress a conception of education as a process, I hasten to add that many other thinkers have done likewise. John Dewey, in 1916, distinguished broad educational processes 'which everyone gets from living with others' from the 'deliberate educating of the young' (Dewey, 1963, 6). But his stress was on the 'intentional agencies', particularly schools, which he believed to be specially necessary in 'an advanced culture' where 'much which has to be learned is stored in symbols' (p. 8). Lawrence Cremin, another member of Teachers' College, Columbia University, speaks of an 'ecology of education' for which we must look:

> beyond the schools and colleges to the multiplicity of indi-
> viduals and institutions that educate — parents, peers, siblings,
> and friends, as well as families, churches, synagogues, libraries,
> museums, summer camps, benevolent societies, agricultural
> fairs, settlement houses, factories, radio stations, and television
> networks. (Cremin, 1976, 29)

Cremin is also notable in that he recognises the sphere, political education, in which such an 'ecology' is specially important. Wishing to 'avoid claiming too much for education' he neverthe-less points out:

> when seeking the sources of social stability and change (and
> especially of social reform and resistance to reform), one must
> consider the possible contributions of all the institutions that
> educate, bearing in mind that the decisive elements may still lie
> elsewhere. (Cremin, 1976, 36-7)

It is, perhaps, a measure of the difficulty of elaborating such an 'ecology of education' that no one appears to have seriously attempted to do it. Marxist writers like Gramsci, members of the Frankfurt School, and the English historian, Edward Thompson, have given important pointers. Rachel Sharp notes:

> However important the role of schooling, other institutions or
> apparatuses as well are involved in these processes. Any syste-
> matic account of the ideological function of education has to
> locate education within a more comprehensive theoretical
> framework which takes cognizance of the complex ideological
> mediation occurring within such institutions as the family, the
> media, the churches, and trade unions, as well as within the day-
> to-day routines of capitalist work processes and within the
> forms and practices of the capitalist state. A whole network of
> institutions and practices articulate with those which charac-
> terize what is normally understood as schooling. (Sharp, 1980,
> 116)

Sharp also repeatedly criticises other writers for their lack of consideration of political economy (56, 59, 74, 85, 122). But she does not herself venture beyond 'the politics of schooling'. To move the discussion forward an attempt must be made to see just how these various agents of education relate to each other and who learns what from which, when. Clearly, the family, of particular type, is the first agent to impinge on the great majority of babies, and equally clearly the types of family and their values and conceptions of their teaching role are different in today's capitalism from families in other societies, present and past. Membership in a London West Indian Rastafarian group of unemployed youth teaches quite other from membership of a group of Italian Australian youth of the same age in the eastern suburbs of Melbourne, Australia. What we need is an 'ecology of education', which will embrace and if possible *explain* them both. In the following sections an attempt will be made to sketch out the shape of that ecology, to look at some of its major constituents and the questions which need to be answered if we are to construct what Marx once called 'the natural science of man' (*CW*, 3, 304). To begin with let us look at problems on the psychological level.

The Psychological Level

The co-operative, self-conscious and self-determining society of Marx's vision makes certain assumptions about human beings which its opponents have questioned. IQ testers suggested that the majority of us are too stupid to make the necessary wise decisions. Others hold that we are too weak, too selfish, or too individualistic to act together in the wider interest. It is necessary, therefore, for any study of Marx and education to consider whether what is now known about human psychology confirms or denies the possibilities which Marx set out.

A problem which I shall leave aside is the relation between the biological and the psychological levels, the problem which expresses itself in the arguments about nature and nurture. Instead I shall begin by looking at studies of learning, especially because of the emphasis which I give to this concept in the definition of education. Unfortunately the results of a busy century of study are disappointing. Topics have been carefully limited: memory and rote learning (Ebbinghous, 1885), skill learning (Bryan and Harter,

1897), classical conditioning (Pavlov, 1927) and trial-and-error learning (Thorndike, 1898; Hull, 1943; Skinner, 1938).[4] The limitations of much of this work, not to say its myopic view, have been ably dealt with by Charles Taylor (1964). It has caused many to lament that:

> learning theory has dealt very little with learning from meaningful verbal discourse . . . Even when we consider the field of what is known in the trade as 'verbal learning', we find that the interest is primarily in how well people can learn lists of arbitrary verbal associations and in what factors influence that kind of learning. (Carroll in Ripple, 1971, 324-5)

> Although no one denies the influence of environment upon cognitive development, the fact of the matter is that we actually know very little about changing the intellect of the child. (H. Clarizio and Clarizio *et al.*, 1977, 48)

> Yet, over thirty years later, [after Merriam had set the aim of study], we know next to nothing about 'political socialization' — the process by which people selectively acquire the values, attitudes, interests or knowledge that fit them for particular political roles and make them take these roles in characteristic ways. (Eulau *et al.*, in Rieselbach and Blach, 1969, 134-5)

In the last few decades, largely stimulated by the work of Jean Piaget which belatedly reached the English-speaking world, a deeper approach to learning has developed. Lawton and Hooper note that 'the special relationship between language and logical thought processes remains unknown or conjectural' (in Siegel and Brainerd, 1978, 191).

Ausubel's distinctions help to clarify thinking about learning. He distinguishes between two processes within different dimensions of the learning process. The first distinction is between *reception* and *discovery learning*. The second is between *rote* and *meaningful learning*. He points out that 'expository verbal instruction, or reception learning, can be either rote or meaningful depending on the materials to be learnt and/or the circumstances. Discovery learning is, by definition, always meaningful, involving as it does some kind of problem-solving stage' (Ausubel, 1963, 15-24). Ausubel also distinguishes three phases of the 'meaningful reception learning' process: a perceptual phase; a learning-retention phase; and a reproduction of retained information phase (1963, 50). The perceptual phase he sees as influenced by 'attitudes, motivations, expectations and cultural frames of reference'. This schema is similar to that noted by Rose in his discussion of memory and the brain. Rose describes learning as a change of brain state during the formation of a new memory and suggests it consists of at least two processes and an entity: i.e. learning and recall, and some kind of memory trace. He also draws attention to such phenomena as 'attention, arousal, motivation, and sensitivity to the rewarding or aversive stimulus offered as a learning incentive' (Rose, 1976, 232, 258). Like the psychologists cited above, Rose is unable to claim great progress. Speaking of the brain as a complex system of pathways he adds: 'such pathways do not yet allow an approach to the major brain functions of learning and memory, drive, motivation or consciousness' (1976, 136).

The old approaches of regarding the human mind, 'whether of hereditary or experiential origin, as fixed and irreversible from an early age', while discredited, refuse to lie down (A.D.B. Clarke, 1978, 251). A.R. Jensen, beginning with his article in the *Harvard Educational Review* (1969), has been a leading figure in the renewed controversy over 'heredity *versus* environment', prompting McVicker Hunt to comment:

> of course, both are important and it's the interaction between them that counts. Actually, I dislike using the term 'environment'; I much prefer to use the term 'experience', for it's not the environmental circumstances *per se* that influence development, but the changes that occur in an organism as it makes efforts to cope with its environment. (Pines, 1979, 67)[5]

In his book, *Intelligence and Experience* (1961), McVicker Hunt draws on work in conceptual development, animals learning to learn, neuropsychology and on programming electronic computers to solve problems to conclude that 'with such a conception of intelligence, the assumptions that intelligence is fixed and that its development is predetermined by the genes are no longer tenable' (1961, 362). A.D.B. Clarke cites Mischel (1977) who develops 'what others have called the transactional model of man' (Clarke,

1978, 254). Behaviour is determined by multiple factors and there is: 'continuous interaction both within the person and the situation . . . [W]e continuously influence the situations in our lives as well as being affected by them in a mutual organic interaction'. Mischel also advocated the need 'to develop a taxonomy of environments'. It might seem attractive to see certain environments as critical, causing a more permanent change in mental structures, but the identification of these would seem to be only possible on a *post hoc* basis without possibilities for prediction.

The bulk of studies carried out by Piaget or inspired by him have been in the area of what might be called the logical operations of thinking. Piaget's own interest lay in the nature of knowledge itself and, according to Furth (cit. Brown and Desforges, 1979, 19), he devoted himself to child psychology in the belief that this would provide him with the necessary understanding of the former. Eschewing the methods of testing and statistical processing employed by the intelligence testers, Piaget and his collaborators developed a more qualitative, clinical style which they came to call 'critical exploration' (Inhelder, cit. Brown and Desforges, 163). The theory offered to explain the development of thought is one of *stages.* Brown and Desforges note, in their critical study, that: 'these stages have a necessary and invariant sequence, stemming originally from physical action but moving by a complex process of reconstruction to increasingly sophisticated mental structures' (1979, 19). Nathan Isaacs, in an earlier critical comment, makes the point that a major outcome of Piaget's work is: 'the dominant psychological fact or law that thought is action internalised and so turned in *operation,* and that the growing organisation and structure of our thought-world simply reflects the cumulative operational thought-work done by us' (Isaacs, 1959, 43).

Piaget's theory sees the child moving through four major stages: the sensory-motor from approximately 0-2 years; the preconceptual from approximately 2-7 years; the concrete operational from about 7 years; and finally the formal operational stage which normally begins during the early teens. As Pinard and Laurendeau note 'Piaget's system naturally invites one to adopt extreme attitudes of acceptance or rejection' (Elkind, *et al.,* 1969, 121). Piaget is criticised for his method, for his treatment of language-thought correspondences, for an inadequate account of individual differences and for his account of the effects of experience (Flavel in Brown and Desforges, 163). For the educator a major issue remains that of maturation versus experience, of the role which education can play in what is clearly a process of 'slow inward evolutionary growth' (Isaacs, 36). Perhaps further light will be thrown on these questions if the distinction taken into Piagetian theory from Chomsky by Flavell and Wohlwill is developed. This is the distinction between competence and performance (Brown and Desforges, 92). A competence model: 'gives an abstract, purely logical representation of what the organism knows or could do in a timeless, ideal environment' (Elkind, 71). Performance, or the 'automaton model': 'has the job of describing a real device that could plausibly instance that knowledge or skill, and instance it within the constraints (memory limitations, rapid performance, etc.) under which human beings actually operate'. According to both Flavell and Wohlwill (1969) and Brown and Desforges (1979) Piaget's theories are competence rather than performance models, though the latter note this is a 'matter of contention' (93).

In addition to a study of logical operations both Piaget and others have been concerned with what might be loosely called values. In 1932 Piaget wrote *The Moral Judgement of the Child* in which he set out from a study of children's games to investigate 'what was meant by respect for rules from the child's point of view' (Piaget, 1965, 7). This work was taken further in the late fifties and sixties by Lawrence Kohlberg who established a series of six stages of moral reasoning through which he claims children do and must pass during development.[6] Kohlberg see justice as the central principle toward which his stages tend. Moreover, the stages are seen as 'structures of moral judgement' (Kohlberg, 1977, 55), a 'general guide to choice rather than a rule of action' (Kohlberg, 1971, 58). They are, he insists, 'metarules — rules for the creation and evaluation of rules — rather than first-order rules' (Kohlberg, 1971, 60).

Kohlberg claims lineage with John Dewey in recognising moral thinking as developing as an *active* process (Kohlberg, 1977, 53), and not simply as the internalising of social rules in some form of passive process. His stages range from a preconceptual stage where the subject is responsive to rewards and punishments, through stages of convention, conformity to outside standards, to an autonomous, principled level where moral values are seen as to some extent apart from the authority of the groups holding them.

Loevinger and Blasi, in a book on ego development, look at some of the ongoing research projects which are also relevant to our concerns. Robert Selman is working on growth in reasoning about interpersonal relations (Loevinger, 1976, 436). John Broughton is working on children's development of what he calls 'natural epistemologies' (441). Augusto Blasi is working on the development of responsibility (446). A number of workers aim to change the mental development of the subjects they are studying (453), something which combines education with research and perhaps brings us nearer to understanding real-life situations.

The only comfort for the future which can be drawn from all this is that the more dogmatic pessimists have been shown to have no proof for their assertions and some have been discredited. But that is still a long way from understanding, much less from being able to assist confidently in the learning process.

The Psychology of Lucien Seve

Largely ignoring the work of psychologists and turning his critical attention instead on humanists and structuralists within the French Communist Party, Lucien Seve finally published his ideas in the monumental *Man in Marxist Theory and the Psychology of Personality*.[7] Since the book addresses precisely the problems of how human beings learn, and, moreover, bases itself on a detailed examination of Marx's writings as they concern the question, it is fitting to examine it here.

As Timpanaro points out, one of the virtues of this long and often repetitive book, is its 'interpretative honesty' (1975, 212-13). In the two chapters which explore Marx's writings liberal citations allow us to judge for ourselves his interpretations, 'readings' which he reminds us should be objective.[8] Seve shows how Marx, in the 1844 *Manuscripts*, is still limited by an abstract concept of man, but overcomes this limitation already in *The German Ideology* (1845-6). Seve concentrates his analysis on this latter work and on *The Grundrisse* (1857-8) and *Capital* (1857). In attempting to construct from this analysis a 'marxist conception and practice' of psychology, Seve takes as his key Marx's sixth thesis on Feuerbach, written in 1845: 'Feuerbach resolves the essence of religion into the essence of man. But the essence of man is no abstraction inherent in each single individual. In its reality it is the ensemble of the social relations (*CW*, 5, 4). Seve comments on this: 'In other words the essence of the human individual is not originally within himself but outside in an excentric position in the world of social relations' (Seve, 138-9).

Supporting this assertion Seve notes such passages as that in *The Germany Ideology* where Marx writes: 'the real intellectual wealth of the individual depends entirely on the wealth of his real connections', and 'circumstances make men just as much as men make circumstances' (*CW*, 5, 51, 54). From such beginnings Seve (302) sets out to construct his own conceptual framework for a theory of personality conforming with historical materialism.

The personality is conceived as divided into an infrastructure and superstructure. The former Seve defines as 'the ensemble of activities which produce and reproduce the personality in whatever sector' (336). The superstructure, while not directly contributing to this, nevertheless, 'plays a *regulating role* in relation to these processes' (350). At the level of the emotions the superstructure is an 'ensemble of *spontaneous controls* which are essentially of internal origin' (350), presumably linked with the biophysiological level of organisation. At the same time the superstructure is also the level at which 'voluntary control' operates (351).

In describing the working of both the infra- and superstructures Seve defines a number of basic concepts. The first of these is the *act* which is conceived as an item of behaviour which 'does something' socially (304-5). It is:

any behaviour of an individual, at whatever level, considered not only as behaviour, i.e. related *to psychism*, but as concrete activity, i.e. related *to a biography; in other words, considered in relation to the fact that it (later) produces a number of consequences* not only immediately for the individual himself but for society ... (311)

Related to the act is the concept of *capacity.* 'The act presupposed the capacity... and the capacity itself increasingly presupposes the act, which can be divided into *manifestation* and *production* of capacities' (331). Capacities are defined as: 'the ensemble of "actual potentialities", innate or acquired, to carry out any act whatever and whatever its level' (313). Seve prefers the term capacity to that of aptitude, so common in educational writings, as he regards the latter to have 'both an innatist and socially relative sense' (312).

Acts are seen as related to two other basic concepts: need and product. Seve argues that '*need* cannot *by itself* [play] the part of a *basic* concept in the theory of the developed personality' (315), though it may do this at the animal level. At the human level there is an activity-need-activity series which can also be read as need-activity-need, but which really requires explanation as a historical, developmental whole. That the forms and norms of needs take on a profoundly social character has long been recognised. More important is the way in which they are developed and reproduced with a *margin of tolerance*, a radically new structure of motivation (318).

Finally we come to the concept of *use-time* (l'emploi du temps). This is 'the system of temporal relations between the various objective categories of an individual's activity' (334). Real use-time is to be distinguished from both empirical and ideal use-time since it has a qualitative aspect depending on the nature of social, abstract activity. That is, real use-time is objective, to be distinguished from both how one appears to live at the level of appearance, and how one aims and strives to live (334-6). As Seve remarks, 'use-time is the real infrastructure of the developed personality' (334) and the degree to which this is individually or socially controlled is one of the important questions both for the development and the expression of personality. In this connection Seve distinguishes between *optative use-time*, or primary superstructural time, and real use-time (350) and formulates a view of the voluntary controls of the personality as: 'not essentially through *direct interiorisation* of social institutions and values but through their assimilation *on the psychological basis of the abstract personality*' (351). Linking voluntary controls with the abstract personality and spontaneous controls with the concrete, both are at one level endogenous and psychological, and at another, deeper level social, exogenous. Seve adds:

> The superstructural psychological contradictions between spontaneous and voluntary controls, between the desired act and the act which is required, are not *original* contradictions, as the mystifying ideology of the metaphysical contradiction between 'nature' and 'culture', 'individual' and 'society', imagines; beyond their relative specificity they are the reflection of the infrastructural contradictions between concrete and abstract personality, between self-expression and alienated labour, i.e. in

the last analysis they also bear witness to class contradictions. (352)

Returning to the infrastructure, Seve illustrates what he refers to as 'the topology of the real use-time', admittedly 'very schematically and hypothetically' (346). He illustrates this with a diagram divided into four sectors. Horizontally it is divided into Sector 1, 'the set of acts which produce, develop or specifically determine capacities', and Sector 2, 'the set of acts which, only making use of the capacities already existing, produces some effect which the exercise of these capacities makes it possible to attain' (313). Vertically it is divided into the concrete personality on the left, the 'ensemble of direct, personal, and particularly consumer activities', and the abstract personality on the right, 'the ensemble of social, but alienated, productive activities' (346-7). Seve sees as particularly significant the opposition between these last two.

Diagram 1

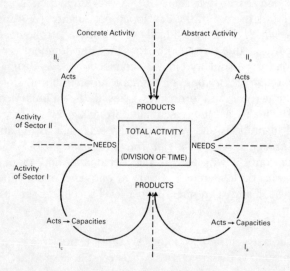

Seve proceeds to give examples of what such diagrams might look like in the case of (1) a child of school-age; (2) a student who does not work to pay for his studies; (3) a factory worker not engaged in militant activity in his spare time; and (4) a retired elderly person carrying out a few small social tasks (348-9).

Diagram 2

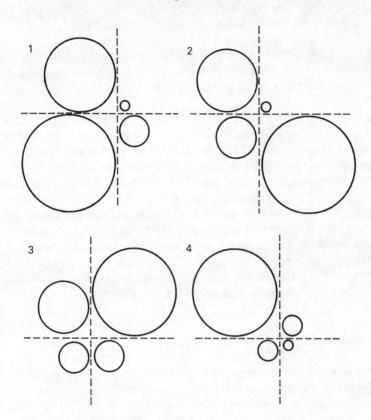

Evaluation

It is easy to dismiss all this, as Paddy O'Donnell does, as simply part of the 'esoterica of French [Communist Party] hermeneutics' (1981, 10). It is also true that his concepts are for the most part crude borrowings from Marx's economic concepts, 'off the peg' as O'Donnell puts it. But the discussion of use-time and of the distinction between concrete and abstract activity is thought provoking precisely about those questions of importance for education for radical change.

As Timpanaro acknowledges, one of Seve's values is in his recognition of human beings as biological as well as psychological and social. Seve speaks of:

the transition from living beings bearing their essence in themselves as a biological heritage to others bearing their essence outside themselves as a social heritage (191), and

social individuality itself develops within biological individuals who as such are not at all the product of the social base and its contradictions but of a quite distinct reality. (144)

He speaks of character, temperament and nervous type as the 'essentially physiological structure of individual psychism', but in the developed human being he sees this as overlaid and dominated by the socially derived elements (213). However, in another place he qualifies this when he mentions death and 'the relative contingency of the singular course of biography' (256). Timpanaro goes further in noting the importance of 'the various social and cultural sub-groups' to which human beings belong and asks for the whole frame, from the social in all its educational, teaching-learning aspects, through the psychological to the biological level (1975, 217). Only when these are all recognised more clearly can the interactions of the separate layers be worked out.

Psychoanalysis

In view of the influence which psychoanalysis, and especially Freud, has exerted on 'western marxism' it is necessary to make some brief comments here.[9] The positive side of psychoanalysis is, of course, that unlike many other schools of psychology it has recognised the psychological level of organisation. But, as Seve and Timpanaro have both pointed out, it has shown a 'lack of interest in economic and social facts' (Timpanaro, 1975, 53). Its concentration on the persisting effects of infancy and often mono-causal approach amount to a form of reductionism almost as dangerous as the physiological psychologies which they ignore (Seve, 382). But it is open to misunderstanding to suggest, as does Timpanaro, that 'it may be that Pavlov will have more to tell us than Freud' (Timpanaro, 1975, 54).

Habermas is one of those 'western marxists' who turns to Freud to 'represent a structure that Marx did not fathom' (Habermas, 1972, 281-2), namely Habermas's concept of 'reflective knowledge'. Important as this concept might be for some future society in which communication, in Habermas's conception, can become the rule, as a present means of understanding the personality it leaves too much to the imagination. This emerges in a passage in which Habermas betrays no hint of criticism:

> Only the metapsychologically founded and systematically generalized history of infantile development with its typical developmental variants puts the physician in the position of so combining the fragmentary information obtained in analytic dialogue that *he can reconstruct the gaps of memory and hypothetically anticipate the experience of reflection of which the patient is at first incapable. He makes interpretive suggestions for a story that the patient cannot tell.* (Habermas, 1972, 260, emphasis added)

Here we see the analyst putting words into the patient's mouth and no comment is made. This is not the only place where Habermas unintentionally makes clear in his description the more than tentative nature of the hypotheses he is embracing. This passage also accepts uncritically the special importance of 'infantile development', an importance still highly problematic. It recurs in the following passage where only the almost imperceptible 'if' heralds a warning:

> But if the natural basis of the human species is essentially determined by surplus impulses and extended childhood dependency, and if the emergence of institutions from structures of distorted communication can be comprehended on this basis, then power and ideology acquire a different and more substantial role than they do for Marx. (Habermas, 1972, 283)

Those who have followed the account of ideology in Marx's works cited here may wonder what kind of 'reading' Habermas has been applying. While there is no doubt that many of his comments on education have been stimulating I do not find this flirtation with Freud helpful and must disagree with Frankel that Habermas has made a 'major contribution to the understanding of learning processes' (in D'Cruz and Hannah, 1979, 197). Though we begin to see the macro, political-economic and social level and the micro, psychological level more clearly in their separation we have yet hardly begun to put them together.

Attainment Testing

Attainment testing is concerned, not with understanding the learning-teaching process, but with attempting to discover what students have learnt, what they know. Both oral and written forms of attainment testing were developed long before capitalism and mass schooling developed. Its use in selecting civil servants in China has a long and well-documented history. But with the development of late capitalism and the 'diploma disease' it has become more pervasive and taken new forms, most recently employing the new high technology capitalism has provided.[10] While some tests can be regarded as in the interests of those tested, perhaps helping them to gauge their own progress in learning, a majority of them are employed for governmental and administrative purposes: to select people, to check and control people.[11] Both their purpose and the methods employed must raise serious doubts in the minds of those with the imagination to envisage a different society.

Here I want simply to introduce two of the larger and widely commented upon tests, study of which reveals the difficulties, and the dangers of uncritically relying on the experts. The first test was entitled 'Equality of Educational Opportunity' and was carried out by the US Office of Education. It is usually referred to by the name of the principal author of the report published in 1966, Professor James S. Coleman of Johns Hopkins University. Approximately 645,000 children from grades 1, 3, 6, 9 and 12 from some 4,000 schools in 50 states and the District of Columbia were involved. They were given standardised tests in reading, writing, calculating and problem solving. The report points out that these do not measure students' intelligence, attitudes or character, but rather skills that 'are among the most important in our society for getting a good job and moving up to a better one, and for full participation in an increasingly technical world' (Report cit. Silberman, 1971, 63). Silberman points out that the study owes its existence to a section of the 1964 Civil Rights Act which directed the US Commissioner of Education 'to conduct a survey . . . concerning the lack of availability of equal educational opportunity for individuals by reason of race, colour, religion, or national origins'. This survey was to be reported to the President and Congress within two years (Silberman, 71). Not surprisingly, the results showed: 'students from minority groups — Indian Americans, Mexican

Americans, Puerto Ricans and blacks — scored substantially below white students . . . [and] the disparity either remains the same or widens as each group goes through school' (Silberman, 63).

In the furore which followed the report various groups re-analysed the data, including staff members and consultants for the US Civil Rights Commission Report on *Racial Isolation in the Public Schools*, members of the Harvard University Seminar on the Equality of Educational Opportunity Report, and Jencks and others at the Center for Educational Policy Research. Criticisms included problems with sampling, the statistical techniques employed and errors in handling the data. However, in the end it appeared that the general force of the findings was confirmed. Jencks commented: 'In particular, and contrary to what some critics have argued, the net effect of the report's various errors was to *under*-estimate the importance of family background and *over*-estimate the importance of school in determining achievement' (cit. Silberman, 72-3).

Silberman went on to add that the Coleman Report's 'most important and controversial conclusion', that the effect of the school on students' achievement was minimal while variations in family background 'have substantial impact' was supported by evidence from elsewhere. He cited the Plowden Report of 1967 in England and a study by J. Burkhead of Syracuse University in the US (Silberman, 73).

The second study is the long series of tests of different school subjects conducted in various countries under the auspices of a 12-nation consortium, the International Association of the Evaluation of Educational Achievement (IEA). Known for short as the IEA Surveys, the project was launched at a meeting of researchers at the UNESCO Institute for Education in Hamburg in 1958 and the major reports were published between 1973-5 (Husen, 1979, 371). Subjects tested included science, literature, reading comprehension, English as a foreign language, French as a foreign language, civic education and mathematics. In all 21 countries took part in at least part of the programme and 'standardised tests [were] administered to strictly comparable samples of students from one nation to the next' (Inkeles, 1979, 386).

In an interesting critical article Torsten Husen from the University of Stockholm, first director of the IEA, sets out the original conception which he admits to have been 'a rather simplistic conceptualization':

We wanted, first, to develop internationally valid measures of students competence in the key subject areas. Second, we wanted to measure the 'input' of money, teacher competence, teaching materials, teaching time, and method of instruction in the educational process. Finally, these inputs had to be related to 'outputs' in each country in terms of student achievements and attitudes. Then we would be in a position to determine the relative importance of various input factors. (Husen, 380)

He refers approvingly to the 'more sophisticated methods of multivariate analysis' used in such studies as the Coleman Report, research for the Plowden Commission and the Jencks study (Husen, 380) and adds:

The straightforward paradigm with representative samples and strict quantitative and standardized methods to test hypotheses uniformly over a number of age levels and countries seemed at the time to be self-evident. We never seriously considered an alternative strategy, for example, limiting ourselves to a selection of a few schools and classrooms that could be subjected to *intensive, qualitative observations.* We certainly expected too much from the broadly collected information that was obtained by questionnaires from the students about their home background and from the teachers about how they taught. (Husen, 382, emphasis added)

Inkeles, in his article, adds to the criticism. But neither of them deals with the structural factors which make such studies attractive even when arguments against them are already known. These include the ease with which they generate considerable data which can then be handled statistically, appearing objective in the process. The inter-governmental, hierarchical nature of the UNESCO system means that large sums of money can, or could, be mobilised. This is a temptation to the inflation of projects beyond what the real state of the art should allow. Returning to the educational level of criticism, there is the temptation, given these surveys, to use their dubious findings in spite of doubts when they fit the case one is arguing.

I have singled out these two examples because they have been used in argument about society and have not met the same sustained criticism as the field of aptitude and intelligence testing has. The whole field of testing is an important and controversial one, clearly reflecting the political economic and social realities of today.

Notes

1. Two places in Marx especially bring out these ideas: the Theses on Feuerbach (*CW*, 5, 3-5 and, revised by Engels, 6-8) and that passage in *The Holy Family* where he and Engels comment on French materialism (*CW*, 4, 130-1). The latter ends frustratingly with the comment: 'This is not the place to assess them', i.e. propositions like 'If man is shaped by environment, his environment must be made human.' The present book is in part an attempt at assessment.

2. Writings on the People's Republic of China prior to 1966, and even after, were full of examples of such faith, whether motivated by pro- or anti-communist feeling. One example is *The Making of a Model Citizen in Communist China* by Ridley, Godwin and Doolin.

3. Lawrence Cremin, who limits 'education' to 'deliberate, systematic, and sustained effort', is one who fears a definition 'so inclusive as to be meaningless' (Cremin, 1976, 29). One of his reviewers, Eisele, disagrees: '[E]ducational questions can be asked about any historic event, and any historic institutions or event can be viewed as potentially educational — able to be described in educational language' (Eisele, 1980, 28).

4. References to key personnel and research are from J. McV. Hunt in Elkind *et al.* (eds) (1969, 32).

5. Both the science and the politics of IQ have been nicely dealt with by L.K. Kamin (1977).

6. For an introductory criticism see Crittenden in D'Cruz and Hannah (1979). More will be said below.

7. French edition (1974), English (1978). The blurb on the latter hails it as having 'rapidly become recognised as the key book to have been published in developing a science of human personality based on historical materialism. It has no rivals in its range and coverage'. The last is true, again a reason why it cannot be ignored here.

8. Seve makes telling criticisms of Althusser's method of 'symptomatic reading' (73, 163).

9. Perry Anderson (1979, 57-8, 82-5) outlines the connections, setting them in the more general framework of western marxism's 'most striking single trait ...', the constant presence and influence on it of successive types of European idealism' (56). See also Timpanaro in New Left Review, 1976.

10. A most useful survey of the older literature on testing is given in C.M. Fleming (1958, 168-91). This includes the problem of the subjectivity of marking.

11. A revealing example is given in Whyte (1960, 183). An American company was about to promote someone when it decided, unexpectedly, to test him beforehand. The testing consultants warned of instability and the man was not promoted. When six months later he had a nervous breakdown the company was relieved to find their testing vindicated!

7 THE SOCIAL STRUCTURES

Marxist discussion has attempted to relate ideas to the social structure, using the concepts consciousness, ideology and class consciousness already introduced above. While this section will concentrate on the actual social structure in particular countries today it will begin with a brief comment on major writings on class consciousness and ideology.

Consciousness is discussed in terms of the relation of ideas to lived (perceived) reality. Given membership of a particular class, religious sect, national or ethnic group how does one perceive the world? What are the particular educational influences which these different environments exert? What role do members play in the educational process? Are they producers of knowledge, transmitters (teachers, parents), or is their role purely that of learner? Clearly, there are group expectations: importantly, expectations of jobs and expectations of power. If one is born into one of the lower classes one does not expect to become a lawyer or a doctor or to become prime minister, whereas these would seem quite natural to someone born into an upper-class family. Born into the upper classes, one is accustomed to seeing power wielded and early wielding it oneself. Born into the lower classes one learns powerlessness young. Which is not to say that no one from the lower classes ever becomes the exception. Similarly, certain classes have distinct class ideologies, e.g. the petty bourgeoisie, or an ideology may be associated with a particular kind of job, e.g. trade union consciousness and factory work (Lenin). This again is not to say that every member of that class or that job will embrace that ideology, or that if someone does embrace it they will embrace it fully. All of which is too general to be of any use. Both as teachers and as political activists we need a much more concrete analysis if 'real communication' is to occur. It is also important, and on this writers on Marx and education have not always been clear, whether one is writing about general, social tendencies, or whether one is concerned with the education of a particular individual.

Those who have applied Marx's idea in a mechanical way have, however, taken the phrase 'social being determines social consciousness' to apply literally to individuals and on this basis have expected certain classes to be progressive or socialist while others have been written off as reactionary. A similar mechanical approach has been to expect social change to come through the prior mass conversion of individuals to a particular world view, or 'socialist consciousness', and to search the social structure for the likely candidates for such conversion. A more careful reading of Marx shows his position to have been very different. In the famous passage where he spoke of what the proletariat, because of what it is, would be compelled to do, Marx added that 'a large part of the English and French proletariat is already conscious of its historic task and is constantly working to develop that consciousness into complete clarity' (*CW*, 4, 37). But that did not mean expecting or requiring any mass identity of ideas as a precondition to revolutionary progress. On the contrary, as he wrote years later, the 'real conditions' of the working class are reflected 'in their heads in the most diversified forms, more or less phantastical, more or less adequate' (Fischer, 1970, 150; Marx-Engels, *W*, 32, 671).

Political activists, particularly socialists, have been interested in class consciousness, a term which is used in a number of senses. Miliband suggests four (in Meszaros, 1971, 22-3). Firstly, individuals may have an accurate perception of the class to which they belong. Secondly, individuals may, in addition, be conscious of the immediate interests of that class. Thirdly, they may also have the will to advance that interest. Miliband's fourth usage is for members of the working class having 'a specific commitment to the revolutionary abolition of the capitalist system'. Miliband notes the high degree of class consciousness commonly found amongst members of 'privileged' classes. People in intermediate positions in society are often not class conscious in these senses or identify with classes different from their own.

Istvan Meszaros (1971, 121) adds another distinction, between contingent (stratum-consciousness) and necessary class consciousness, both arising in response to experience. The former 'perceives merely some isolated aspects' of reality while the latter has the total, long-term situation in mind. It is 'consciousness of the necessarily global character of any viable historical alternative to the established order of productive relations'. In converting these consciousnesses into practice, Meszaros argues, it is not having some 'homogeneous *psychological bond*' that is important, but having 'the available programmes and institutional forms' which 'more or less self-conscious', or class-conscious people can relate to. Such programmes need to take account of the complexities of the social structure, the varying interests of different groups and their likely perceptions.

Poulantzas and Olin Wright are two writers on class who have attempted to deal with the connection of a group's social place and its ideas or beliefs. Both demonstrate the lack of an elaborated conceptualisation of education and a workable distinction between the social and individual psychological level. Poulantzas, who incorporates the ideological into his definition of social class (1975, 14), carefully distinguishes himself from 'the historicist problematic' which he particularly associates with Lukacs (1973, 60, 195-206), but also with others like Bourdieu (1973, 61). His objection to seeing ideologies as pure reflections of the physicho-social conditions of existence of the class is sound (1973, 203) and his discussion of the dominance of different regions of ideology (moral, religious, juridical, etc.) illuminating (1973, 210-21). But when it comes to why certain groups adopt a particular ideology at a particular time there is silence. We are told:

> Bourgeois ideology, of course, also exerts its effect within the working class. (1975, 288)

> We cannot rule out the possibility of whole sections of the petty bourgeoisie not only adopting working-class positions, but even placing themselves on the actual terrain of working-class ideology. (1975, 289)

Why 'of course'? What makes for this 'possibility'? Are these in some sense necessities resulting from some structural quality, in which case this needs spelling out, or are they accidents occurring within the limits of the available, class-determined ideological structure? The view of education set out here would suggest the last.

The confusion in which the present state of understanding of educational questions leaves one is well exemplified by the section in Wright (1978) on 'Immediate and Fundamental Class Interests' (pp. 88-91). Fear of being accused of subjectivism runs through the section like a sore, when it is a nettle that should be firmly grasped:

> To talk about the objectives of the class struggle is very similar

to talking about the *subjective motives* or the class *consciousness* of class actors. In general, I prefer to use the expression 'objectives' since it does not have the psychologistic overtones of either subjective motives or consciousness. (p. 88, n. 72)

Wright tries to handle the problems with the concepts class interests and class capacities. Class interests are: 'hypotheses about the objectives of struggles which would occur if the actors in the struggle had a scientifically correct understanding of their situations' (p. 89). This Wright believes to be neither an 'ahistorical, moralistic' nor a 'normative claim', though it may be a 'somewhat oversimplified' one. The point is, he is talking about 'the translation of objective interests into subjective motives', and this is an educational question. He speaks about 'if workers had a scientific understanding of the contradictions of capitalism' (89). His class analysis is to further his belief that 'to define a position as located within the working class is to say that such a position can potentially sustain socialist objectives in class struggles' (89).

Wright defines class capacities as 'the social relations within a class which to a greater or lesser extent unite the agents of that class into a class formation' (p. 98). He sees these as divided into structural capacities, links 'which are generated directly by the structural developments of capitalist society', and organisational capacities, or links 'which are constituted by the conscious organization of the members of that class' (p. 99). His example of the former is the concentration of workers in the factories during the historical development of capitalism, but he warns that this does not mean that 'workers within highly collective, industrial labour processes will necessarily be the most militant' (p. 99 n. 85). Rather, structural capacities 'condition the possibilities for successfully realizing class interests within those struggles' (p. 99 n. 85). Neither of these concepts, class interest nor class capacities, seems to take us on to new ground. Only when class analysis is combined with much more concrete investigation of how ideas arise, are transmitted and take hold within different groups of people, will there be the possibility of more fruitful theorising, but that will require much more serious attention to education.

The Social Classes

Something more must first be said about the polar classes, capitalist and working class (bourgeois and proletariat) whose importance was emphasized in the section on Marx above. These are the appropriators and the producers of surplus value, the peculiar capitalist form of the surplus product. The proletariat, this special class 'whose conditions of life necessarily drive it to social revolution' (Engels cit. Draper, 1978, 36) consists of those workers who produce surplus value in the process of commodity production. This includes many white collar and mental labourers as well as the blue collar industrial workers who are usually referred to as working class. But it excludes many other wage-workers whose conditions are essentially similar, but who do not contribute to the production of surplus value.[1] Draper, emphasizing that Marx's view of the proletariat in no way implied any 'honorific aura' (1978, 34), goes on to stress that calling the proletariat a 'revolutionary class' is to stress its 'historical potential' (1978, 51). The only certainty is that the communist dream cannot be produced without them. Marx's reasons for assigning the proletariat this potential can be summarised as: (1) their conditions of life lead them to organise; (2) their interests, unsatisfied by capitalism, lead them to struggle; (3) their struggles tend to push further than the limits imposed by capitalism; (4) their conditions of struggle tend to produce a high degree of militancy at critical times; (5) it is the only class with the 'social weight and power' to carry through the necessary changes (Draper, 1978, 41-7). Draper sums these points up by saying: 'Marx's theory asserts that *only the proletariat, by the conditions of its existence, embodies a social programme pointing to an alternative to capitalism*' (1978, 47).

This view of the proletariat as the, or even a, revolutionary class has been challenged increasingly from within the ranks of socialists, including those who claim to support Marx's analysis in other aspects. The latest of these is Andre Gorz's *Farewell to the Working Class* which combines a Hegelian parody of Marx's writings on the proletariat with descriptions of the present and calls for a future which only occasionally acknowledges its similarity to what Marx himself wrote. In a parody of a well-known passage from *The German Ideology* Gorz writes of today's 'neoproletariat':

a growing and more or less numerically dominant mass of people moving from one 'job' to another. Learning trades they will never regularly practise, following courses without outlets or practical utility, giving them up or failing them because 'after all, what does it matter', they go on to work in the post office during the summer, to pick grapes in the autumn, to join a department-store staff for Christmas, and to work as a labourer in the spring ... (Gorz, 70)

Is it a certainty they have no class feeling? Maybe. But what will they be compelled by circumstances to do? Gorz himself supplies some of the answers in his discussion of job sharing and working shorter time for the same money, ideas completely consonant with the Marx which he cites on another point (Gorz, 95-6; Marx, *CAP*, 3, 958-9).

The capitalist class, has frequently been ignored by education sociologists, or is said to have perished as a class in the 'managerial revolution' and the era of widespread shareholding. Marx frequently referred to capitalists as 'simply personified capital' pumping out surplus value from the worker (*CAP*, 3, 959; 1019-20). He contrasts the authority the capitalist 'dons as manager and ruler of production' with those of former exploiting classes, owners of slaves or serfs. Authority has become economic rather than political or theocratic (*CAP*, 3, 1021) just as exploitation, through the expropriation of surplus value, has become disguised.[2] This does not mean that one cannot identify members of the capitalist class, whether the owner-employer of the small factory or retail shop employing wage labour, or the director of one of the multinational conglomerates (Mandel, 1968, 233-6; 411-19; 539-41).

An important member of the non-polar classes is the petty bourgeoisie. This consists strictly of owners of their own (small) means of production which they work typically without other than family labour. They may be shopkeepers, small merchants or tradespeople such as carpenters or tailors working on their own account. Marx brought out the paradoxical nature of this class of commodity producers falling outside the system of capitalist production in an illuminating section of *Theories of Surplus Value* (TSV, 1, 408, cit. Draper, 1978, 291). Draper points out the distinction between this class and the small bourgeoisie with whom they are easily confused. The latter are primarily employers of labour whose surplus value they expropriate. In practice the distinction can be a fine one, and one which is not infrequently crossed. (Draper, 1978, 289). The rural petty bourgeoisie, the peasantry, continues to be an important class in such late capitalist countries as France and Germany.

In Search of Reassurance

In recent decades a number of attempts have been made, within a Marxist framework, to define classes more strictly and to look especially at the non-polar classes. In part this has been an exercise in despair at the failure of the socialist movement, in part a function of new understanding, or understanding by new groups on the left, of the social systems of the USSR, Eastern Europe and China, and in part it reflects the pressures of 'academic marxism'.[3] I shall concentrate here on two major accounts: those of Nicos Poulantzas in France and Erik Olin Wright in the USA. But first two quotations from Marx to remind us that he was well aware of the trend towards a growth of 'the middle classes', so often hailed as a refutation of Marx's ideas. Both quotations come from those sections of *Theories of Surplus Value* where Marx discusses certain ideas of Ricardo and Malthus.

What he [Ricardo] forgets to emphasise is the constantly growing number of the middle classes, those who stand between the workman on the one hand and the capitalist and landlord on the other. The middle classes maintain themselves to an ever increasing extent directly out of revenue, they are a burden weighing heavily on the working base and increase the social security and power of the upper ten thousand. (*TSV*, 2, 573)

His [Malthus] supreme hope, which he himself describes as more or less utopian, is that the mass of the middle class should grow and that the proletariat (those who work) should constitute a constantly declining proportion (even though it increases absolutely) of the total population. This in fact is the *course* taken by bourgeois society. (*TSV*, 3, 63 cf. Draper, 1978, 621-3)

Poulantzas begins his book, *Classes in Contemporary*

Capitalism, with the statement that classes are 'groupings of social agents, defined principally but not exclusively by their place in the production process, i.e. in the economic sphere' (14). Emphasising that 'political and ideological relations' are also important he re-shapes the definition to read:

> The class determination, while it coincides with the practices (struggle) of classes and includes political and ideological relations, designates certain objective places occupied by the social agents in the social division of labour: places which are independent of the will of these agents.

He goes on to distinguish 'structural determination' of place with the particular 'class position' adopted by a particular class at a particular time, giving as example the labour aristocracy where it takes up a bourgeois position at a particular place and time (15). He carefully distinguishes between the agents, the individual members of the various classes and the class as a place in the class struggle (17), repeatedly emphasising that it is the latter his analysis is concerned with. Finally, he defines *fractions* and *strata* within various classes, groups distinguished by particular economic, political and ideological relations, and social *categories* for certain groups which cut across classes. Categories include the state bureaucracy and 'the intellectuals, defined by their role in elaborating and deploying ideology' (23).

Poulantzas bases his classification at the economic level on Marx's distinction between productive and unproductive labour, the former being labour which in the capitalist mode of production produces surplus value (209-23). On this criterion, correctly, he follows Marx in distinguishing the working class (proletariat) from the 'wage-earning class', a wider group which includes those working in the 'sphere of the circulation and realization of surplus-value' (94). It is his next step which is so controversial! He chooses to identify the unproductive wage-earning classes with the traditional petty bourgeoisie, calling them the *new* petty bourgeoisie. He justifies this by the debatable claim that they 'nevertheless have the same effects at the political and ideological level' (205).

Poulantzas finally describes three fractions of the new petty bourgeoisie which he sees as having an 'objectively proletarian polarisation':

1. the great majority of lower-level workers in the commercial sector; state and service personnel 'affected by the introduction of machinery' and 'mechanization of labour'; and employees in the service sector such as restaurants, cinemas or lower-level health workers.
2. 'the subaltern agents of the public and private bureaucratized sectors, i.e. 'office workers'.
3. engineers and technicians (i.e. what the British distinguish as technologists, or tertiary educated technical personnel). Acknowledging their status as productive of surplus value, Poulantzas separates them from the working class (proletariat) they are 'involved . . . in the political relations of management and supervision of the labour process' (239) and more importantly, in 'maintain[ing] political and ideological relations of subordination of the working class to capital' (242).[4] Nevertheless, 'in recent years the forms of struggle of this fraction have distinguished it from the various groupings of intermediate engineers and managers' and stamp its nature as 'ambiguous' (326).

Wright, while acknowledging Poulantzas's work as 'the most systematic and thorough attempt to understand precisely the marxist criteria for classes in capitalist society' (1978, 31), prefers a different solution. He objects to the use of productive and unproductive labour to distinguish the working class from the 'new petty bourgeoisie'; to Poulantzas's handling of political and ideological factors; and particularly to the classing together of the new with the old petty bourgeoisie. He argues that 'the ideological divisions between the two categories are at least as profound as the commonalities' and that 'while ideological relations may play a part in the determination of class position, they cannot neutralize divergent class positions [determination] determined at the economic level' (44).

Wright's solution to these objections is to rename what are essentially the same groups as 'objectively contradictory locations within class relations', or 'contradictory class locations'.[5] Using the criteria of control of labour power, control of the physical means of production and control of investments and resources, Wright identifies three such contradictory locations. These are managers and supervisors located between the bourgeoisie and proletariat; small employers located between the bourgeoisie and the petty bourgeoisie; and semi-autonomous employees located between the petty bourgeoise and the proletariat (1978, 87-8). Wright also identifies groups (confusingly using the term position where Poulantzas uses determination) outside the 'social relations of production', but which seen to differ in conceptual level from those identified by the latter as categories. These are 'such positions' as 'housewives, students, pensioners, people permanently on welfare' (88). Wright reveals his interest in preferring such an analysis at the beginning of his essay when he writes: 'Above all, it matters for developing a viable socialist politics how narrow or broad the working class is seen to be' (1978, 31).[6] On such a basis he estimates US working class in 1969, i.e. the 'non-supervisory, non-autonomous employees' to total in between 41-54 per cent of the population, with another 25-34 per cent at 'the boundaries' of the working class (87). However, similar estimates of the working class and those fractions of the petty bourgeoisie 'with an objectively proletarian polarization' would hardly do much worse!

The 'Educated Classes'

Two groups much talked about today must now be dealt with: the middle class and the intellectuals. The middle class(es), of which the intellectuals are usually seen as a part, is often an honorific, self-applied. Marx and Engels used the term in the singular when writing in English in the then British sense of the bourgeoisie (Draper, 1978, 290; cf. 613-27). But in the modern usage of the term it refers to different groups which relate themselves to the two polar classes in different ways, and is of no scientific value. But at the level of appearance it certainly has force. John Welch, in a book of heart-searchings by members of the American New Left, articulates widely felt attitudes. Himself of working-class origin, he comments: 'I never recognised myself nor my family in any of the New Left descriptions of workers' (Walker, 1979, 185). Writing of the 'terrific sense of class hatred' in the USA he says:

> I learned, growing up, that there's Us and Them, ordinary people and 'rich people'. These rich people look down on our sort, and we hate them. Now, in the US we never see the people who are really rich, so those people I called 'rich' were actually the 'upper middle class'. The Scarsdale people, the PMC [professional-managerial class — Ehrenreichs' term]. They were the bosses that we saw; they were the schoolteachers

who acted like missionaries bringing 'culture' to the heathen. They tried to teach us to shut up and be obedient, and they tried to interest us in the elements of the 'finer' culture outside. We made them miserable and they complained: 'How did I get stuck teaching these dummies, why can't I get a job teaching in a *nice* suburb?' (Walker, 186)

This repeats a point made earlier: the real capitalist class is for most people, including most academic sociologists, invisible. Barbara Ehrenreich, writing later in the same book, adds a further dimension to this gut class hatred. Researching with Deirdre English in 1974-8 on different professionals who 'had come to have a defining influence on women's lives and work' she comments: 'it seemed that they had their own class interests' (p. 318). Finally, Sandy Carter brings out the bitterness of women against social workers ('She makes me feel so stupid' [p. 112]) or working-class members of left-wing discussion groups against their middle-class comrades ('The other working class person and I didn't ever say much. When we would talk, we'd always feel stupid' [p. 113]).

Turning to intellectuals, Draper points out that Marx preferred to talk about the 'role of *educated people* (the so-called "educated classes")' and with 'educated recruits of bourgeois background who aspire to specialize in the manipulation of ideas, or conceive this to be their special contribution' (Draper, 1978, 481, 489). Marx deals with their class position in those sections of *Capital* and *Theories of Surplus Value* where he discusses productive labour, i.e. that labour which produces surplus value. In the former he refers to the school teacher who is proletarian in so far as he works in a 'teaching factory' devoted to producing profit for its private proprietor. (*CAP*, 1, 644). Marx uses the same example when he speaks of those cases where 'production cannot be separated from the act of producing . . . all performing artists, orators, actors, teachers, physicians, priests, etc.' Here, he says, 'the capitalist mode of production is met with only to a small extent, and from the nature of the case can only be applied in a few spheres'. He goes on to show that where it does the teacher, actor, etc. are 'productive labourers', 'wage-labourers' *in relation to their employers*, and therefore members of the proletariat (*TSV*, 1, 410-11; Draper, 1978, 489-93).[8]

Like the 'middle class' the term intellectual has no scientific validity. Examination quickly reveals it covers a number of different strata, important in a number of different ways for education. For example, sections of the creative artists and certain scientific and technical personnel are concerned with the production and often the distribution of knowledge. With teachers there is uncertainty in using the term and some prefer the related term usual in Soviet and Eastern Europe, the intelligentsia. This refers to all those who have been certified at the specialised secondary or tertiary level of schooling. For many of these, including low-level technical and office workers, the term intellectual would be quite inappropriate.

Talcott Parsons sees the intellectual as a 'social role category', as a person expected 'to put cultural considerations above social' (Rieff, 1969, 4). He contrasts those who have found their place in the universities with the 'creative' and 'performing' artists, until recently, at least, outside them and the further 'asymmetry' between the humanities and the sciences (1969, 18). He allows himself a touching expression of faith in the importance of intellectuals, 'even in the pragmatic, "tough-minded" United States', seeing them as being or becoming 'strategically the most important [groups] in American society' (1969, 19).

Edward Shils takes an even more individualist and elitist position, seeing intellectuals as those few persons 'in every society . . . with an unusual sensitivity to the sacred'! (Rieff, 25). He also notes the importance of the modern university in increasing the numbers of intellectuals and, alongside this, the incorporation of them into organised institutions (Rieff, 36-7).

Dahrendorf likens intellectuals today to the court jesters of former times, standing apart from society's social ranks, 'not at all affected ... by its gradations and careers, its privileges and petty quarrels'. Such a comparison, unfortunately, would seem to fit rather few of those usually embraced by the term (Rieff, 49-52).

Much more useful as a model for attempting to understand the complexities of the intelligentsia as a group, or as he prefers to call it, a social category, is Regis Debray's *Teachers, Writers, Celebrities*, originally entitled *Le Pouvoir intellectuel en France* when it appeared in 1979 (x). In his short introduction to the English edition Francis Mulhern sets it within the tradition of writings on the intellectuals going back through Sartre, Aron, Nizan and Benda. 'It lies', he says, 'uneasily among its predecessors.' In contrast to a largely ethical tradition, Debray sets out to: 'discover the structured tendencies of intellectual behaviour in successive cultural production-systems and to show how these dictate the posture of the intelligentsia in given political situations' (ix). This makes the book a model for the kind of analysis which requires to be conducted in other countries of late capitalism where, as Mulhern suggests, things are similar but not the same.

Debray is describing the 'aristocracy of intellectual workers', those who '*create* as opposed to those who administer, distribute or organize, those who invent as opposed to those who repeat' (1981, 23). Itself hierarchically ordered. Debray gives pride of place to those who are able to obtain access to the means of mass communication. These 'high intelligentsia', he points out, are 'socially authorized to express individual opinions on public affairs independently of the normal civic procedures to which ordinary citizens are subject' (32). In all Debray estimates there were in 1978 between 120,000 and 140,000 members of the French intelligentsia as he defined them, a mere 0.65 per cent of the active population of 21,775,000.

While focusing on the present, the media cycle, as he dubs it, Debray looks back over two other periods when other institutions were dominant. Between 1880 and 1930 Debray sees the university as the dominant institution for the intellectuals. But the *teacher* declined and the *author* rose (50) and 'the publishing cycle (1920-60) took over' (60-78). Significantly, Debray describes the present state of the universities as one in which they have been 'industrialised and made to submit to the inexorable laws of productivity and profitability' and where 'the diploma market has fallen in line with the labour market' (44).

It is a great strength of Debray's book that has writes both at a 'philosophical and theoretical' level and at what Mulhern describes as the level of 'mundane affairs'. One could also say he chooses the most illuminating level of *abstraction*. In another book which has received attention two other writers have been less helpful: George Konrad and Ivan Szelenyi, *The Intellectuals on the Road to Class Power*. Written under conditions of repression in Hungary, the book argues a transition of 'the intelligentsia' from an estate under 'traditional redistribution (Western European feudalism)', through being a stratum under 'free-market capitalism' to being a class in conditions of 'rational redistribution' (1979, 64), which seems to some extent to include late capitalism as well as the systems of the USSR and Eastern Europe which these authors have particularly in mind. They write: 'it is permissible to speak of a class position of the intelligentsia only in societies where, in keeping with the principles of rational redistribution as a mode of economic integration, intellectual knowledge by itself confers the right of disposition over the surplus product' (63).

In view of the fact that large numbers of other people have, in capitalism, the 'right' to shares in the surplus product this does not seem convincing. One might also take a rather closer look at 'intellectual knowledge'. Might it not rather be acceptance by and passage through certain institutions rather than possession of either knowledge or skills which is the real criterion of power? Without more comparative, concrete studies it is hard to take these questions further. We need to know such things as:

how are the intellectuals and other middle strata related to other social groups and how does that affect their intellectual production?

how do they see their social function and how do others see it?

how do these groups relate to the major political-intellectual issues of our time?

how are they organised, if they are organised?

how are they trained?

what are the social origins and connections of these groups and how does that affect their intellectual production?

It has already been noted that the growth in these intermediate strata is a major feature of late capitalism. At the end of this section some indications of their numbers and proportion relative to other classes will be given.

The Aristocracy

Only a minority of the advanced capitalist countries today support an aristocracy with a monarchy at its head. Japan, the Scandinavian countries, the Netherlands and Britain in their different ways have developed this ancient estate into a modern capitalist asset. While attacks on the monarchy surface from time to time in such places as the British Parliament there is generally a conspiracy of silence, where there is not outright adulation. From the Chartists through to today's Labour Party leaders, apart from an attempt now and then to claim the English revolution as their heritage, serious discussion of the monarchy and hereditary privilege is, where possible, avoided.[9] Ralph Miliband (1973) is one of the few even to recognise the existence of such a class, much less to analyse their significance. Anthony Sampson is more informative, if not on the theoretical level, describing the family, expert in 'the art of survival' (1982, 3-13), and the other families, many of whom are hardly surviving (24-9).

Engels, who from his contacts in the Chartist movement commented that 'the English working-man respects neither Lords nor Queen', went on to observe that although republican a Chartist 'rarely or never mentions the word', preferring to use the term 'a democrat' (*CW*, 4, 518). Marx made a number of comments on the historic links between the aristocracy and the English bourgeoisie, especially in his articles for the *New York Daily Tribune* (*OB*, 346-7, 353-5; *CAP*, 1, Chapter 27). He claimed that already under Henry VIII the landed estates of the big landed proprietors were 'not feudal but bourgeois property' (347). Doreen Massey and Alejandrina Catalano, writing about *Capital and Land* in Great Britain in the decades since the Second World War, commented that aristocratic landholdings 'are *at the individual level* in no sense the remains of a former "feudal" ownership'. Rather, they have been bought from the proceeds of 'court offices, minerals, or trade' (1978, 72).

Does this close association of wealth from land rent and capital (commercial, financial and industrial) justify the silence on the left? So far as education is concerned, certainly not. As Miliband put it:

> The unifying and socially emollient role of the British monarchy, for instance, has long been recognised and understood, never more so than since the coming into being of 'popular politics'. And it is the same recognition which was largely responsible for the decision of the American occupying power in Japan at the end of the war to maintain the imperial institution, since this, it was felt, 'was an instrument to ensure the smooth transition during limited revolution directed from above, an inhibition preventing revolutions from below'. (1973, 189)

It is perhaps typical of our present society that the most open discussion of the reactionary influence of the monarchy has been made in respect of Japan, an Asian country and one defeated in war with the USA and her Euro-Australasian allies. But even there the criticisms were quickly muted as the US occupation forces found preservation of the monarchy necessary for the strengthening of capitalism against threat from the left (Halliday, 1975, 244; Livingston *et al.*, 1973, 2, 11-17). The Japanese system of tennoism (emperorism), constructed alongside the building of capitalism in the middle Meiji period Halliday, 40) was a system in which the school, with the Imperial Rescript on Education of 1890 and the imperial portrait, played a well-documented role (Passin, 1965).

Ethnic Divisions

To the individuals in many of the countries of late capitalism the recent migration of workers has come as a surprise, were they to reflect on their own past they would see it as an often-repeated process in human history. The countries of Western Europe are themselves places of settlement of previous migrations and nations like the English a blend of Anglo-Saxon and Norman ethnic groups, to mention only two. What is new are the forms of migration and the political climates making for new expression on the level of ideas. Pluralism and multi-culturalism express both new ideologies and new forms of consciousness and a change from previous policies of assimilation. They provide some politicians and academics with a new bandwagon, and ethnic groups with a weapon for manoeuvre in what is usually a difficult and even hostile world.

In the aftermath of the Second World War migration differed from the movements which had earlier peopled the Americas, Southern Africa and Australasia. Some 30 million people migrated to Western Europe alone, resulting, after some had left again, in a net increase in population of 10 million between 1950-75 (Castles, 1984, 1). In Australia in 1981 almost three million people had been born abroad, 1,348,000 of them Anglophones, 1,086,716 Europeans and 360,900 Asians (Lever, 1984, Table 1.3). Not only are the gross numbers large, but job and other opportunities dictate that settlement is uneven, usually concentrating in particular cities and parts of cities.

The reason for migration have varied. Some people returned from former colonies to their metropoles. Others were refugees.

But the greatest number were migrant workers encouraged to fill the bottom of the labour market in the then expanding capitalist economies. A majority of these saw migration as a temporary phase in their lives, but large numbers ended by staying as conditions in both their former and new homelands changed. Their role in the restructuring of the economies of Western Europe is discussed in broad terms by Castles (1984, 20-39). Constance Lever Tracy (1984) examines in closer focus the role of immigrant workers in the Australian working class, concentrating particularly on the city of Melbourne.

The educational aspects of migration range widely. The migrants are both teachers and learners. They are also used as 'materials' by reactionary forces within the host countries who would use them as scapegoats. Castles devotes a chapter to 'Racism and Politics' (190-212) in which he gives examples of hostility which range from jokes told against foreigners, through discrimination in housing, legal inequalities, to physical attack and even murder. Britain, France, Switzerland, Sweden, the forms are different but the 'escalation of racism' as the World Council of Churches called it, is taking place. In West Germany, on which Castles concentrates, *Rassismus* has a long history. In the present it feeds on unemployment, fear of youth portrayed as a threat to law and order and on anti-Turkish feeling dating from the defeat of the Turks before Vienna in 1683! Racism is a major ideological tool of various neo-Nazi organisations which are active. But Castles warns that all this 'does not imply that all Germans, or even the majority, are racists' (201). Many realise that racism poses a threat to Germans as well as the immediate victims. It also encourages the development of racism among some of the migrants, for example, right-wing Pan-Turkish groups in West Germany (222).

Both Castles and Lever Tracy relate ethnicity to class and class consciousness. The former reminds us that 'the nascent cultural expression' of foreign minorities in West Germany is not a simple transplant from the homeland, but arises in response to the migration experience, to 'poverty, exploitation and class struggle' (Castles, 217). Critical of 'the erosion of popular culture, the disintegration of the family, the coldness of social relationships, [and] the weakness of moral and ethical values' the foreign migrants wish to preserve their language and other aspects of national identity from their countries of origin (228). Among the youth born of migrant families, as many as 50 per cent of whom may be among 'the never employed' (Sivanandan) Castles notes a 'growing political consciousness and militance' (214). Lever Tracy, studying a group of non-Anglophones unable to move out of 'the working class core', found 'elements of a working class counter-culture' which included the values of participatory democracy and international solidarity based on 'substantial social and cultural resources and international networks' (455-6).

The Empirical Picture

It would be useful were educators to have data on the numbers of people in each of the classes we have been discussing and their relative proportion in the society. Unfortunately these figures are difficult to obtain. Since the categories are controversial different sources provide different classifications. Official statistics are collected with quite other considerations in mind. One is, therefore, bedevilled by the difficulty of reconciling groups based on employment category and income stratification with criteria of class. The figures cited give both an example of the problem and at the same time a rough idea of the relative size of the categories under discussion.

In the USA, Wright (1978, 86) gives the following percentage distribution of the economically active population in 1969. Beginning with the polar classes, the bourgeoisie is 1-2 per cent and the proletariat 41-54 per cent, depending on definition. The petty bourgeoisie Wright estimates as 4.5 per cent. The remainder fall within what Wright defines as the 'contradictory locations within class relations'. These are top managers, middle managers and technocrats, 12 per cent; bottom managers, foremen and line supervisors, 18-23 per cent; both falling between the two polar classes. Finally, there are small employers, 6-7 per cent, positioned between the bourgeoisie and the petty bourgeoisie; and semi-autonomous employees, 5-11 per cent between the petty bourgeoisie and proletariat. The Ehrenreichs, supporting their attempt to define the professional-managerial strata as a class (n. 7) use the US Bureau of Census figures to show the huge growth of this group between 1870 and 1930. Engineers; managers (including some manufacturers); social, recreation and religious workers other than clergy; college faculty; accountants and auditors;

government officials, administrators, inspectors; and editors and reporters totalled 39,900,000 in 1870 and 123,100,000 in 1930, a growth of 308.5 per cent (Walker, 1979, 18). Westergaard and Resler, whose concern is mainly with different forms of inequality, devote some attention to what they cite as a 'quite misleading' point: that 'nearly half the working population now are in non-manual jobs' (1976, 291). While this may be true for 'a majority of working women', 'over three in every five men are still manual workers'. The figures they cite are unfortunately all in percentages of occupied men or women which makes them difficult to handle and compare. David Weir (1973) cites figures from Bain, Bacon and Pimlott to show that white-collar workers in Great Britain (managers and administrators; higher professionals; technicians and lower professionals; foremen and inspectors; clerks; and salesmen listed separately) increased from 3,433,000 in 1911 to 9,461,000 in 1966, i.e. by 276 per cent. Branson and Miller use the Australian Council of Educational Research occupational categories for their study of class-based inequality in secondary schooling and draw attention to the high degree to which 'ownership of the [Australian] means of production', and therefore capitalist class, continues to reside outside Australia (1979, 81-4). They are not concerned with either the size of the various categories or changes in these. German (Federal Republic) statistics distinguish such categories as manual worker (Arbeiter); salaried employee (Angestellte); public official (Beamte) and self-employed (Selbstandige). These occupational categories are translated by sociologists into strata under various terms (Dahrendorf 1977, 86-107). One often cited classification is that by Dahrendorf which distinguishes the following strata (as a percentage of the population: elites (Eliten) — the plural stressed, 1 per cent; manager-beaurocrats (Dienstklasse), 12 per cent ; middle class (Mittelstand), 20 per cent; worker-elite (Arbeiterelite), 5 per cent; working class (Arbeiterschicht), 45 per cent and lower class (Unterschicht), 5 per cent. In addition he sees a 'false' middle class ('Falscher' Mittelstand) of 12 per cent standing alongside the working class and poking up alongside the base of the middle class proper. These are the salaried employees, the new middle class, typically of the tertiary sector, such as the waiter and the salesperson. Another writer notes the growth in white-collar workers in industrial employment in Germany (the FRG) between 1907 and 1970 from 8 per cent to 23 per cent of all workers, or a rise of 288 per cent (Cipolla, 1976, 1, 241).

For France there is the useful study by Jane Marceau (1977). She uses the following classes, regrouping the categories of the Institut National de la Statistique et des Etudes Economiques (INSEE) which are given in parenthesis below alongside her terms.[10]

Bourgeoisie, upper class (*classe superieure*): (2) *patrons* of industry and commerce; (3) liberal professions and *cadres superieurs*.

Middle class (*classe moyenne*): (4) *cadres moyens* — middle and lower management; (5) white-collar workers, artisans and shop-keepers.

Working class (*classe populaire*): (0) farmers; (1) agricultural workers; (6) manual workers.

It will immediately be apparent that this classification confuses property owners with non-property owners, both at the top and bottom of the scale. However, this is compensated for when Marceau goes on to cite data on the structure of the active population where the minor categories are given separately. This reveals the following proportions in 1968: employers, 10 per cent; liberal professions, 5 per cent; *cadres moyens*, 10 per cent; white-collar workers, 15 per cent; manual workers, 38 per cent, service personnel, 6 per cent; farmers, 12 per cent; farm workers, 3 per cent; and others, 3 per cent (1977, 31). Relevant to the growth of 'the middle classes', Marceau notes that between 1954-69 salaried persons increased from 62-74 or 76 per cent of the working population.

Particularly interesting from our point of view is the study by Baudelot, Establet and Malemort on *La petite bourgeoisie en France*. They see the petty bourgeoisie divided into three fractions. The first, the workers in commerce and services, in 1968 totalling 1,171,000. The second, middle and higher functionaries in the public service, 1,194,000 persons. The third, middle and higher management in capitalist production, distribution and exchange, totalling 1,180,000 (p. 256). A feature of their study is the attempt to work out for different examples the quantity of surplus value which has been redistributed to them, the major reason for their defining these groups as petty bourgeoisie (they do not, of course, see them as *producing* surplus value). The surplus value ranges from 55.4 per cent of income of the higher administrative cadres through 47.9 per cent of income of engineers to only 6.9 per cent of income of primary school teachers (1975, 234). I am not aware of any discussion of this point. If it is accepted as economically sound there is the further problem for education of what difference it makes. The recipients will only be aware of their relative position on salary scales, the level of appearance rather than essence. Revelation of their essential position would be unlikely to make any difference to either attitudes or behaviour.

Learning in Society

The social structure outlined above is the framework which structures people's lives, but it is far from exhausting the groupings and organisations to which they belong and which have important educational significance. Among these are religious organisations, professional organisations, trade unions and political parties. Robert Jungk (1976, 191-2) has listed a number of organisations which have developed in recent years in the social field which challenge some of the older types. He has classified them according to what he sees as their main aim. They are:

(1) *Predominantly Material aims*:
(a) Rent- and housing-communities, neighbourhood groups.
(b) Shopping communities.
(c) Car pools.
(d) Holiday communities.
(e) Kindergartens.
(2) *Predominantly mental aims*:
(a) Therapeutic groups.
(b) Group marriages.
(c) Encounter- (Sensitivity-) groups.
(d) Meditation groups.
(e) Mutual protection of inward-looking communes ('islands').
(3) *Political and world-ideological aims*:
(a) Citizens' initiatives.
(b) Cadre- and action-groups.
(c) Socialist communes as examples and 'bridgeheads'.
(d) Child shops.
(e) Agricultural communes.

(f)   Ad-hoc associations for mutual help.
(4)   *Predominantly occupational aims*:
(a)   Planning offices.
(b)   Media production groups.
(c)   Medical group practices.
(d)   Pensioners' study groups.

Such a classification gives a good idea of the range of organisations which now exists. In practice, of course, many of the categories overlap and there is often overlapping membership of different organisations. Of educational interest is the nature of the ideologies, worldviews, and other ideas propagated intentionally and unintentionally by these organisations and the degree to which these overlap or conflict with one another, and with those of more traditional organisations. It is also significant how many people, of what social class and age, belong and are active.

In order to illustrate the kind of studies which need to be done I shall briefly discuss some of the studies which have been made of 'community action' and 'social work' in England, and on 'volunteer programmes' in the USA.

Community action was defined by the Community Work Group sponsored by the Gulbenkian Foundation in 1970 as follows:[1]

> Community work is essentially about social change; about the redistribution of power and scarce resources; about the inertia of large institutions; about conflicts of interest between different groups in the community; about how the activists and the inarticulate may both have a proper say in decision-making processes that affect them; and about the extent and kinds of decisions that people wish to make, or contribute to making, themselves. (Smith and Jones, 1981, 155-6)

These are precisely the kind of issues relevant to Marx's vision of the future, however little that may have influenced the Committee of 55 chaired by Lord Boyle. But to go on: social work is generally conceived rather differently, but in recent years some social workers have moved nearer to the 'community action' ideals. Mike BrakeRoy and Bailey, in the introductory chapter to their *Radical Social Work and Practice*, explain that definition is not easy and that many professional workers 'steer clear of the question' (1980, 7). They note that 'social work as an institutional process can simultaneously assist people and render them less able to help themselves' (1980, 9). They warn that in the depressed conditions of Britain in the eighties: 'social work's traditional role of mediation between the rich and powerful and the poor and deviant may become replaced by an insistence on its social control function' (1980, 17). While combatting this trend radical social workers must help people 'to understand their position, and their feelings, and [give them] insight into their motivation' (1980, 24). While social workers need a 'radical political perspective and a radical concept of psychology' they need to be careful not to use or manipulate their 'consumers'. 'The commonsense view is that most social work consumers are too damaged or "inadequate" to be involved' in self-help activities (1980, 19). 'The powerless' must not be put in a 'confrontation in which they lose considerably, and which leaves the social worker unscathed' (1980, 23). Thus while social work hardly redistributes power it can sometimes give some confidence and self-respect to those from whom it has been taken and in its radical form it aims to give both understanding and some element of self-determination, perhaps by bringing those with common needs and problems together (1980, 25), to those who seek its help.

Both community action and radical social work have understanding of one's situation and control over one's life as central concerns. Both involve co-operation between the expert and the layperson, with an emphasis on breaking down the distance between them through genuine communication. It is cause for regret that few presently available reports of either have been written with education in mind and make explicit the teachings and learnings involved. In Germany Wolfgang Beer set out a range of possible learnings resulting from a decade of citizens' initiatives (Buergerinitiativen). These numbered between three and four thousand and involved as many as one and a half million West Germans (Beer 1978, 7, 51-70). Beer sees joining in such an initiative as often a political break and a heightening of self-consciousness (56). It may provide an experience of solidarity (58); one may learn particular information and skills (60); one may acquire a critical understanding of the workings of the political process (60); women may learn to take their own initiatives (66); there may be readjustments in relations between men and women within the family (66); and it may help overcome the social isolation from which many suffer, and also bring people into contact with people with whom they would normally not mix (68).

This last is very important and one worth further examination. While fruitful co-operation of different types of people (different classes, different races, different religions or political affiliations) may make for better understanding it is also true that contact can reinforce prejudice. This is often forgotten by well-meaning liberals anxious to promote racial understanding!

One of the important factors affecting what people can learn is the nature of the leadership given. Strong leadership is required to achieve agreed goals and there is often reluctance on the part of both leaders and led to attempt any changes which might jeopardise success. In addition, learning may either not be a goal, or one not given very high priority, and the concept of rotating leadership appears still to be very new. The comments of Butcher, Collis, Glen and Sills are interesting here. On the basis of four case studies of 'community groups' in north England they conclude that there was a tendency: 'for an elite to set the organisational ball rolling in the first instance, and for more or less the same elite both to become the group's initial leaders at its formation and to maintain this leadership role over time' (Butcher *et al.*, 1980, 185). They add that 'Michels' "iron law of oligarchy" . . . seems from this evidence to hold for community groups as much as for political parties' (1980, 186). While they suggest this 'is probably regretted by most readers' they go on to say: 'Oligarchy may not therefore be an unmitigated disaster; indeed for certain critical periods, particularly in task-orientated groups, it may be requisite' (1980, 188).

Key figures in many of the groups are paid community or social workers and their behaviour can be decisive for learning. The guidelines of the Association of Community Workers make clear they attach importance to such learnings. They see the role of community workers as being:

> to help organisations and groups within the community (geo-graphical community or community of interest) to identify their own needs and their own interests, and to act in consort to influence policy and get resources to meet those needs and to develop the confidence and skills to achieve their own interests in a way that will lead to the improvement and greater fulfil-ment in life for themselves and for other members of their com-munity. (Butcher *et al.*, 1980, 215)

Perlman and Gurin distinguish four major purposes of community work: strengthening community participation; enhancing coping capacities; advancing interests of disadvantaged groups; and improving social conditions and services (1980, 216-17). Butcher *et al.*, point out that depending on whether the emphasis is on social relationships or the social environment, strengthening community participation, and therefore, I would add, learning to lead, assumes a high or low priority (1980, 217).

McConnell, reporting on the Strone and Maukinhill Informal Education Project in Scotland, writes of the role of the 'community educationalists'. They should be 'catalysts helping people to diagnose, clarify and implement their own goals' and not 'leaders inspiring people with their goals'. He concludes that: 'for SMIEP the relationship to participants, whether it be the committee or others involved, was one of dialogue and respect between equals' (Smith and Jones, 1981, 193). But such a role, especially for social workers, is not easy. 'Getting alongside people', as John Hart commented, 'will directly threaten some definitions of professional practice' and may bring about 'conflict between social workers and some employing authorities' (Brake and Bailey, 1980, 63).

A very different approach is put forward by Marlene Wilson in a book published by Volunteer Management Associates of Boulder, Colorado. This is the enlightened business management philosophy of late capitalism applied to social work. Scott Myers's *Every Employee a Manager* is cited approvingly (Wilson, 1976, 81-2) and the 'right to be involved in planning and evaluating the program they participate in' is granted to every volunteer (186). Managers shall be *enablers* (25, 32) and must know how to delegate work (34). But these are means to predetermined ends and the job of the manager is to direct and control. Wilson's ideal managers are the kind 'who make things happen' (27). They: '(a) define the problem; (b) analyse the problem; (c) develop alternative solutions; (d) decide on the best solution; and (e) convert the decision into effective action' (1976, 29). Their 'actual functions' are: (1) planning, (2) organising, (3) staffing, (4) directing and (5) controlling (30). Chapter 6 is devoted to that stumbling block of all efforts to obtain real workers' control: 'designing jobs and recruiting to fill them' (101). The limitations on learning in such an atmosphere are well known. More subtly than the 'authority-orientated' methods which Myers and Wilson both criticise, these methods sap people's confidence and limit their talents. They contribute to the society of spectators, to the passive (silent?) majority about which the managers then complain when excusing their insistence on doing the managing.

The knowledge and skills required for even such a limited objective as provision of a pedestrian crossing on a dangerous street can be quite considerable. Part of these must be inputs at the beginning, often by the community or social worker. Other things are learnt in the course of the action. The dice are loaded in favour of the already-schooled and division of labour tends to perpetuate present inequalities. Leo Smith, talking about problems of public participation in local government decision making, notes a number of difficulties. Reports are written in language which only a minority are used to. 'Communication skills' needed for 'thinking about and discussing alternatives, identifying the further information needed and making choices' have not been developed (Smith and Jones, 1981, 18). Public meetings require time and skills of 'public speaking and debate; not to mention confidence in standing up to people with authority in the locality' (1981, 18).

Many of the actions described bring out the possibilities of learning about the functioning of both representative government and the behaviour of especially local government officials. But while the issues are analysed by those who write up the experiences it is seldom clear how those who took part perceived them. For example, Butcher *et al.*, describe how inaction to challenge a compulsory purchase order on houses in the Glodwick area of Oldham 'the long-standing loyalty of many local residents to the Labour movement' seems to have made them reluctant to 'challenge or attack council decisions and policies' (1980, 165). In the case of the Senior Citizens Action Group of Cleaton Moor, Butcher *et al*, write that 'the role of councillors as spokesmen and advocates for particular community interests' is a 'jealously guarded' one 'which they found threatened by the Community Development Project's attempts to encourage self-organisation among local people' (1980, 38). Experience with negotiating over tenancy agreements in a London borough brought the following comment on the importance of local government officials:

Although we were dealing with a number of skilled, shrewd and highly ambitious politicians the officers always controlled events. They succeeded in prolonging the debate for years when it could have been sewn up in months. They blocked progressive provisions in the agreement contrary to the wishes of the councillors and ourselves . . . (Smith and Jones, 1981, 205)

But there is little in all this to suggest that the lessons were clear, were openly discussed (since they were tangential to the objectives of the actions), or in most cases were learnt. Only in the case of the Islington Council does the writer say: 'many people have realised how powerless community action is if the council is not at all sympathetic to their needs and aspirations. The struggle for control of the Labour Party has intensified and recruitment is increasing . . .' (Smith and Jones, 1981, 94).

Learning who to trust and particularly to trust in oneself to act, however, is probably the most difficult thing to learn for it involves old loyalties and often networks of friendship and relationship. At the same time, there are many testimonies to other learnings in these situations, from skills like the collection and presentation of information, through lobbying and going on deputations, so the organising of meetings and marches. What is not always clear from the sources is how many people were affected, what ages and what class of people. But this must suffice for now. I hope I have demonstrated the significance of such organisations for the kind of learnings necessary for self-conscious and self-determining human beings in Marx's sense. I shall return to these questions below when other types of organisation and grouping will be examined.

Notes

1. For an account of the concept of surplus value see Marx, *Value, Price and Profit*, Freedman's *Marx on Economics*, pp. 70-93, or such introductions as Mandel's *Marxist Economic Theory*, Chapter 3.
2. It was transparent that a slave or serf was being exploited, but in the wage relation, 'a fair day's wage for a fair day's work', the division between paid and unpaid work is unseen, if frequently 'felt'.
3. Erik Wright begins his book (1978, 9) with the comment that 'as a graduate student in sociology' he was constantly expected to frame his ideas in particular ways if non-marxists were to 'take those ideas seriously'.
4. He notes that in certain cases engineers and technologists/technicians 'form the main labour force and hence do not exercise tasks of direction and supervision over other works' (242). This group is Serge Mallet's 'new working class'.
5. Two points might be made here: Wright admits that 'in a sense, of course, all class positions are "contradictory locations"' (p. 62); and Poulantzas, in his detailed analysis, brings out precisely similar phenomena, e.g. in discussing engineers and technicians.
6. 'How its relationships to other classes is understood' (Wright, p. 62) would

seem to be catered for similarly by various other classifications.

7. This they do largely on functional grounds: this group's 'major function in the social division of labor may be described broadly as the reproduction of capit: list culture and capitalist class relations' (Walker, p. 12).

↑. In his introduction to the Penguin New Left Review edition of Marx's *Capital*, Vol. 2, Mandel (pp. 42-3) claims that Marx changed his mind about 'so-called "immaterial goods"': concerts, circus acts, prostitution, teaching, etc.' ever being productive labour. He notes the lapse of time between the writing of *Theories of Surplus Value* and Vol. 2 (1861-3 and 1867-70). But even in the earlier manuscript there is a contradiction between pp. 157 (exchange with capital versus revenue) and 172 (persistence or non-persistence of a commodity). Marx also commends Adam Smith for not open[ing] the flood-gates for false pretensions — hardly a good argument on the scientific level if sound on the political! He admits Marx 'does not explicitly contradict' the possibility of immaterial goods being commodities in Vol. 2. but argues (1) that Marx's definition of a commodity stresses its physical nature — which it does; and (2) if commercial travellers or book-keepers can't be productive 'obviously' nor can teachers. But this last is to ignore that in Vol. 2 Marx is discussing the contribution of various people to the production and distribution of some commodity jointly produced by *other* people. In the case of 'immaterial goods' the singer, teacher, etc. *is* the producer. For Marx the real distinction remains the exchange against capital or revenue (Mandel, 43, n. 48). Instances of immaterial commodity production were for Marx rare and relatively insignificant. Only had he lived to edit his own manuscript could we be as confident as Mandel as to what he *really* thought!

8. As readers will recall, Debray was the author of *Revolution in the Revolution*, and was arrested by the Bolivian authorities in 1967.

9. Fenner Brockway's *Britain's First Socialists*, seeking authority for *democratic* socialism, mentions without comment the demand of the Levellers for the abolition of the House of Lords and the Monarchy (146). Tony Benn (1980), himself born an aristocrat, is equally reticent in essays which lay claim to Leveller inheritance.

10. The numbers are the INSEE code numbers.

8   THE POLITICAL STRUCTURES

The political structure includes all those institutions normally included under the term *the state*:[1] the government, the administration, the military, the police, the judiciary and sub-central or local governments and parliamentary assemblies. In addition there are other institutions, most obviously the political parties and various pressure groups. At the supra-national level there are a large number of institutions like the United Nations Organisation or the European Economic Community which have different relations with, and impingements on, the nation-states. All of these, in ways which I shall suggest, play an important part in people's political education. I would add, their reality plays a much stronger educational role than any teaching about politics which may occur in the schools.

The particular form of these institutions varies widely among the different metropoles of late capitalism. Britain, Japan and a few smaller countries are monarchies. The Federal Republic of Germany, the USA, Australia and Canada are federations. Britain and the USA have essentially two-party parliamentary systems whereas Germany and France have each a number of different political parties. Voting in elections is compulsory in Australia, failure to vote resulting in a fine, whereas in England and other countries it is voluntary. Only at a high level of abstraction is there a sufficient unity for writers like Miliband to speak of 'the western system of power'. Frankel is right to stress the variety, the 'very non-identical nature of state institutions' in the different capitalist countries, and the need to analyse 'the specific conflicts between and among classes' which express themselves through these various institutions (1983, 18-19). This is as true for education as it is for political understanding.

Any consideration of the educational effect of the political system must begin with consideration of the way in which particular groups and individuals relate to particular aspects of the system. Job holders and aspirants to jobs will be likely to have a somewhat different attitude and understanding of the system from others, especially from any who are excluded from such jobs (cf. the Berufsverbot in the FD Germany). Activists in the political parties are likely to view the system differently from members of the so-called silent majority.

All this is to consider what people may learn from experience of the political system, whether that experience is intense and participatory or slight and uninvolved. One must also recognise that the state and other institutions of the political system are themselves intentional teachers, not simply through control of much or all of the school system, but through various other channels as well. This intention expresses itself as much through the secrecy system which has already been discussed as through any positive propagating of values and information. Perhaps of greatest significance is the way in which the state and other institutions of the political system serve to educate the emotions. Patriotism, loyalty, respect for authority, these are all encouraged by the pomp and ceremony of state, the flag, by the costumes worn by judges and other state officials on solemn occasions, and a host of other symbols. Their conservative power has been recognised by people at both ends of the political spectrum and either fostered or attacked in consequence. But, as with other education agents, effects are not direct and automatic, though many talk as if they were. For example, in the current concern for law-and-order, a concern in which the truth is elusive and interest plays games, certain conservative elements call for schooling in political institutions in a manner which shows uniformed optimism for its outcomes.

The Class Nature of the State

Therborn stresses that the class character of the state is expressed through the 'social content of the actions of the state' rather than in from what class come the various members of the state institutions (1978, 132). However, if one is to fully analyse the complexities, and particularly to understand the educational implications, then it *is* necessary to consider the individuals who make up the state institutions as well as 'the actions of the state' which result from their individual actions.

One of the important educational problems for the left is to obtain experience in 'running the country'. All revolutions have shown the difficulties which new leaderships have experienced and their weakness compared with members of families previously experienced in leadership positions. In order to take meaningful decisions understanding is required, and such understanding clearly comes best from doing or standing very close to the doers. This gives considerable advantage to those who already hold power, both economic and political. From this point of view writings like C. Wright Mills' *The Power Elite*, or the earlier classic in this genre, *Tory MP* by Simon Haxey, with its analysis of 'the Cousinhood', take on a new significance.[2] It is not a question of 'back-stage string-pulling' or 'lining one's pockets', or such jibes. It is a question of the monopolisation of experience and the knowledge that goes with it which is educationally important.

The Public Service

The public service here means the central and local state bureaucracy, known in Britain as the Civil Service and local government. Its members are known variously as public servants, *fonctionnaires*, or *Staatsbeamten*. Such a service normally consists of a number of divisions: workers, clerical staff, executive officers and an administrative grade. Only the last is concerned with initiating policy and it is these about whom most is written. Educational questions include the link between recruitment to the public service and certain kinds of schooling; the moral-political ideas of public servants; and the role of public servants in informing, or not informing, the public they are supposed to serve.

The evidence for Britain and France shows that recruitment to the public service is heavily biased towards the upper classes of society. For Britain, data from the immediate period after the Second World War shows that 55 per cent of entrants to the administrative grades came from the 'public or fee-paying schools' (*Eighty-fifth Report of HM Civil Service Commissioners*, 1953). In 1977, 86 per cent of top British civil servants were graduates of Oxford or Cambridge, as were 13 out of 18 of the major senior permanent secretaries of departments (Sampson, 1982, 176, 178-9). A high proportion went to public or fee-paying schools. In France, where recruitment to the senior ranks is through the Ecole Nationale d'Administration (ENA), the picture is similar. Studies show a high proportion of students and successful candidates to come from families of the upper classes. In addition, many civil servants have close relatives who are also civil servants (Marceau, 1977, 135, 133, 84-5).

One of the interesting educational questions is what happens to recruits from other than the upper classes, e.g. that 3 per cent, sons of skilled working-class fathers who were allowed entrance to the Ecole Nationale d'Administration in 1945-51 (Marceau, 1977, 135). Since there is no direct evidence in this case one can only conjecture from evidence elsewhere. One might expect the pressure to 'fit in' and 'belong' to result in exaggerated conformity and conservatism.

The mythology of public service is of being neutral and unpolitical, simply doing what the elected politicians decide. Miliband cites a French authority on that point. He writes: 'the establishment of an absolute separation between the political and administrative sectors has never represented much more than a simple juridical fiction of which the ideological consequences are not negligible' (Meynaud, cit. Miliband, 1973, 48). The same writer commented on 'the acceptance of dominant ideologies' and of planning being simply a 'means of consolidation of capitalism' with certain public servants 'never losing an opportunity to exalt the merits of private initiative and free enterprise' (Miliband, 114). This is no doubt reinforced by the transfer from public servant to lucrative posts in private industry on retirement. Anthony Sampson, giving a number of recent examples in Britain, comments that 'by his mid-fifties [the senior civil servant] will be searching anxiously for directorships' (1982, 181).

What is involved here is a pervasive atmosphere in which problems are considered within a framework of assumptions about the rightness, rationality and naturalness of capitalism. It is not that there are no disagreements or rivalries. There are certainly plenty of those. But they do not disturb the final consensus which must exert a powerful restraint on anyone who might wish to do or even think differently. Given the fundamentally pro-capitalist nature of Labour and Social Democratic governments to date the outcome of a real challenge has yet to be tested (Miliband, 108-10).

One interesting counter to what has been said is the recent phenomenon of public servants leaking certain secret information to the media. The threat of human extermination by nuclear war has so penetrated human conscience as to override the kind of conservative professional pressures I have been describing. It remains to be seen whether this is an exceptional feature or part of a broadening expression of genuine concern for the extension of genuine democracy and open government.

The Political Parties

These are obvious political educators, both of their membership
and the wider public. They are producers of large quantities of
'teaching materials' in the form of books and pamphlets, leaflets
and now television programmes. Most political parties have youth
organisations or sections connected with them which are educationally interesting. The field is vast and heavily documented and
would take our discussion too far to pursue here.

The Law

Included in this term here is the judiciary proper, lawyers and solicitors (in the English sense), the police, prisons and those organisations concerned with intelligence and surveillance, such as the
CIA and FBI in the USA, or MI5 and the Special Branch in the
UK. Following Althusser these are often referred to as the
repressive state apparatuses, in contrast to agents of legitimation.
But this is too sharp a distinction. For some people the law helps to
legitimate the social status quo. The educational considerations are
many and complex and can only be suggested here.

While a truism, it needs to be said that people's attitudes to the
law depend on their experience. For large numbers in the affluent
metropoles of late capitalism contact with the law comes little
nearer than the traffic policeman or the television crime thriller.
Media sensation may be reinforced by experience of robbery or
even terrorism. The court is likely for them to be a divorce
court, or, more rarely, jury service. The educative effect of
such experience is rather different from that of a trade unionist or
political activist involved in picketing a strike or street demonstration. These may not only witness a different face of the police,
but also get arrested and brought before a court in rather different
circumstances. Other workers may be injured and have to use the
courts to try and obtain compensation. Or there are the youths
who suffer police harrassment because of their youth and the
image which has been built up of them, or the youths who get into
trouble with the police for using the streets as their playground
(Corrigan, 1979, 137).

It is probably true to say that the most significant educational aspect of the law is that a majority of people are profoundly ignorant of it. This is only partly because many activities which affect people go on in secret. The screening and security checking for job purposes which Miliband refers to (1973, 111) have surfaced, in part perhaps because of the deterrent effect which it is hoped they will have on others. But the formidable apparatus of official secrets acts, laws against conspiracy, sedition, or even vagrancy which exist in different countries ready to be used for political purposes when necessary remains for most people a closed book (Bunyan, 1977, 5-57). The system of D-notices issued by the Services, Press and Broadcasting Committee in England affects what the public is allowed to learn, but is itself little known (Bunyan, 9-10, 188).

At a different level the law as legislation has an educative effect where it is seen to support or prohibit something on which public feeling is aroused. The decisions of the US Supreme Court in the field of civil liberties, black schooling or the teaching of evolution have all provided 'teaching' material of an important kind. They are examples of the complex nature of the legal process in modern capitalism which, as Engels long ago remarked, 'must not only correspond to the general economic position' (*SW*, 1, 385).[3] Law also, on another level, shapes the school system and much else concerned with access to information, as has been noted in the section above on knowledge.

The Armed Forces

The armed forces are that other arm of 'the repressive state apparatus', prepared, as Tony Benn, looking back over British history, reminds us, as much for 'domestic repression' as for foreign war (Sampson, 1982, 250). As with the public service there is the myth of neutrality, of a non-partisan attitude. But the slightest acquaintance with military writings or speeches corrects that illusion. Formerly there was a clear preference for aristocratic values among the officer class expressed clearly in the stereotype of the Prussian Junker. More recently capitalism and trade have become more acceptable, the more so that lucrative posts in industry have become freely available to ex-officers.[4] As weapons have become increasingly technical there has been more and more contact between industry and the armed forces, themselves concerned with international trade in arms (Sampson, 1977).

The question is, of course, much more than just what values the officer class holds, or from what class they are predominantly drawn or enter on leaving the service. It is a question of what role the military play in political affairs. C. Wright Mills has argued that the growth of the military-industrial complex has led in the USA to the military becoming a power group of equal strength with the civilian government and the leadership of the capitalist corporations. But Miliband disputes this, at the same time recognising the strong influence which military thinking has on all aspects of public affairs (1973, 122-3). He stresses that the metropoles of late capitalism 'have been characterised by a high measure of civilian predominance over the military' (1973, 118). Discussing the events in Germany after the First World War, the attempted Kapp *putsch* of 1920 and the events in France around the Algerian War, Miliband draws attention to two counters to a more direct military role. The first is 'the hostility and potential resistance of the organised labour movement' (120) and the other is that so far no government has been sufficiently left to make military leaders 'feel a sense of total political and ideological alienation' (121).

The military are significant educationally in a variety of ways. At one level they are involved in the production of knowledge. Military personnel take part in think tanks, act as advisors to government and economic bodies and produce reports, articles and books which enter into the general store of knowledge, some secret and some open. The military also act as teachers, having military schools for initial and retraining purposes which involve a great variety of persons, nationals and foreigners. One area of teaching which has featured in recruiting advertisments in at least England is that given to the military themselves. 'Join the Army and Learn a Trade' points to the specialised arms where various engineering skills, electronics, or learning a foreign language for intelligence purposes can have civilian spin-off later on. Officers like to advertise themselves as having experience in handling men when applying for civilian jobs.

The military have had direct influence on youth in the schools where, depending on time and place, there have been military cadets. Such youth movements as the Boys Brigade or the Boy Scouts have been strongly infused with military values (Wilkinson, 1969). More pervasive moral-political values and particularly emotional education may occur through membership in the forces or having relatives or close friends who are. The educative effect of the military is an elusive question to pursue, but there is little doubt that many in high places believe it to be important. Hence such of the pomp and ceremony of state involving the military, the wearing of military uniforms by leaders of major capitalist nations and the particular way in which memories of wars are officially handled. The reactions of many English to the recent Falklands' War needs balancing with the kind of evidence Miliband cites on attitudes. But such questions, vital as they are, will remain finally testable only in practice. Theory may be able to do little more than note that they are there.

Estimates of the numbers of persons involved must take account not only of the size of the armed forces at particular times,[5] but also of the replacement rate, i.e. the number of people in the population who have passed through the armed forces. It must also consider the length and particular nature of this exposure. Service in Vietnam or Northern Ireland must teach different lessons from service in NATO. The difference between serving as a regular and being a conscript, or between being an officer or one of the other ranks is significant, but is often not taken into account when generalisations about militarism are being made. Then there are organisations of reserves, ex-service personnel who spend short periods training with the regular forces, maintaining skills and, importantly, attitudes. Social clubs for former members of the armed forces may play a part in keeping certain moral-political attitudes active. They may or may not have an impact on later generations, in part depending on how exclusive they are with membership and privilege.

The ideals of the military have found a place within the school systems of at least some of the countries of late capitalism, in the form of cadet corps. Class divisions within the school system may be reflected in distinctions in the military cadets, e.g. during the Second World War in the English public schools there were officers' cadet corps, whereas in the local grammar schools pupils aspirations were limited to non-commissioned ranks!

R. Kolkowicz, writing on the Soviet military and the Communist Party, contrasted what he called 'natural' military traits with traits which he thought were desired by the party. He gave the former as: elitism; professional autonomy; nationalism; detachment from society; and heroic symbolism (Kolkowicz, 1967, 21). The key point at issue for those looking towards a radically different society is surely whether the armed forces are part of the working people, the people armed (as in Switzerland?) or whether they are the disciplined tools of the ruling class, 'theirs not to reason why'. 'Elitism' and 'detachment from society' both bear on this point.[6] Questions of conscious discipline and responsibility (the latter an issue at the Nuremberg Trials after the Second World War), and education concerning these, are more pertinent than ever with today's threat of nuclear extinction. A book which illustrates the dangers of the contemporary military mind regarding detachment is that by British Brigadier Frank Kitson (1971). Kitson begins by admitting the difficult problem of terminology (1971, 2) and settles for a definition of *subversion* stressing government and legality:

> Subversion, then, will be held to mean all illegal measures short of the use of armed force taken by one section of the people of a country to overthrow those governing the country at the time, or to force them to do things which they do not want to do. It can involve the use of political and economic pressure, strikes, protest marches, and propaganda, and can also include the use of small-scale violence for the purpose of coercing recalcitrant members of the population into giving support. (Kitson, 3)

'Illegal measures' remain undefined, like the sinister 'enemies' lurking in the background throughout the book (51, 85, 86), and instead all kinds of political activities regarded as legal and normal by democrats in the countries of late capitalism are specified. Kitson's political understanding is further revealed in the passage on p. 67 where, with hindsight on 'any counter-subversion or counter-insurgency campaign' (Malaysia, Kenya, Cyprus?) he asserts: 'it is easy to see that the first step should have been to prevent the enemy from gaining an ascendancy over the civil population, and in particular to disrupt his efforts at establishing his political organisation'.

He notes the problem that the government may not recognise the threat, and adds: 'in any case in a so-called free country it is regarded as the opposite of freedom to restrict the spread of a political idea'. Communism is then given as the ultimate example, an idea which threatens to stamp out freedom and put the government's foreign policy in the hands of 'another power such as

Russia or China'. To avoid such fate, Kitson argues, 'the army should become involved . . . in an advisory capacity' and the whole apparatus of information-gathering, with which Kitson deals in some detail, be utilised. In case one has doubts he adds: 'There is no danger of political repercussions to this course of action, because consultation can be carried out in strictest secrecy' (68). After all this it is hardly reassuring to read:

> There is of course an element of truth in the idea that an effec-
> tive domestic intelligence system could be used to jeopardize the
> freedom of the individual if it fell into the wrong hands, but the
> anger posed by subversion unchecked by good intelligence is far
> greater. (Kitson, 71)

It is noteworthy that the question of information gets such empha-sis. But even more noteworthy is the fact that a book embodying this view of politics was recommended by the then Chief of the General Staff 'for the soldier of today to help him prepare for the operations of tomorrow' (Kitson, xi).

Consideration of views like those of Kitson reinforces the importance, in any total view of the educational process in society, of situating the military in the creating and reinforcing of political attitudes and behaviour. At the highest level there is participation in various think tanks and briefing meetings where information is exchanged and policies may be worked out which then spread down through the society as sanctified wisdom. There is also the network of military schools, many of these important for the dominant teaching role exerted by the forces of the USA.

A number of academic studies have tried to discover the effect of service on military personnel. One of these was undertaken in the Federal Republic of Germany. The paper surveyed various expections before reporting the study's findings (Lippert, *et al.*, 1978). Some critics expect the soldier to become uncritically accommodating and, after discharge, better able to conform to the requirements of capital in the workplace. Others expect the 'authoritarian personality' to be strengthened. Military and politi-cal leaders have other expectations. One military document declared: 'The requirement of service in the Bundeswehr creates a significant potential for democratic and civic awareness — not only for the soldier himself, but also for his immediate surroundings, his family and colleagues' (cit. Lippert, 227). Both a government

White Paper and a retired general are cited as expecting military training to provide 'democratic and civic awareness' and 'basic concepts of democracy and the state'. Apart from the generality of such statements there is little chance of their being empirically substantiable. Nor are Lippert and his co-authors much more helpful. In a carefully designed study they attempted to test the following hypotheses: (1) military service leads to a destabilisation of existing systems of orientation for the draftee; (2) military service develops or strengthens democratic awareness for the draftee, and (3) military service provides the draftee with military motivation (228). Discussing their detailed and complex results they remark; 'no unified planned socialization takes place during the period of military service' (237). Since their study was of draftees over a period of only one year I do not find that surprising. Now would I find 'strengthening democratic awareness' easy to measure. Rather, it would seem more useful to proceed quite differently, through participant observation and related methods to establish more concretely what was taught and the detailed ideological positions held by particular young soldiers, their families and their former and later workmates. Nevertheless, this is not to say that Lippert's findings are of no interest.

Moral-political Education

In this section I want to look at a number of academic approaches to moral-political education, as a learning and as a teaching process. First some general points. It should be recognised that in one form or another, whether in Christian Europe or Confucian-influenced Japan, moral-political questions have dominated schooling from its earliest beginnings. Only in the present stage of late capitalism, with its confusion and conflict of values are many schools fearful of these questions, allowing them to be handled unconsidered and unconsciously, often the province of a 'hidden curriculum'.[7] Moral-political questions may be handled as religion, politics, social studies, or, unlabelled, in the literature, history and other courses. It is only recently that the coupling of moral and political has been made explicit (Price, 1979; van Ijzendoorn, 1983).

Many studies of moral-political learning have been carried out under the title of political socialisation. Roberta Sigel defines this as: 'the process by which people learn to adopt the norms, values, attitudes and behaviours accepted and practised by the on-going system' (1970, xii). She emphasises that such a concept includes more than simply knowing and automatically doing. 'The individual so makes these norms and behaviours his own — internalises them — that to him they appear to be right, just, and moral.' While such a definition allows for different political systems in which the individual may range 'from obedient passive subject in one system to active participating citizen in another' it does not seem to allow for questioning of norms and values. The 'well-functioning citizen is one who internalizes society's political norms and who will then transmit them to future generations'.

Easton and Dennis (1969) cite a variety of definitions of socialisation and political socialisation which includes 'consequences', usually of a conformity type, and comment they regard this as inappropriate and even hazardous for research (1969, 26). Their own definition: 'those developmental processes through which persons acquire political orientations and patterns of behaviour' (1969, 7) sees political socialisation as neither 'inherently conservatising' nor 'destabilising' (1969, 37). The outcome of this complex and lifelong process can be either or both depending on the state of the political system, what is being transmitted and what the learners gain from their experience (1969, 7).[8]

Ted Cohn is one of those who, fearing 'political revolution with its attendant cataclysmic social and economic consequences', and in spite of doubts of the efficacy of education, looks to a form of social-political education as an aid in 'the creation of more just egalitarian democracies' (Cohn, 1983, 1). This he bases on the ideas of Habermas, Kohlberg and Rawls. Kohlberg's position is significant. He sees 'the only philosophically justifiable statement of aims of moral education' as one 'in terms of the stimulation of moral development'. This he conceives of as 'the encouragement of a capacity for principled moral judgement' and of 'the disposition to act in accordance with this capacity' (1971, 41). He also sees what he regards as stage six-type moral thinking as providing the necessary principle by which we can 'resolve the problem of the conditions under which it is morally right or obligatory to violate the law' (1971, 62).

Marx began by recognising that existing societies are deeply riven by conflicts of interest. He viewed many of the processes of socialisation, or political education, as ideological. Embued with a deep moral purpose, he eschewed moralising, rather seeing human betterment through a process of 'revolutionary practice' in which people would gain real understanding and would change them-selves in the process of trying to change their situation.[9] Marx's vision of communism as the transcendence (Aufhebung) of human self-estrangement requires, as Meszaros points out, the making of moral questions fully conscious (*CW*, 3, 296; Meszaros, 1970, 284-5). The morally good is at the same time an inner need. Freedom is 'the realisation of man's own purpose' (Meszaros, 1970, 186; cf. Kamenka, 1972, 26-31, 155-60).[10]

Studies of Learning

The studies I shall discuss in this section are on outcomes rather than on the actual learning process itself. The learning process, so far as significant social learnings are concerned, appears to lie in the 'too difficult' category for most researchers. Hess and Torney state that 'political socialization *apparently* follows several models' (1967, emphasis added). But they deny these are 'explanatory models', regarding them intead as: 'devices for examining the atti-tudes the child brings to the socialization process and the ways he utilizes experience in the development of political roles' (1967, 19). Yet identification and the cognitive-developmental model clearly are explanations. But we are still far from any definitive understanding, or indeed much more advanced than common-sense. It is little wonder then that the latter slips into writings which purport to be more than that.[11] Furthermore, the sensitive nature of the subject matter exacerbates the normal difficulties of the study methods employed and one needs to be particularly atten-tive to the nature of the sample population, the questions asked and the very small amount of time over which data were usually gathered.[12] One might be forgiven for preferring a good novelist to much of what goes under the name of social science!

One of the better-documented studies of 'the socialisation of children [as distinct from adolescents or adults] in the area of politics' is that carried out in the late fifties and early sixties by David Easton and Robert Hess in the USA (Easton and Dennis, 1969, viii). Some 15 pilot studies were conducted in schools involving nearly six thousand children and over five hundred teachers. From these a questionnaire of some 40 pages length was produced. It employed pictures and other aids to suit the age of the children questioned and students in different grades answered fewer or more of the questions. Tests were administered in classrooms by one of the test administrators who travelled to the different cities in groups of four. In the final test just over 12,000 children took part. Hess and Torney, using the results in their book, *The Development of Political Attitudes in Children* (1967), see their analysis as concerned with 'the process by which an individual child is prepared to become an adult member of the political community' (1967, v). This they expand as 'a sense of involvement in political life', that is 'interest, or subjective engagement, and overt or active participation in fulfillment of interest'. Easton, writing with Dennis in *Children and the Political System* (1969), attempts to link the data with systems theory in order to discover when and how 'support for political authority arises in the American political system'. They speculate that this arises in childhood, much earlier than other investigators have suggested, and that 'this early source has profound consequences for the functioning of political systems' (Easton and Dennis, viii). Judgement of that claim must be seen against the kind of questions asked.

In the final, multiple-choice type test children were asked such questions as 'who is my favourite of all (father, president, policeman)?; who makes the law (Congress, president, Supreme Court)?; who does most to run the country (Congress, president, Supreme Court)?; or why do we have laws (to punish people; to run the country; to keep people from doing bad things; to keep people safe)? (Hess and Torney, 43, 35, 51). On such evidence Hess and Torney felt confident to use expressions like 'a firm attachment to the country' (219), 'faith in political authority figures' (213), and 'trust in the political system' (215). Easton and Dennis speak of the building up of: 'diffuse support on which, if later experiences do not deflect the child, authorities and others in the system may subsequently call' (276). It is hard from all this to see how Cohn can cite this work as showing that 'by ten years old they [children] are capable of demonstrating a high degree of political understanding' (1983, 6). On the contrary, the exciting glimpses into the actual thinking of the children allowed by citations of scripts from interviews during the pilot studies suggest a far from high degree. But they hint at ways of thinking which require detailed, qualitative study like that employed in other studies by Kohlberg and Connell if we are to make any progress in understanding the process of learning to be moral-political. It is interesting that both Hess and Easton seem to have realised the limitations of their method at the time (Hess and Torney, 97; Easton and Dennis, 421).

A decade later, in 1970-1, a much more ambitious testing of civic education was carried out by the International Association for the Advancement of Educational Achievement. One of a number of tests of school subjects, the test was administered to school students at age 10 years (in Germany, Israel, Italy, Netherlands), age 14 years (Finland, Germany, Iran, Ireland, Israel, Italy, Netherlands, New Zealand, USA) and 18 years (Finland, Germany, Iran, Ireland, Netherlands, New Zealand, Sweden, USA). Questions were framed to elicit information on cognitive, perceptual and effective aspects of civic education and on such background matters as students' leisure interests, exposure to mass media, and political discussion with peers and adults (Torney *et al.*, 1975). Five attitude scales were used which dealt with what Oppenheim calls 'support for democratic values' (1975, 26). These were separately labelled anti-authoritarianism, tolerance and civil liberties, women's rights, value of criticism and efficacy/responsiveness. Support for these values expressed rose with increasing age in all countries tested. At the same time there appeared to be an inverse relationship between 'support for democratic values' and 'support for the national government' (Torney, 1977). A danger is that since these results are what one would like to believe one is encouraged to ignore the limitations of the research method employed.

The great merit of Connell's *The Child's Construction of Politics* is that it provides lengthy extracts from the tape-recorded interviews with the 119 Sydney school children who are its subjects. The introduction expresses an empirical approach, while the final chapter admits to having made 'some use of' previous studies, 'particularly the classic studies of Piaget' (1975, 228). A major argument is that children construct their own interpretations of the political world (1975, 1). Connell comments: 'I was impressed with the . . . attractively casual way they treated the "social influences" that were supposed to be moulding their outlooks' (1975, 1). Yet when Connell comes to 'reflect' on his findings in the final chapter he is forced to admit that in a sense 'all of the children's ideas about politics are derivative' (1975, 230). He argues for the need for 'concrete historical analysis', yet has chosen not to attempt it. His final conclusion is that, considering the 'general tenor and total content of the interviews, we must be impressed by the conventionality, the lack of *realised* freedom, in them' (1975, 239). Thus 'the established political order is safe' — [for the time being at least] — for what of the challenge' (1975, 240).

What Connell's book brings out nicely is the way in which this sample of Australian children think about various questions: the confusions of premier with prime minister; the role of England's queen and America's president; or the nature of the Vietnam War. Connell documents the increasing order with age, but cannot convince the unconvinced that they witness stages of development. He speaks of 'the familiar class-linked pattern' of support for political parties, but slides between status and class without clear definition of either and assumes for calculation that all children in the same district belong to the same class! (1975, 65)[13]

The work of Lawrence Kohlberg is of special interest to us because it has been taken up by Habermas and some members of the political left. He began with a study of 'the development of moral judgement and character' of a group of 75 boys, originally ranging from 10 to 16 years of age. He followed them up at intervals of three years until in 1971 they were 22 to 28 years old. Tests consisted of moral problems and the boys' answers were analysed for the kind of moral thinking/reasoning they applied to work out their answers. From this and studies in a number of other countries (Malaysia, Taiwan, Mexico, Turkey, Israel, Honduras and India) Kohlberg claims that as young people develop their moral reasoning passes through a number of stages. These stages, Kohlberg insists, imply invariant sequence whatever the culture, though the speed through the sequence may be different for different children and youths. The stages are 'structured wholes', total ways of thinking, and must not be confused with attitudes (Kohlberg, 1971b, 167-71). The stages can be briefly characterised as:

Stage 1: Obedience and punishment oriented.
Stage 2: Instrumental hedonism and exchange.
Stage 3: Orientation to approval and stereotypes of virtue.
Stage 4: Law and order orientation.
Stage 5: Contractual-legalistic orientation.
Stage 6: Universal ethical principle (justice) orientation.[14]

In this work Kohlberg is claiming both that this is how people actually do think, and also that (stages 5 and 6) is how they ought to think. He sees moral reasoning developing alongside and in some way connected with development of cognitive thinking. His definition of the moral is 'principles of choice for resolving conflicts of obligation' (1971b, 215) and he specifically shuns any 'claims about the ultimate aims of men, about the good life, or about other problems which a teleological theory must handle' (1971b, 214-15). He sees his work as confirming the tradition from Kant to Hare in that the stages are increasingly universalisable from 1 to 6. 'The claim of principled morality', he wrote, 'is that it defines the right for anyone in any situation' (1971a, 46).

There are a number of problems with Kohlberg's work. The first particularly concerns the problem of learning. Not only are individuals not consistently operating at one stage, but when it comes to wider studies it is clear that stages 5 and 6 are relative rarities in some cultures. Among middle-class urban boys tested in Taiwan and Mexico the great majority of statements made fell into stages 3 and 4 and less than 10 per cent into stages 5 and 6 — all at age 16. In two isolated villages in Turkey and Yuicatan stages 1 and 2 remain important at this age while stages 5 and 6 'are totally absent in this group' (1971a, 37-8). Granting Kohlberg's powers of interpretation, and this is always in doubt with Piaget-type experiments (Crittenden in D'Cruz and Hannah, 261), there still remains the very small data base on which the work is founded. Yet, considering the inconsistency under experimental conditions, would we really be wiser had we evidence of girls' thinking, or even comparative sampling of the major countries? Kohlberg's optimism avoids the question of the relation of thinking to doing and is on a par with much of the thinking on political socialisation discussed above.[15]

One other work needs to be mentioned here: Paul Willis's *Learning to Labour*. The book is a powerful description of the moral-political learning of a small group of British 'non-academic working class boys' (Willis, 1977, vii). Here I wish only to draw attention to Willis's analysis of these learnings in terms of what he calls 'penetrations': 'impulses within a cultural form towards the penetration of the conditions of existence of its members and their position within the social whole' (1977, 119). These penetrations are glimpses of the truth through 'blocks, diversions and ideological effects' which do not crystallise out at the individual level in conscious, expressible understanding (1977, 121-2). The penetrations Willis discusses are an '"opportunity-costed" assessment of the rewards of the conformism and obedience which the school

seeks to exact from working class kids' (1977, 126); an assessment
of the nature of available work ('most work in industry is basically
meaningless' (1977, 127); and a 'real penetration' of difference
between possibilities for individual social mobility and possibilities
for the class as a group (1977, 128-9). One wishes there were
more studies like this.

What Is Taught

It is a truism that everything is moral-political and no perspicacity is
required to see the role of literature, history or economics in
expressing values. Then there are such topics as nuclear physics or
the mathematics of stocks and shares or other commercial trans-
actions. All of this requires consideration, but this section will confine itself to those subjects directly intended to educate in this area.

In the course of preparing the research for the IEA Civic Education study, national centres in the different countries concerned
(England, Federal Republic of Germany, Finland, Iran, Israel,
Italy, Sweden and the USA) provided materials from which an
analysis of what was being taught could be prepared. Sources
included public laws and official statements of intent or content, examples of civic education examinations, summaries of textbooks and teaching materials and data on time spent and numbers
of students and teachers (Torney *et al.*, 32-41). From these the
International Civic Education Committee prepared a 'set of
themes which were agreed upon as common to all participating
nations':

Cognitive content:
1. Constitutional framework.
2. Meaning of concepts related to citizenship, such as
patriotism, duties, authority.
3. Historical development of country.
4. Governmental structure, organisation and institutions at
different levels.
5. Political processes including election, political parties and
voting.
6. The legislative, executive and judicial branches at different
levels.
7. The bureaucracy and civil services.
8. Foreign affairs and international organisations.
9. Government and the economy, including taxation.

10. Government and social services, including welfare.
11. Communication and mass media.
12. The social sciences and methods of problem solving.
13. Man as a social and interdependent animal.

Affective content:
1. Understanding rights and obligations, respect for others, tolerance, loyalty, belief in equality, respect for law, willingness to defend the homeland.
2. Support for the democratic way of life: belief in freedom of the individual, right of citizens to express dissent, right to be represented; willingness to participate by voting.
3. Appreciation of world interdependence and amity.
4. Respect for government and for national tradition without ethnocentrism.
5. Respect for diversity in moral and religious values, as well as respect for political opposition.
6. Interest in current events and social problems at national and international level.

Behavioural content:
1. Willingness to obey the law, pay taxes, accept military obligations, participate in patriotic rituals.
2. Participation in group decision making by joining, leading and voting in groups.
3. Practising tolerance and showing respect for others.
4. Demonstrating logical and critical thinking ability in problem solving.
5. Reading newspapers and learning from current sources of information such as radio, books, magazines and television.
(Torney and Oppenheim, 41-2)

Torney and Oppenheim note differences of emphasis in materials from the different countries (1975, 40-1), but the real problems lie elsewhere. Schools, for all the protestations about critical thinking and the like, tend towards the safe and defensible. Greenstein noted topics which are 'probably considered too controversial and "subjective" to be dealt with in the classroom' (1965, 98). Describing teachers' questioning in the FR Germany, Dumas and Lee comment: 'Despite current references to the method of critical thinking, we observed no open discussion of controversial public issues, an observation that was reinforced as generally valid by several of the national authorities whom we interviewed' (1978, 87-8). While some of the timidity stems from attacks by such bodies as the Australian Society to Outlaw Pornography (STOP) and the Committee Against Regressive Education (CARE) whose spokeswoman, Mrs Joyner, is reported to have said: 'Children don't go to school to learn to think' (Scott and Scott, 1980, 55), there are complex social conflicts at work on which such organisations feed (Nelkin, 1982).

A brief description of political education in schools in a selection of the countries of late capitalism reveals the variety which exists on common themes. It bears witness to a point made earlier, the faith which authorities still place in ancient symbols, and testifies also to the strivings of teachers and others to bring up new generations to more enlightened values — both in defiance of any evidence that their efforts make any difference!

In Sweden the basis for current teaching of civics was laid down by statute in 1962 and 1964, when the 9-year comprehensive school was established. Civics is linked with religious knowledge, history and geography and with the natural sciences in blocks of time which allow 'pupil-activating and individualised working' (Ronnas, 6) and an interdisciplinary approach. This is aimed to ensure that 'pupils' conceptual world is kept together as far as possible in work at the school' (National Swedish Board of Education, lgr, 69, 5). The curriculum for the comprehensive school speaks of 'respect for the pupil's human dignity' and attempts to balance both 'the needs of the individual and the demands of society (ibid, 4). Beginning with 'how people live and work together', the civics syllabus moves from the home in the early years outwards until in the senior years it prescribes study of 'certain important social questions'. These could include: 'traffic, environmental control, the total defence, and the use of tobacco, alcohol, and drugs' (Swedish, lgr, 69, 1(4), 1). The religious syllabus, while remaining heavily Christian biased, has, since 1962, moved away from sectarian teaching for belief to a wider conception of information and understanding. This now includes, at the senior levels of the 9-year school, information about 'the Jewish religion. Islam, Hinduism. Buddhism and the religions of the natural peoples' (Swedish lgr, 69, 1 (6), 2).[16] It also allows at this level for 'other views of life and attitudes to existence than the religious' and attempts to deal with 'essential questions and trends of thought in modern ethics and philosophy' (ibid, 1).

Moral-political education in Japan is of special interest for several reasons. As the only advanced capitalist country in Asia it does not share the European Christian democratic tradition. Very explicit moral-political teaching and ritual formed an important part of schooling in the period leading up to and during the Second World War, and under the US occupation after the war conscious efforts were made to democratise this teaching.[17] Marxism is also strongly influential in wide circles in Japan, including the Japan Teachers' Union (JTU or Nikkyoso) (Halliday, 1975, 250, 410, n. 50). There are thus widely differing and strongly felt opinions about the subject as well as a tradition which has resulted in a capitalism somewhat different from that of other centres.

Symbolic of the values which the democratic movement in Japan rejected after the war was the Imperial Rescript on *The Great Principles of Education*, written for the Emperor in 1879 and regularly read in ceremonies which had deep religious significance (Passin, 1965, 154-5). Confucius was recommended as the best moral guide; pupils were warned of the dangers of 'indiscriminate emulation of Western ways'; and appended notes on elementary education recommended that classroom portraits should be of 'loyal subjects, righteous warriors, filial children, and virtuous women' (Passin, 1965, 227-8). The final note emphasises the class bias of the teaching: 'Agricultural and commercial subjects should be studied by the children of farmers and merchants so that they return to their own occupations when they have finished school and prosper even more in their proper work'. One is reminded of Victorian England and upper-class warnings about educating people 'above their station'.

The Imperial Rescript was recognised as having 'lost its validity' by mild resolution of the Diet in 1948 and the equally notorious ethics course was replaced by an American-style social studies course (Halliday, 1975, 243). But in 1952 the Ministry of Education began advocating a return to a separation of morals from history and geography. Courses of ethics were reintroduced in the primary school in 1956, but without textbook or examination (Anderson, 1975, 113; Halliday, 1975, 246). Occupying one hour a week they paralleled a continuing social studies course which in 1971-2 ranged from two hours per week in grade 1 to four in grades 4-6 (Anderson, 1975, 114). At the junior high school level a morals course occupying one hour per week was also separated from the social science course (Anderson, 1975, 129). At the non-compulsory senior high school level ethics remains part of a social studies course which also includes political science-economics, Japanese history and world geography. The ethics course is worth 2 credits towards the total of 85 required for graduation and the course is compulsory (Anderson, 1975, 163, 168-70).

Examination of the content of the morals courses for primary and junior high schools described in Anderson does not explain the concern expressed within and without Japan. Platitudes like 'to persevere to the last for the realisation of right aims' or 'to understand that courtesy is necessary in collective life' (Anderson, 1975, 115, 137) seem harmless enough, even worthy. Nor need there be, apparently, any fear of students learning, if Anderson is to be believed. He writes of the junior high school course:

> Despite valiant attempts by the school authorities to win students' acceptance of the moral values of patriotism and good citizenship, and despite frequent Ministry workshops for morals teachers to increase class effectiveness, the course cannot be called a success. It still troubles the teachers . . . They are not enthusiastic about teaching it. Generally the students are bored.

He goes on to make a familiar point:

> To be effective, the course will probably have to come to grips with controversial or personal problems, such as the rights of young people in a traditional family, changing patterns of sex behaviour, arranged marriages vs. love marriages, the examination torment, student participation in school policy and government, political issues and the like. *These the Government would reject as leading to radicalism however, and few teachers would be prepared to handle them objectively.* (Anderson, 1975, 139, emphasis added)

More disturbing to democrats and those farther left is the content, not of the morals course, but of the social science and Japanese history courses. Already in the 1968 materials for the guidance of teachers of grade six Japanese history it was advocated: 'it is necessary to guide children so that they will have a deep understanding and reverence for the Emperor . . . and let them realise the significance of the national holidays . . .' Speaking of the teaching on myths and legends the materials went on:

> Care should be taken so that interest in details should be
> avoided, but by utilizing the accounts of historical personalities
> and stories, the children should be guided to think of the rela-
> tionship of the imperial family and the nation which is reflected
> in history . . . (Anderson, 1975, 118)

Much of the controversy about these courses has been about the
content and censorship of textbooks. One of the important legal
cases was that of Ienaga Saburo, Professor of Japanese History at
Tokyo University of Education, who in 1965 sued the Ministry of
Education for censorship. In July 1970 a Tokyo district court ruled
in his favour, limiting the right of the Ministry, but an appeal was
made (Livingston *et al.*, 537-51; Halliday and McCormack, 186-
90).

Equally interesting is the Federal Republic of Germany. Both
Germans and foreigners have been anxious to understand how
such a nation could succumb to Hitler's fascism (naziism) and,
following the 1945 military defeat, move towards a different,
hopefully democratic society. The first of these questions occupied
the Frankfurt School of marxists, one of whom, in his period of
exile in the USA, was to produce that classic socio-psychological
study of political education, *The Authoritarian Personality*
(Adorno *et al.*, 1969).[18] In 1967 Adorno was, with Ludwig v.
Friedeburg, to write a foreword to an important empirical study of
the second question (Becker *et al.*, 1970).

Responsibility for school curricula rests, not with the Federal
government, but with the eleven states (Laender) which also
publish textbooks and other materials. After the Second World
War new civic education courses were begun which varied from
state to state and were known under such names as Sozialkunde,
Gesellschaftskunde, Staatsbuergerkunde or politische Bildung. In
the primary, or Grundschule, Heimatkunde courses introduce
pupils to local history, geography and legends, and Sachkunde
courses relate the local community to elementary history, geography, politics, economics and natural science (Dumas and Lee,
1968, 33). Sozialkunde, favoured particularly by the American
military government as a means of re-education in democracy after
the Second World War, is described by Dumas and Lee as con-
sisting of lessons on the rights and responsibilities of citizens; the

structure and functions of German governmental institutions; a comparison of Western democratic with marxist political and economic systems; and such social problems as overpopulation, environmental pollution, or social inequality (1968, 66). In 1960 a course integrating history, geography and Sozialkunde was recommended for the two final years of the gymnasium by the Permanent Conference of State Ministers of Culture. A number of themes around which this could be done were suggested, but in practice there is 'considerable variation' between states (Dumas and Lee, 69-70).

The time spent on the different courses varies with pupil age-grade and between states. In the Bavarian Grundschule (1975) Heimat- and Sachkunde together occupy three and four hours respectively in grades 1 and 2 and grades 3 and 4. Religious instruction is also given for two hours per week in grade 1 and three hours in the other three grades. Together they occupy some 21 to 29 per cent of the weekly timetable which ranges from 23 to 25 hours. In the gymnasium in Hesse the separate courses of geography, history and Sozialkunde occupied 6 to 7 hours per week, while the Gemeinschaftkunde which replaced them in grades 12 and 13 occupies only 4 hours per week.

In two states somewhat radical proposals for politische Bildung have been proposed. In Hesse the curriculum guide, published under Social Democratic auspices in 1972, is known as the Rahmen Richtlinien. Highly controversial, this framework proposed a common programme irrespective of social class and type of secondary school; merging of history, geography and Sozialkunde curricula; a critical examination of social, political and economic institutions — critical being used in the sense of critical thinking of the Frankfurt School of marxists; and the unified course, or Gesellschaftslehre, was to be based on a prescribed set of basic concepts (Dumas and Lee, 48-52). The Richtlinien proposed in 1973 for North Rhine-Westphalia has proved less controversial, partly by having history and geography as distinct, if reduced subjects in the curriculum. Originally closer to the curriculum guide in Hesse, it has been revised to remove elements opposed as 'socialist'. Objectives are set out along American, behaviouristic lines and a number of alternatives are offered for each theme or topic. The following brief extract gives something of the flavour of the 'learning aims' set out.

1. The ability, by means of thinking in alternative political terms, to recognise dependencies:

(b) The ability to establish the basic values, norms and interests within controversies.

2. The ability, via partisanship, to exercise the right of self-determination in political conflicts:

(a) The ability to offer an opinion after careful analysis of a political theme. (Dumas and Lee, 54-5)

History is obviously a sensitive vehicle for moral-political teaching and for some time after the Second World War that war and National Socialism and Adolf Hitler proved difficult for schools to handle. According to Dumas and Lee a new generation of teachers and 'increasing interest' in the Nazi period contribute to more confident teaching.

The subject is dealt with in some depth in most German classrooms, and it usually does not fail to include even the most difficult of topics, the Nazi concentration camps and the massive exterminations of the Jews. However, it also is clear that even today the approach generally taken to the study of this period is that of an examination of how and why Hitler was able to gain power, followed by an objective recitation of the events that followed his coming to power. Potentially controversial or explosive issues are carefully avoided. (Dumas and Lee, 65)[19]

Religious instruction, while not considered by Dumas and Lee as part of political education, does include 'moral precepts' as well as 'religious dogma' (1968, 84). Taught separately for Protestants and Roman Catholics, it is compulsory until an age which varies from state to state. In Bavaria and the Rhineland-Palatinate those who withdraw must take an ethics course instead (Dumas and Lee, 84-5).

In all the courses described the traditional German emphasis on the memorisation of information is predominant. Dumas and Lee comment:

One teaches that certain political and economic practices and institutions are right and others are based upon a false doctrine. Rarely, in our experience were these viewed as values and attitudes — rather this is additional knowledge to be mastered. (1968, 83)

One cannot help wondering whether their assumption that the USA is different would stand up to similar examination. But there is little reason to doubt their comment that:

> despite current references to the method of critical thinking, we observed no open discussion of controversial public issues, an observation that was reinforced as generally valid by several of the national authorities whom we interviewed. (1968, 87-8)

Political education in the USA is of interest because of the extremely advanced form of capitalism in that country and also because of the influence of US education on the school systems and mass media of other countries. Reference has already been made to attempts to export forms of political education to Germany and Japan during the occupation periods after the Second World War. Books and other teaching materials originating in the USA are widely used, not only in the English-speaking countries, but also in such areas as Scandinavia where English is widely used and the comparative cost of producing native language materials is high. Other and less formal examples of influence would repay study.

The requirements for political education are laid down by statute in many of the states, whose responsibility education is. A majority require a specific course in civic education for 13 and 14 year old students. Of the 50 states more than 40 require instruction in the United States constitution. More than 30 require study of the state constitution and US history. More than 20 require state history, US government and education in respect of the flag. Sixteen to eighteen states require the Declaration of Independence to be taught, together with such things as the principles of representative government and the duties of citizenship, democracy and American institutions (Torney *et al.*, 1975, 39). Foster has identified three styles of such curricula: (1) 'conservative', with an emphasis on an historical approach, which he claims is 'even today the predominant mode of instruction'; (2) a 'middle-of-the-road' style, combining 'references to current events and contemporary problems with the study of history'; and (3) 'liberal', along lines developed by designers of the 'new social studies' courses in the 1960s (Foster, 1977, 46-7).

An aspect of political education which has received increasing attention is referred to by Udom (1982) as 'economic socialisation'. In the school classroom this appears in curricula which stress free enterprise, economic theory or consumer education (Udom, 29-36).[20] Economic Education, a body set up in 1948 as a result of a New York University workshop and funded by the Committee for Economic Development (Udom, 24-5; Hertzberg, 1981, 72-3). Udom betrays the usual naïve enthusiasm for the efficacy of the courses he describes. 'It is difficult to imagine', he claims, 'any preparatory course in citizenship roles that could have more impact on citizens than economic socialisation beginning at an early age'!

In the business world a great deal of education in business economics is conducted by the various schools of business in the universities, of which that at Harvard is perhaps the best known. How much this spills over into the schools below the tertiary level is uncertain, as is also its dissemination among the broader public. This would make a useful study. One such school with expressed broader aims is the Institute for Constructive Capitalism in the Graduate School of Business in the University of Texas at Austin. This Institute 'strives to improve communication between the private sector and society through education', producing studies in enterprise education research.[21] These include research into teaching materials for schools. They also run workshops for teachers, community organisations and business groups.

Education for capitalism is not confined to schools. At least one big firm, Joseph T. Ryerson and Son of Chicago, has inaugurated a plan (the Ryerson Plan) of 'hiring a number of high school teachers each summer to work and learn at Ryerson'. They are given experience in different sections of the corporation, the aim being to give them 'real knowledge of how the free market operates within a free society' to counter the 'anti-business, anti-free-enterprise bias prevalent in many parts of our American society today'.[22]

Another strand of moral-political education which took off in the seventies is based on the work of Kohlberg. Ralph Mosher, introducing a book of papers describing research in this field, instances Watergate, and people's lack of trust in the political leadership and American corporations as reasons why such programmes have been supported (1980, 5-6). Hertzberg cites the discussion this work has generated (1981, 140). For college students Arthur Levine has proposals for what he likes to continue calling a liberal education; one which is 'concerned with basic skills and touch[es] upon the place of its subject matter in the larger world' (1980, 139).

Widespread and conflicting concern has been expressed in the USA over the types of courses provided. Unfortunately, as Hertzberg complains, this has not been based on a sound knowledge of past reform movements. In the social sciences reformers tend to have 'historical amnesia' before the mid-fifties (1981, 169). Mehlinger (1967), a curriculum developer, criticises the conservative-type curricula for their stress on the formal structures of government to the neglect of less formal but significant ones; for the avoidance of controversial questions; and for not teaching inquiry skills (Foster, 47-8; Hertzberg, 1981, 101-19). In 1970 a group at Columbia University, NY, in a book entitled *Civic Education in a Crisis Age: An Alternative to Repression and Revolution*, expressed a fear that 'our schools may be turning out millions of students who are not forming a strong allegiance to a democratic political system' (Center for Research and Education in American Liberties, 1970).

The new social studies courses stress a number of themes. Students were to learn through use of the inquiry method and cognitive content seen as 'obsolete' was to be discarded. Use was made of abstract concepts developed in the social sciences, following the ideas of Jerome Bruner. Courses were to be interdisciplinary, 'cosmopolitan, cross-cultural, and international' (Foster, 47). One of the courses to attempt to put these principles into practice was called *Man: A Course of Study (MACOS)*. This was developed between 1963 and 1970 by the Education Development Center with a grant of $4.8 million from the National Science Foundation. It was intended as a year-long course for the fifth and sixth grades and it used films, tapes, games and other modern teaching devices to interest the students. Fundamental questions about human society were explored through a focus on the Netsilik Eskimos, a traditional hunting society of the Pelly Bay region of Canada. At the same time, for political reasons, the course was linked to the biological curriculum, salmon, herring gulls and baboons being studied to stimulate thought about human behaviour. Dorothy Nelkin, describing the course, writes:

> MACOS does not avoid controversial issues. The course
> includes discussions of religion, reproduction, aggression, and

murder, for it is built on the assumption that it is necessary to deal with such problems in a thoughtful and reflective manner. 'Oversimplification and dogmatism are twin enemies of creative thought'. In controversial areas, teachers are advised to encourage their students to cultivate independent attitudes and warned that the questions raised by the course often have no clear-cut answers. (Nelkin, 1982, 49)

With descriptions of the Netsilik practice of senilicide and infanticide and students being required to 'explore relationships among their families and friends' it is small wonder that the course ran into opposition and bans (Nelkin, 50). Nelkin's study is valuable for bringing out the complexity of this opposition. It included not only fundamentalist Christian and anti-evolutionist believers but people disillusioned with science and technology or resentful of the erosion of local power by distant 'bureaucracies' or 'experts' (Nelkin, 167-73).

Conclusion

The studies of political learning mentioned do nothing to advance our knowledge of what are the significant influences in political education, and little to enlighten us on values and beliefs held which really motivate behaviour. Teaching seems equally unpromising. In the rare situations where a genuine attempt is made to be critical there is little evidence that lessons are regarded as other than schooling, the artificial exercises which intrude into the 'real life' of students. In addition, teaching is largely within the liberal-individual framework, though, as in the USA, this can be more overtly pro-capitalist. It seems unlikely that genuine alternatives to the pressing problems of our time are very frequently raised. Finally, there is the recurring problem of the individual and the social levels of organisation. Learning and teaching is aimed at the individual and there seems to be little discussion of the relationship of these two levels on which the solution of social problems depends.

Notes

1. Two important books on the state written in the marxist tradition are Miliband (1973) and Therborn (1978). The latter reviews a variety of marxist views on the state, including those usually referred to as Eurocommunism. Boris Frankel (1983) is useful for criticism of current marxist theories and for problems he poses. His new conceptual framework, involving *processes* electoral, production, credit and food production) is, disappointingly, theoretically weak.

2. The 'cousinhood' referred to the way in which 53 government members of the British House of Commons were related to members of the Peerage in the 1930s. The same book gives details of the notorious Anglo-German Fellowship. Miliband gives examples of the sharing of personnel between business and government and the essentially upper-class nature of state bodies in various European countries and Japan (1973, 52-9).

3. Therborn, who also notes the sometimes progressive role of the US Supreme Court, probably goes too far in saying 'bourgeois law is not class-specific' (1978, 235). The class biased nature of the law has often been argued, e.g. the well-known New Left Book Club volume, *Justice in England* (1938). Paul Phillips has made a careful study of the writings of Marx and Engels on the law. It is a useful source for study, but unfortunately as Engels might have said of the author, 'he lacks dialectics'!

4. S.P. Huntington reports that 'in the mid-fifties over two thousand regular officers each year were leaving the services for the more lucrative positions in [US] business' (cit. Miliband, 1973, 117-18). The situation is similar in the other metropoles

5. The International Institute for Strategic Studies publication, *The Military Balance 1973-1974*, enables us to compare the size of the armed forces of the following countries with that of their total population.

Nation	Population (in 1000s)	Regular forces (in 1000s)	%
USA	210,900	2,253	1.06
FR Germany	60,100	475	0.79
France	52,000	504	0.94
UK	56,250	361	0.64

Source: Carlton and Schaerf, 1975, p. 197.

6. This was, of course, the point made by Marx in his discussion of the Paris Commune (cf. Draper, 1971, pp. 74, 152). In his first draft he speaks of the 'permanent army that defends the government against the citizens'. William McNeill, writing of the Prussian army of the mid-eighteen hundreds, remarked that Prussian officers 'strove to make the army an effective bulwark of the hierarchic principle of society upon which their own way of life . . . depended' (1982, 246). Reasons for thinking these considerations still apply spring easily to mind.

7. Hidden curriculum is a term apparently coined by P.W. Jackson (1968). See also Dreeben (1968); Kohlberg (1971, 25-30); and Apple, 1979, Chapter 5).

8. Inkeles is another who has stressed socialisation as possibly a 'major vehicle for change' (in Goslin, 1969, 631).

9. Marx's third Thesis on Feuerbach, comment in Draper (1977, 1, 232-4). Kamenka (1972) and Meszaros (1970) write on Marx and ethics from very different standpoints, but make some importantly similar points.

10. I must dissociate myself from Kamenka's remarks about Engels here, but this is not the place to argue that matter.

11. Inkeles is probably overstating it when he writes of 'the massive importance of the earliest years in the development of the individual' (Goslin, 630). Hess and Torney say: '*it seems likely* that the influence of church membership is mediated *at least partially* through the family (1967, 117, emphasis added). Greenstein notes that 'the thesis that the individual's early experiences affect his later political behaviour had received wide currency' (1965, 8).

12. In the apparently more illuminating studies where subjects were interviewed this often did not exceed one hour!

13. While this *might* be true for some countries it is certainly not so for Australia.

14. Kohlberg (1971a, Appendices 1 and 3). See also Crittenden in D'Cruz and Hannah (1979) and Habermas (1979, 77).

15. Kohlberg's optimism is implied in, e.g. his claim that stage 6 thinking 'would in fact be universal to all mankind if the conditions for socio-moral development were optimal for all individuals in all cultures' (1971b, 178).

16. This last phrase is a strange one!

17. This is not the place to discuss the suitability of the label 'fascist' for the pre-1945 regime, but I agree with Halliday's judgement (1975, 133-40) that, while there was a fascist movement in Japan between 1920 and 1945, the term should not be applied to the regime as a whole.

18. See Held (1980, 35) and Slater (1977, 115).

19. See also Bunn (1962).

20. Udom does not explain his order of concepts treated under these three headings (1982, 36). Under 'free enterprise economics' he begins with 'unemployment, inflation, tax, and includes labor/strike and recession'. Under 'consumer economics' he begins with 'overtime, standard of living' and includes 'AFL/CIO'. Udom's study is very valuable for its appended details of state programmes and names and addresses of 'associated agents of economic socialisation'.

21. From a leaflet issued by the Institute. Udom's study is a product of this Institute.

22. From a leaflet issued by the firm. I am indebted to Michael Apple for sending me a copy after I read his citation in *Cultural and Economic Reproduction in Education*, p. 248.

9 THE SCHOOL SYSTEM

It is a major argument of this book that one must choose one's level of abstraction carefully to suit one's problem and that extreme abstraction often militates against an understanding helpful to radical social change. One must, therefore, immediately ask whether to speak of *the* school system in the singular is such an abstraction, or whether there are not significantly different school systems requiring attention. This question should be coupled with the question of how far school systems should be regarded as capitalist, as serving the interests or reflecting the structures of the capitalist mode of production in its late capitalist stage. Definitive answers to these questions require historical and comparative studies beyond the scope of the present work which can only suggest lines of approach and tentative solutions.

The economic boom after the Second World War was accompanied in all the metropoles of late capitalism by a school boom. This was in part the result of demands of labour movements, as in England, and in part the result of the nature and needs of the capitalist economies. The expansion of the tertiary sector of the economy created large numbers of jobs requiring a different kind of schooling. At the same time there was not the demand for juvenile labour that there was in earlier periods of capitalism, and various interests converged to keep youth 'off the streets' by raising the age at which compulsory schooling ended. One must note that raising the school leaving age followed a period in which large numbers of youth stayed on in school beyond the age of compulsion. It would be interesting to know how much this could be attributed to parental expectations and pressure, how much to genuine expectation that this would lead to better job chances and how much to inertia and the feeling that nothing better immediately offered.[1] With individual differences in the different countries this was a common trend, with the USA, the wealthiest and most powerful capitalist country, leading the way.

While the school expansion, through certification, assisted in the limited 'upward mobility' which fractionated the working classes, creating Poulantza's new petty bourgeoisie, it did nothing to create the unified school system which had been the dream of so many social reformers in education. In Britain the upper classes and Labour Party aspirants continued to send their children to the so-called public schools. In the USA, where private schooling becomes class significant only at the tertiary level, a similar class division was accomplished through housing prices which ensured some local elementary and high schools a privileged intake. The European-wide movement for comprehensive schooling, a movement supported by liberal believers in 'equal opportunities for all'[2] and groups extending to the political left of that position, offered little hope of fundamentally altering the situation.

The school expansion and its more recent halt and retrenchment can be understood only when the clash of interests is untangled. To some extent the capitalist class is above the battle, their positions protected and unchallenged. Their role has been as supporters of conservative policies of selective growth, of limiting opportunities to those 'best able to profit from them'. A few of their spokespersons have expressed the usual fears about educating people to be politically discontented or creating a less docile workforce. The main actors in the school scene have been the new middle classes for whom the schools have provided the certificates and often the jobs that followed. For the expansion of schooling, and particularly of the tertiary sector, has created thousands of interesting and generally well-paying jobs. One must add that it has also provided a huge market for publishing, for audio-visual equipment, and now computers. Teasing out the class, ethnic and status interests, the educational from the commercial, is a job which has hardly begun. It would mark progress to have these interests clearly defined and openly recognised.

In this section I shall largely confine myself to a few topics discussed by writers on Marx and education, since my major aim is to shift the focus of discussion from schools to wider educational questions. This is not to imply that marxist writers have not recognised such questions. Bowles and Gintis speak of consciousness developing through 'direct perception of and participation in social life' (1976, 128, cf. 219) and then go on to mention the family in addition to the 'educational system', i.e. schools, as being the institutions 'more immediately related to the formation of personality and consciousness' (129). Sharp, writing about the way in which schools function to 'reproduce the social relations of production', adds that 'however important the role of schooling, other institutions or apparatuses as well are involved' (1980, 116). Writing about 'what is to be done' and the 'struggle for hegemony', she lists the family, trade union, community organisation, political parties and the media (168). Madan sees himself as 'grasping the relations within a totality, the relations between schools, the family, work and politics' (1978, 2) and he included a section on 'The capitalist mode of production' (158-64). But all end in what I see as an overestimation of the school as a site of significant political learning and a place where revolutionary action can take place (cf. Sarup, 1982, 114; Harris 1982, 143-4).

In addition there is the problem that much of this writing is at too high a level of abstraction. In part this may be because for some current interpretations of marxism 'empiricism' is a dirty word. In part it may be because of the delicate nature of the topic. Whatever the reason, such generalisation is harmful to understanding and ways must be found to overcome it if understanding is to be improved. School studies need to be linked with studies of their environment. In addition, these need to be made on a comparative basis internationally. For example, what are the similarities and differences between the education of children of the upper classes in the different countries? What, if any, differences does attendance at a private rather than a state school (USA, West Germany?) make?

The Correspondence Principle

The most widely cited book on the correspondence theory is that by Samuel Bowles and Herbert Gintis, *Schooling in Capitalist America*, published in 1976. The theme was not new, but had been framed differently in the communist and liberal literature before it. These had dealt with the phenomenon in terms of differential access to different kinds and levels of schools. Among the important works in this genre was *Intelligence Testing and the Comprehensive School* (1953) by Brian Simon in England. Liberal thought was directed to various theories of 'deprivation' and questions of social mobility.

Bowles and Gintis state their principle as follows:

The educational system helps integrate youth into the economic system, we believe, through a structural correspondence between its social relations and those of production. The structure of social relations in education not only inures the student to the discipline of the work place, but develops the types of personal demeanor, modes of self-presentation, self-image, and social-class identifications which are the crucial ingredients of job adequacy. Specifically, the social relationships of education — the relationships between administrators and teachers, teachers and students, students and students, and students and their work — replicates the hierarchical division of labor. (1976, 131; 1978, 611)

What they are talking about is 'reproducing consciousness' (126-31). Capitalism requires 'people to be properly subordinate ... and sufficiently fragmented in consciousness to preclude their getting together to shape their own material existence' (130). This, they go on to emphasise, 'cannot be insured by [the social organization of the workplace] alone' (129 and 1978, 60). The family, school and other institutions are also involved in the production of consciousness. As for the family, 'Indeed, it is precisely because family structure and the capitalist relations of production differ in essential respects that our analysis sees schooling as performing such a necessary role in the integration of your people into the wage-labor system' (144 and 1978, 62). As they state in their reply to Sherry Gorelick (1978), their theory is not a 'mirror' theory, consciousness passively reflecting social structure. Rather, they claim that 'the degree of transformation of consciousness occurring through the experience of schooling is mediated primarily by the *structure* of social relations in schools, and this transformation *in part* explains why the correspondence of structures in work and education facilitate the reproduction process' (p. 62, my emphasis), reproduction here meaning both consciousness and the social class structure.

Bowles and Gintis cite evidence that the same types of behaviour are rewarded in both schooling and work (1976, 134), and that personality traits rewarded and penalised in high school and by work supervisors are the same (136-8). They make the already obvious point that a 'class stratification within higher education parallel to the hierarchical relationships of production in the modern corporation' exists. They note the 'multitiered system dominated at the top by Ivy League institutions and the great state universities, followed by the less prestigious state universities, state colleges, and ending with the community colleges' at the bottom

(209). Importantly they note in their final chapter that:

> The educational system, basically, neither adds to nor subtracts
> from the degree of inequality and repression originating in the
> economic sphere. Rather, it reproduces and legitimates a pre-
> existing pattern in the process of training and stratifying the
> work force. (265)

This it does, not in the content, the information transfer process,
'but in the form: the social relations of the educational encounter'
(265). This is that part which has by others been called 'the hidden
curriculum' (Apple, 1979, pp. 82-104).

Bowles and Gintis talk about the 'social relations of production', a marxist concept, and about the (hierarchical) division
of labour. But their analysis is really concerned with income
inequalities, 'individuals whose parents were in the top socio-
economic decile' on earnings (88), and other income groups with
parallel groupings based on the division of labour. True, they make
a clear distinction between 'labour incomes' (wages and salaries)
and 'property income' (interest, rent, dividends and profits) (90)
and draw attention to the very unequal ownership of property
which continues to exist. But they concentrate on 'the vertically
ascending hierarchy of authority' in the 'hierarchical division of
labour' to 'each level' of which 'there is associated a basic wage or
salary' (92-3). The failure to distinguish between class, in Marx's
sense, and the strata Bowles and Gintis actually operate with,
leaves us with essentially liberal goals: removal of inequalities; gen-
eralised development; and 'smooth integration of individuals as
fully functioning members of society' (1981, 45-6), which is surely
not what these writers intend. To point correctly to similarities in
the countries of 'state socialism' (the USSR, etc.) is only to introduce further unsolved problems (1978, 63).

Bowles and Gintis's work has come in for a lot of criticism from
within the radical and marxist educational trend. While some
critics have unhelpfully contented themselves with labelling,
'bourgeois conceptualizations', '"Durksonian" determinism' or
'structural-functionalist', others have attempted to grapple at the
level of argument. Sarup (1978) illustrates both of these
approaches, but mainly the latter. His most extended and
important point is the uncritical use which Bowles and Gintis make
of statistics (173-5). This, Sarup argues, leaves them unable to

justify their rejection of the grosser failings of earlier writers on IQ and educational testing (175). Interestingly, in their *Montly Review* self-criticism, although they list their 'mistaken decision not to articulate fully the underlying theoretical arguments', particularly the question of the state (64), Bowles and Gintis nowhere, to my knowledge, take up this difficulty of evaluating statistics. Sarup's other valid criticism is their neglect of the micro-level, that of classroom interaction and the curriculum. He is right in seeing that any assertions of learnings, of legitimations through effects on consciousness, must take this level into account. At the same time one must add that no book can deal with everything, and in a number of their formulations Bowles and Gintis made clear their recognition of the need to explore such questions too. Finally, two criticisms of Sarup's must be rejected. His attack on their 'deterministic ontology' (178(3)) and assertion that they see 'Man' as 'passive' is not even borne out by the citations he gives. His first (127) comes immediately after mention of 'struggles of furious intensity' and the pessimistic paragraphs from which the second citation is sliced is followed by one which begins: 'But this congruence is continually disrupted' (128). Sarup's second criticism is that accepting Bowles and Gintis's 'over-deterministic picture' leaves 'a problem when one has to explain how radical transformation of society is going to come about' (176-7), and causes 'many teachers [to] find it difficult to locate themselves in' the 'macro-level' analysis (179). This is not really the point. The point is, whether the analysis is correct. If so our difficulties are real indeed and they cannot be just wished away.

Before coming to my own criticism of the correspondence principle let us look at some other influential writers, if not in the same vein, whose work bears on the question. Basil Bernstein (London), whose identification of restricted and elaborated speech variants and socio-linguistic codes in the sixties became a focus of controversy, is one of these (1971, 1-20). He sees his work as concerned with 'the nature and process of social control' and with '*one* interpretation of how the category class is constituted in our consciousness' (1975, 29, 30). He sees his theories as contributing to change, as raising:

the básic issue that we can change the *social* means of the reproduction of class relationships, but not necessarily change the cultural means of such reproduction. It points to the question that although family and school are not themselves major levers of radical change — those lie in economic and political structures — family and education shape mental structures and so forms of feeling and thinking which may militate for or against changes in cultural reproduction. It therefore raises as a major problematic the relationships between social and cultural reproduction. (1975, 30)

All of this sounds promising, and indeed there is much of interest in his work, but his concept of class is quite other than marxist and a poor foundation for the claims he makes on it (cf. Sharp, 1980, 53-9). He uses the marxist term, mode of production, and defines class as 'the fundamental *dominant cultural category*, created and maintained by the mode of production' (1975, 175, emphasis in the original). He also uses the marxist-sounding term, 'ruling class' (1975, 191). But when he is more specific it is clear that it is strata rather than Marx's classes that he has in mind, and particularly that polymorphous group, the middle class. One has, therefore, to read passages like the following with these reservations in mind: 'Class is a fundamental category of exclusion and this is reproduced in various ways in schools, through the social context and forms of transmission of education' (1975, 28). I shall return to this point below.

Another influential writer who establishes connections between 'every institutionalized educational system' and 'the relations between the groups or classes' is Pierre Bourdieu (Paris) (1977, 54). He does this in part through his metaphor of cultural *capital*, a metaphor which owes more to bourgeois economics than it does to Marx (1977, 30). He writes: 'The educational system reproduces all the more perfectly the structure of the distribution of cultural capital among classes (and sections of a class) in that the culture which it transmits is closer to the dominant culture and that the mode of inculcation to which it has recourse is less removed from the mode of inculcation practised by the family' (1973, 80). He uses statistical tables to demonstrate that 'those classes or sections of a class which are richest in cultural capital become more and more over-represented as there is an increase in the rarity and hence in the educational value and social yield of academic quali-fications' (1973, 81). And he asserts that: Institutions of higher education which ensure or legitimate access to the ruling classes, and, in particular, the *grandes écoles* ... are therefore to all intents and purposes the monopoly of the ruling classes' (1973, 85). Unfortunately again, while the name of Marx is frequently mentioned in the texts, we are dealing with an analysis in terms of social strata, the occupational groups of the ISAA: farmers; workers; white-collar workers; craftsmen and tradespeople; intermediate office staff; professional, higher office staff; etc. (1973, 100-4; cf. Sharp, 1980, 70-1). Its value is in what it reveals about the peculiarly French literary culture and schooling, on the upper levels of which Bourdieu concentrates.

For the German Federal Republic a study of the data gives the same picture. Children of the self-employed and officials (Beamte) are largely to be found in the academic secondary schools (Gymnasien) while children of workers go predominantly to the Hauptschulen. A study by a working party from the Max-Planck-Institut fur Bildungsforschung gives figures for 1972-80 (p. 81).

Finally I would refer to another French study, that of Christian Baudelot and Roger Establet. Also making use of the data provided by INSAA they draw attention to the difficulties of converting these to social class (1972, 72). They argue that rather than a unified school system there are two systems: a secondary-superior system and a primary-vocational one (42). They estimate that the child of a worker has a 54 per cent chance of being schooled in the primary-professional system and only a 14 per cent chance of being schooled in the secondary-superior one while a child of bourgeois parents has exactly the reverse chances (81).

Turning now to my own comments, the findings of discrimination over entry, discrimination within the schools and in the granting of certificates and other awards play a significant part in reproducing the class system. But, to repeat, they affect stratification within the working classes, the so-called 'new petty bourgeoisie', rather than between working classes and any bourgeoisie. Were it possible to remove discrimination in the school system one wonders what effect this could have on the class system. In recent decades in many countries the number of young people staying on longer in the secondary schools and taking various forms of certificates previously reserved for the few has greatly increased. The experiences of England and the secondary modern schools' successes with the school certificate and higher school certificate are one example. But who would claim that this has significantly altered the class structure? If it seemed to some to bring nearer the liberal dream of 'equal opportunities for all' at the school level it also carried the dream beyond the school and turned it into the nightmare of greater competition for jobs requiring these certificates, or entry to tertiary college.

Perhaps the benefit of making a clear distinction between class and stratification analysis would be to highlight just what the argument is about and just what can and probably cannot be done. Willis, from a different perspective, recognised this when he said: 'There is no contradiction in asking practitioners [teachers] to work on two levels simultaneously' (186, cit. Harris, 1982, 143).

To close this section I will recapitulate some of the points. First, there is abundant evidence from all the major countries of late capitalism that the schools are to a greater or lesser extent socially segmented. Studies have concentrated on concepts of middle class and working class usually based on parental (father's) occupation and/or income level. Other related studies have dealt with the links between type of schooling and certification and jobs obtained on leaving school. An extension of this aspect is 'the diploma disease' (Dore, 1976). Studies of examinations like the English eleven-plus for entry to secondary school and those granting entrance to tertiary (the French *baccalaureat*) reveal the way in which concepts of class are disguised, converted into feeling of individual blame. An ideology of meritocracy and social mobility sanctify individual rather than class struggle in the liberal dream of a white-collar, well-paid job for all. Need I say, that was not Marx's dream and in the late capitalist reality of the eighties it should not be ours.

Control and Administration

With the student movements of the sixties well behind us it is perhaps not surprising that our selection of Marx-influenced writers have little to say on the way in which schools are controlled and administered. Has experience shown that this is neither an easy or very fruitful area in which to get involved? Has the absorption of student and even staff representation on college committees convinced us that this is not a useful way in which to bring about change? What about secondary and primary schools?

Roger Dale tries to deal with these questions in his 'Education and the Capitalist State' (Apple, 1982, pp. 127-61). He criticises Bowles and Gintis for failing to make clear why the 'needs of capitalist accumulation are expressed in such different forms in different social formations [countries]', and what the implications of this for politics would be (129). However, when Dale addresses education as 'a state apparatus' he does little more than hover above the surface with Offe's distinction between 'bureaucratic' and 'technological' control (140-1). For reasons not explained he then talks about 'the nature of the teaching profession' which he calls 'the substance of education state apparatuses', calling attention to their being 'publicly trained, certified and paid' (142-3). He then denies that they can be regarded as 'ideal type bureaucratic official[s]'. Yet what one should be considering, to fulfil his own aim of finding 'spaces and opportunities for initiating or resisting change in education' (146), surely, is the hierarchy of command of which the teachers are but a part, and a somewhat lowly part at that. Without a concrete analysis of the relationship between schools — and a distinction between different levels of schooling where this is important — and the bodies above them which control them: school governing councils, local education departments and bureaux, regional bureaux, and the central state organs (ministries), one has not really advanced more than half a step from the formulation of Bowles and Gintis with which he began.

At one point it looks as if we are approaching the control organs. Education systems, Dale tells us, are 'legally constituted' (153). He makes the interesting contrast between the positive use of legal proceedings in the USA, e.g. to bring about desegregation, and negatively in England, e.g. to prevent Labour Party plans to make secondary schooling comprehensive. The introduction of a core curriculum is introduced in a paragraph on bureaucratic rule following, and teaching machines are the best Dale can offer as an example of 'technocratic management'. After that the argument moves to control in the sense of social control and questions which really deserve clarification are abandoned.

Sarup, in *Education, State and Crisis*, is concerned with the ideological role of state control of education and does not pause to ask questions concerning the form of administration or management. His mention of the latter term is in connection with Braverman's analysis of changes in the labour process in industry. His only reference to schools is to suggest that head teachers may now have to study management, and that the 'split between administrative/bureaucratic management and practising class teachers is thus widening'. The 'fragmentation and routinization' which occurs in industry is being copied in the schools (36). Then elsewhere he throws in the interesting comment that the apparent move to decentralisation in English schooling can fragment control, so providing 'an effective obstacle to those seeking social change' (64). By example he refers to the way local education authorities frustrated attempts to set up genuine comprehensive schools. This is an argument worth of study and development, but falls outside Sarup's main thrust, the ideological role of state schooling.

Harris, in *Teachers and Classes*, has an index entry for 'administration' which directs the reader to 'bureaucratic-type activities'. Under the latter we are told that:

the very structure and functioning of schooling (under capitalism) parallels the social relations of production under capitalism. There are controllers and the controlled. The controlled have no power over the production process and have to accept it, and the rules which come with it, as given. (1982, 84)

The controlled Harris has in mind here are the pupils who must 'acquiesce in their lack of control' and who are thus prepared for lives in industry under similar 'alienating' conditions (1982, 84). He goes on to talk of teachers' activities divided between 'police-type' and 'bureaucratic-type' (96-7), seeing teachers as the 'political agents of capital' in performance of these two types of activity. When Harris talks about the role of the state it is support of ideology he has in mind and apart from casual reference to such things as legalising '"Family Trusts"' (102) or 'controlling and sorting children for employers' (103) he does not explore.

The term bureaucratic, which I have discussed elsewhere, is used by numerous writers to refer to school government. But in this context it is usually used imprecisely and means little more than disapproval of a system in which those at the bottom of the hierarchy have little or no control over setting the rules they have to enforce and obey. Rather than general denunciation, specific exploration of the different models in operation, both between different kinds and levels of schooling and between different countries of late capitalism, are necessary to open the way for real change (Dale in Apple, 1982, 146). Such aspects as employment security, a professional orientation to work and methods of job evaluation need to be seen in the light of studies of modified bureaucratic theory (Clegg and Dunkerley, 1980, 163-9). Perhaps even more important are questions about the building into rules, regulations and managerial styles of an interest in control for its own sake and the transmission of this through business studies and courses in administration (Clegg and Dunkerley, 252-5, 537-9).

The hierarchy which I have mentioned several times without defining runs from the taught at the bottom, at the classroom level of teacher-student interaction, to the country's legislators at the top. Its form varies widely and is often contrastively examined as 'centralised' versus 'decentralised' (e.g. Archer, 1979), though these terms need care since a 'decentralised' unit like the New York Board of Education administers a population comparable with that of Australia or the Netherlands (Holmes, 1965, 181). But equally important is the division between state and non-state control (often religious) and their interaction. For in none of the countries of late capitalism are non-state schools free of some form of state regulation and in most cases many, if not all, receive considerable state subsidy.[3] Evaluation, for our purposes, is required of the powers of the different levels and divisions and the possibilities these allow for the development of genuine communication and participation of those interested. I will try and spell out some of the meanings which I consider important in this formulation below. One of the difficulties any investigation of these questions faces is to get behind the formal patterns of how it is supposed to be, to the realities of how it actually works (Clegg and Dunkerley, 225-7). The latter is often shrouded in rumour and secrecy and guarded by fears of libel action or victimisation.

Genuine communication here means an exchange between different levels of the hierarchy involving sincerity, truthfulness and at least an attempt to understand each other's discourse. In practice this ideal seldom seems to be attempted. In some cases there are limitations on direct communication between levels. All too often the higher level treats communication from below as an attack to be warded off regardless of substance. Gerald Levy gives examples (Chapter 10).

The interested parties include the teachers and students whose difficulties of communication are considered by Harris (1982). Directly affecting these are school administrators increasingly divorced from the classroom as the size of schools has grown and with it the ideology of control. These may include heads of department, subject supervisors, committees and committee chairpersons and the institution heads and deputies. Immediately above and in a sense outside the school is usually some kind of council on which representatives of other interests sit. Then there is the nature and distance from the local education authority to consider, and the nature of the powers of each of these levels. It is in this arena that the farce of financial control is played out, often involving penny-pinching through the year until near the end when those reponsible suddenly discover credits which 'must be spent', all too often only on large and insufficiently considered items. Mistrust of those at the bottom of the hierarchy in financial matters is only part of a general lack of trust in many parts and levels of school systems which does not normally reveal itself in official reports or theorising but which can only be repaired if openly faced.

Continuing the list of interested parties one must glance sideways at the students' parents. I say sideways since parents have seldom been incorporated directly in the hierarchy. In some schools and systems there are active parents' associations, while in others parents are discouraged from any participation and seen as a threat to teacher expertise. Clearly, in any attempts to democratise education in the grassroots sense I am using, communication and co-operation with parents will be important. At the same time we should, perhaps, ponder two things. One, Nadezhda Krupskaya's comment that children are neither the property of their parents nor of the state, but belong to themselves (1959, 6, 158). The other, the experience in England of the William Tyndale affair where young middle-class and professional families, many of them members of the Labour Party, moved into what had once been a working-class area, and began to take an active part in school affairs (Gretton and Jackson, 1976, Chapter 2). Roger Dale has argued that one consequence of this is 'the likelihood that the progress of parent participation in schooling w[ill] be articulated in a conservative rather than any kind of progressive or radical philosophy of schooling' (Dale *et al.*, 1981, 310). The marxist vision is of co-operation in the maximising of freedom for all interested parties. In the long struggle to achieve this it will be necessary constantly to question the aims of those concerned in order to bring out the 'hidden agendas' and reifications of interest through which the educatory aims of schools are constantly displaced.

Another group which appears increasingly to be organising itself as a separate interest group is that of the professional education administrators. Strongly organised in the USA, it is represented by the National Association of Governors and Managers in Britain. Any analysis of their role needs to separate tertiary from the other levels of schooling. It will be interesting to see with what groups administrators ally themselves and what, if any, divisions in their ranks become significant. Some might well look to the upwardly mobile Labour Party parents who featured in the William Tyndale affair (cf. Bacon in Dale *et al.*, 1981, 404).

Teacher trade unions are clearly an important element in the struggle for democracy. But like the wider union movement they have not seen this as a major goal of their work. Engaged in struggles to improve the working conditions of teachers and the conditions for study of students, the question of democracy has all too seldom found expression. The British National Union of Teachers passed a resolution at its 1971 conference calling for staff representation on boards of school governors and local education committees and for school councils to be considered which would reduce the power of head teachers. But faced with implementation of democratic measures, or pressure from the rank and file movement within the executive, action appears to have been distinctly conservative.[4] One of the problems is membership of the particular union which often gives it a particular bias, head teachers, or women teachers from mainly non-state schools being examples which come to mind. The division of interest between head teachers and others has bedevilled the British NUT over many years and is part of the wider question of modern trade unionism. 'Responsible' unions are those whose officials side with employers and the state in organising the corporate society, and this means stifling rather than encouraging rank and file democracy.

Finally, to return to students, something must be said about arguments over allowing them a role in the democratic process. Taking tertiary school students first, the arguments against their inclusion have included their ignorance, their short-term membership of the institutions concerned and the confidential nature of much of the decision making process of which they are also the object (student evaluation especially). These arguments were countered in the late sixties (e.g. Stedman Jones in Cockburn and Blackburn, 1969, 49-52), but at least in British practice that followed, students, like non-professional staff in the universities and colleges, settled for less (Moodie and Eustace, 1974, 196-207).[5] The inclusion of students of secondary and primary school age has probably nowhere been seriously considered by other than a small minority. In the late sixties and early seventies there was some organisation. In England a National Union of School Students and a Schools Action Union were formed. The President of the former, writing in *Radical Education* in 1974, denied being a 'pupil-power' organisation and said 'what we hope to achieve is a situation where parents, teachers and students are working together'. Their aims included co-operation with teachers in deciding curricula and schools run by councils of 'students, teachers, parents and non-academic staff' on a 'community' basis (*Radical Education*, 1, autumn, 1974, 15).[6] In Australia the anti-Vietnam War movement seems to have stimulated students to form similar organisations, in Victoria, e.g. the Secondary Students Union. In 1972 that Union called protest stoppages over 'inequalities in schooling opportunities and the need for democratisation in school government'. It also drew up a wide-ranging bill of rights for students (Bessant and Spaull, 1976, 183).

The complexities of trying to understand the administration process are nicely illustrated in the collection of papers edited by Elizabeth and Michael Useem, *The [US] Education Establishment*. The title and the accompanying cover blub suggest a conspiracy theory approach. The blurb asks 'Who really runs America's education system?' and goes on to refer to 'trustees, school boards, administrators, and local businessmen [who] have a tenacious grip on school practices'. But the editors draw attention to the article by W.W. Charters in which 'he argues that it remains to be demonstrated empirically that board members are guided by occupational and class loyalties in setting school policies'. They cite other researchers who 'have found that in some cases school board members who are identified with the middle or upper class hold more liberal and progressive views on education than those drawn from the working class'. The editors also refer to studies showing how 'business notables', while having far from absolute control, can do much to influence school politics informally. Most usefully, they conclude that while '[n]othing approximating a coherent, conscious elite controls public education, yet the organizations, groups, and positions most involved in setting educational priorities are generally not accountable to students, parents, or the community at large. Turning to Britain and the universities, the study by Moodie and Eustace draws attention to the diverse interests represented by 'laymen' on university councils: commerce and industry; scholarship and education; and moral and social purpose (115). They speak of 'the value of the intelligent, experienced outsider' who can bring particular and different expertise and who, with time available, can serve on committees which academics would prefer not to (118-19). Their study, couched necessarily at a fairly high level of abstraction, shows the value of case studies like those on Warwick University (Thompson, 1970) or the Hornsey College of Art (Students and Staff, 1969). Everyone in capitalist societies is influenced by bourgeois ideology to some extent and a conspiracy theory approach is not likely to be the best, which is not to deny that conspiracies often exist! Only by focusing analyses on particular policies or problems and the structural forms which hinder and facilitate these can we learn best how to change in desired directions. To think that obtaining representation of students or women, or reducing representation of other groups, such as businessmen or professors, will necessarily change anything is to delude ourselves.

Academic Freedom

The issues which come together under the concept of academic freedom are variously connected with problems of school control and adminstration and will, therefore, be discussed at this point. Speaking about external threats to freedom Elizabeth Schneider identified five levels of interest groups within the universities which might be affected: 'trustees, administrators, faculty as a whole, individual teachers, and students'. Affected areas might include 'faculty hiring or promotion and student selection or student funding' (in Kaplin and Schrecker, 1983, 221). Other threatened areas include research: the choice of research topic, funding and other support, or the publication and otherwise distribution of findings. In addition there is the possibility that the threat to freedom arises within the institution, or, especially in the case of schools other than universities, from within the administration system or governing bodies.

There is, not surprisingly, difference of opinion about the meaning which should be given to the topic. In the Conference on the Concept of Academic Freedom held at the University of Texas at Austin in 1972 William van Alstyne argued strongly for a distinction between general civil liberties which should apply to everyone regardless of employment or employer, and those special freedoms required by the nature of the academic pursuit (in Pincoffs, 1975, 59-85, 125-30). He drew attention to constraints which the latter places on those seeking its protection. He claimed a strong ethical pressure for 'exceptional care in the representation of that [academic] "truth"' the research into and teaching of which is protected (76). Knowing falsification of results and plagiarism frustrate claims to freedom and require accountability. John R. Searle argued rather for a general theory, in which the university is seen as 'an institutional embodiment of the general social values of free inquiry and free expression' (Pincoffs, 93) and a special theory, resting on a claim that knowledge is valuable and that the university is 'an institutional device for the advancement and dissemination of knowledge' (Pincoffs, 89). Amelie Oksenberg Rorty, in the same debate, saw 'our dilemma' in wanting:

> to assure academics and intellectuals freedom from external interference with their professional activities, while on the other hand, we want to avoid placing judgment in the hands of a self-perpetuating academic elite, which must form their judgments following existing standards of competence. (Pincoffs, 103)

She points to the difficulties the original thinker must have with established, necessarily conservative, standards. 'Placing the burden of proof on change and transformation generally initially cripples all but the most rhetorically mellifluous or sophisticatedly ambiguous theories' (104). While this argument speaks for the conservative nature of one's academic peers any arguments for judgement by the wider public must take into account the 'greater scope [that would allow] to the tyranny of fashionable and arbitrary judgements' (106). Bertell Ollman, while admitting that academic freedom as an ideal 'opens up a little space' for people to defend themselves against reactionary attacks, argues that under capitalism the universities should primarily be seen as performing rather a repressive role (Kaplan and Schrecker, 55, 52-3). This operates at three levels: that of government attempting 'to keep radicals or Marxists out of the university'; university administrators refusing to hire or give them tenure; and departmental faculties

202 The School System

initiating or supporting such actions on conservative interpretations of standards (52). At the same time he remarks on 'the
striking development' of recent years, that of 'a growth in the
number of radical scholars and the increased legitimation of radical
scholarship'.[7]

Following Marx there is no question of defending some abstract
notion of academic freedom. Indeed, one does not have to be
either a reactionary or a marxist to recognise certain necessary
limitations on unrestrained freedom of expression. Elshtain, using
the example of Robert Faurisson's recent denial of the Nazis'
practice of genocide, points to 'the vantage point of scholarly
authority' from which his assertions can be combatted. She argues
for a belief in 'some truth to be found' on which that authority can
be based, and therefore, it follows, though she does not state it,
'shoddy' scholarship and 'warped interpretation of highly selective
material' must in some circumstances be denied academic
authority (Kaplan and Schrecker, 173). The problem is to set the
limits, especially after the experience of the Nazi period and the
experience of the USSR. Some of the arguments are rehearsed by
Bedau in 'Free speech, the right to listen, and disruptive interference' (Pincoffs, 191-211 and Pasch's reply, 212-34). I would
suggest only constant questioning of whose interest is involved,
who is saying what and who is preventing what from being said
and done can bring about that general enlightenment required for
a better society. For that reason study of the record so far is helpful.

The United States has a well-documented history of cases.
Whether Edward Bemis, dismissed from the University of Chicago
in 1894 for connections with striking Pullman railroad workers, or
Scott Nearing, fired from the University of Pennsylvania in 1915
for publicly opposing the use of child labour in coal mines was the
first radical to suffer (Ollman in Kaplan and Schrecker, 45), the
charge in both cases concerned the essence of capitalism. The dis-
missals in New York in 1940 were of communists, as were those a
decade later in the McCarthy period. In 1978 Joel Samoff was
denied tenure by the University of Michigan and Ollman himself
prevented from becoming Chairman of the Government Department of the University of Maryland, both for being marxists
(Ollman, Kaplan and Schrecker, 46, cf. notes to Ellen Schrecker,
40-3; *Critique*, 14, 109-20). Interesting light is thrown on the
limitations imposed by one's colleagues' conventional views of

what and how one should study by the case of Richard M. Pfeffer who was denied tenure by the Political Science Department of Johns Hopkins University in 1978. He had taken a year's sabbatical leave on half-pay to work in a factory and then write up his experiences in a book which did not meet with the approval of his colleagues when it appeared! Like others before him, and perhaps rather naïvely, he took the side of the workers and became a union activist (Pfeffer, 1979).

In Germany, which has a particularly unpleasant history of repression, radicals were again attacked in the seventies under what has been called the Berufsverbote (employment-prohibition). This began with a decision in January 1972 of Federal Chancellor Brandt and the premiers of the various states (Länder) that 'members of "extremist organisations" as "enemies of the constitution" [should] not be let into the civil service' (*IMSF*, 22, 7). According to the working committee of the 'Initiative to do away with the Berufsverbote' by June 1975, 171 teachers, 86 university teachers and 18 'social educators' were among 330 victims of whom the committee had detailed knowledge. Some, like Professor Horst Holzer, University of Bremen, Silvia Gingold, 29 year old teacher in Hesse, or F. Konrad, tenured teacher in Bavaria, were attacked for alleged membership of the legal Communist Party (*IMSF*, 39-40, 45-6, 47). Others, like Wolf-Dieter Narr, Social Democratic Party member and university teacher in West Berlin, were attacked, apparently, for activities with the peace movement (*IMSF*, 40-1). The case of Ulrich Topp, Heidelberg gymnasium teacher and official of the Union for Education and Science is disturbing for its implications for political education in schools (*IMSF*, 49-50). One of the better documented cases is that of Peter Bruckner, social psychologist in the Technical University of Hannover, suspended in 1972-3 and again in 1977. His case stimulated publication of a 352-page volume of articles in his support by distinguished scholars throughout Germany, though one must add that many others were silenced by fear (Krovoza *et al.*, 1981, cf. Bruckner, 1972).

The other countries of advanced capitalism are not free from their cases of academic repression, but I shall leave it there. Broadened beyond the scope explored in these paragraphs to that of freedom for all citizens to be informed on those issues essential to their lives, I believe we have one of the most significant failures of the process of education in the countries of advanced capitalism.

With a technology which would allow everyone to take an intelligent, informed interest in these matters we have a political economic system which uses technology to befuddle us and deprive us of genuine information. That it is, and has been, worse elsewhere and at other times is no comfort.

To sum up, following Marx one would want to ask of present administrative systems the degree and ways in which they reflect the purposes and styles of capitalism and thus militate against the deeper purposes of education. One would look for ways in which present structures might be altered to facilitate transition to a more co-operative and democratic structure in the future. But changes will not be possible without changes in the wider, political-economic structures of society. In tertiary schools, and to a lesser degree in secondary and primary levels as well, much of the hierarchy is defended on the grounds of the certification function which schools perform. With a different political economy the competitive nature of this certification would also change. Were everyone guaranteed a decent basic wage and hours of work adjusted to those already required in *today's* conditions, with their tens of millions of unemployed and glut of consumer goods, it would be possible to do things very differently. With conditions of work more equal between jobs (guaranteed decent pensions, holidays, flexible hours) those for whom teaching and research are a career rather than a vocation might more easily see their place elsewhere and the quality of schooling be further raised in consequence. With shorter hours more people would be able to participate in the kind of work they enjoyed and the present waste of talent could be overcome.[8] The present system of ranks (professor, senior and principal lecturer and the rest), already inappropriate, could be replaced by the simple distinction between trainees and trained.[9] This would then end the present highly negative practice of 'publish or perish' and similar cosmetic activities required for promotion or even survival in one's job. A simplified administration could be evolved, incorporating rotation of jobs and delegation of decision making. All this is not to underestimate the difficulties, particularly in the transitional period. Changes over the last two decades have shown that with our psyches, and unchanged institutional structures and objectives, committees are often simply time-wasting, and the replacement of professors by lower ranks no more than a change of face. But that is no argument against further changes, including those which would make those already forshadowed a genuine change for the better.

Discipline, Order and Management

The problems and concept cluster which lie behind these words have played a central role in schooling from the beginning. Complaints by teachers, parents and other social groups about the school teachers' failure to discipline their charges are not confined to the more conservative periods of late capitalism, though their vehemence at these times might make one think so. Nor is there sound evidence available on which we can judge the extent to which 'ill discipline' is a greater problem today than before, though many think it is. Part of the difficulty is, as so often, a lack of clear definition, of conceptualisation. Comparisons are near impossible since never before in history have so many young people stayed at school for so long. There is also a problem of over-generalisation, of treating schools in all their variety as School. Some of the writers whose work I shall examine here have introduced new ways of looking at these questions, but much more needs to be done before we have the understanding necessary for a new and sound practice.

Typical of the liberal approach of the forties and fifties is that of Sir Percy Nunn, former Director of the University of London Institute of Education, whose book, *Education: Its Data and First Principles*, was widely used in teacher training in England. He distinguished discipline from order, seeing the latter as 'the maintenance of the conditions necessary if school life is to fulfil its purpose'. Significantly he added that order 'is most effective when based on imitation and the routine tendency'. Discipline he saw as internal, as 'the submission of one's impulses and powers to a regulation which imposes form upon chaos, and brings efficiency and economy where there would otherwise be ineffectiveness and waste' (p. 250). His writing is full of unexamined social assumptions and undefined ideals further exemplified in the following passage: 'The discipline a child gains at school from his teachers and his comrades is of the same character. It is a directive influence, which shows him the better way and stimulates him to make it his own. The discipline of a fine school tradition works in the same way' (p. 251). While to some of us the language sounds archaic I would suggest there are still many schools among us where similar rhetoric is taken for valid today.

Sarup (1982) is the only marxist writer on education to tackle these questions directly. In a chapter on 'The enforcement of discipline' he discusses Michel Foucault's book, *Discipline and Punish* (1975), a book in which Foucault traces, in the years 1760–1840, the evolution of new ideas of social order and ways of treating those who broke it. As Sarup summarises it:

> The classical age discovered the body as object and target of power; it became aware that the body can be used, manipulated, shaped, trained, made to obey. Many of the disciplinary methods had long been in existence, in monasteries, armies, and workshops, but in the course of the seventeenth and eighteenth centuries the '*disciplines*', the insights and techniques of the human sciences, became general formulae of domination. What was new was that by being combined and generalised they attained a level at which the formation of knowledge and the increase of power regularly reinforced one another in a circular process. (p. 15)

Foucault goes into great detail about the ordering of space and time, the architecture of prisons, the timetabling of schools, and school examinations (Sarup, 16, 18; Foucault, 152, 148, 168-9). Foucault notes the failure of prisons to diminish crime. Sarup comments:

> Similarly, we could ask: what is served by the failure of the school? Just as prison, and no doubt punishment in general, is not intended to eliminate offences, but rather to distinguish them, to distribute them, to use them, so, perhaps, schools do not fulfil the function of education — they train pupils for docility and 'usefulness'. (p. 22)

Sarup is critical of Foucault's concept of power, of his apparent attack on 'rational organization as such' (Sarup, 25), and his overemphasis of the similarities of prisons, factories, barracks, hospitals and schools. Sarup maintains that, while helpful in making us think, this overemphasis neglects essential differences. Many socialists, he suggests, neglect the significance of 'the disciplinary mode of domination itself' and simply ask 'that working class kids should have *more* of the *same* type of schooling' (p. 23). Moreover, in the current stage of late capitalism there is increasing unease about the way in which medicine, psychology, the agencies of the welfare state and schools render ordinary people powerless through their assumption of expertise. A part of this is the conception of the norm whose judges the various experts are. Sarup cites Foucault:

> We are in the society of the teacher-judge, the doctor-judge, the educator-judge, the social-worker judge; it is on them that the universal reign of the normative is based; and each individual, wherever he may find himself, subjects to it his body, his gestures, his behaviour, his aptitudes, his achievements. (Sarup, 22-3; Foucault, 311)

Learning to Labour by Paul Willis sets out to understand why working-class kids 'let themselves' get working-class jobs (p. 1) and in the process it tells us a lot about questions of discipline and order. It concentrates on 'a group of twelve non-academic working class lads' from a 'good' non-selective secondary modern school in an industrial midlands English town (p. 4). What concerns us here is not the process by which the group evolved its oppositional style, but Willis's analysis of the school as institution and the 'teaching paradigm[s]'. As in Foucault, Willis notices spacial relations.

> In a simple physical sense school students, and their possible views of the pedagogic situation, are subordinated by the constricted and inferior space they occupy. Sitting in tight ranked desks in front of the larger teacher's desk; deprived of private space themselves but outside nervously knocking the forbidden staff room door or the headmaster's door with its foreign rolling country beyond; surrounded by locked up or out of bounds rooms, gyms and equipment cupboards; cleared out of school at break with no quarter given even in the unprivate toilets . . . (p.76)

Then there is time:

> The careful bell rung timetable; the elaborate rituals of patience and respect outside the staff room door and in the classroom where even cheeky comments are prefaced with 'sir'; compulsory attendance and visible staff hierarchies ... (p. 68)

Willis describes school as 'the agency of face to face control *par excellence*' and adds that 'what successful conventional teaching cannot tolerate is private reservation' (p. 65). Conventional pedagogy is 'tactics for exposing and destroying, or freezing, the private'. Willis sees teaching as 'essentially a relationship between potential contenders for supremacy' which in contemporary capitalist societies relies more on bluff than the 'actual power of direct coercion' (p. 63). 'The teacher's authority must therefore be won and maintained on moral not coercive grounds.' It is based on teaching as an exchange — of 'knowledge for respect, of guidance for control' (p. 64). Individual teachers and different schools play this 'basic teaching paradigm' differently, and, though Willis does not make the point explicitly, with mass unemployment and the increasingly obvious irrelevance of the knowledge exchange he stresses, there would seem to be an increasing tendency for the exchange to break down. Willis notes that in both the old secondary modern schools and the working-class comprehensives it has been common to replace the offer of knowledge, so often clearly rejected, with a moral offering: 'what it is worth the student striving for becomes . . . deference and politeness themselves'. Having 'the right attitude' becomes the slogan for everything (p. 69). Control, such as it is, is maintained through a general lowering of expectations to a more realistic level (p. 70). An alternative to this bending of the 'basic paradigm' is the adoption of aspects of progressive education', individualised learning, attempts to make curricula 'relevant' or team teaching, but adoption in order to strengthen essentially 'control purposes' (pp. 71-2). Willis seems to approach Foucault again when he stresses that whether traditional or modern in approach, the teaching paradigm aims not at 'overcompliance' but on the pupils' willingness to reciprocate, 'willingly and from their own resources' (p. 83). That is, the pupils are expected, within clear limits, to agree to their own domination.

Using a different methodology from Willis, Paul Corrigan studied two boys' schools in the northern England town of Sunderland, one a new comprehensive and the other a much older secondary school. Not starting from a particular hypothesis, and in fact changing his ideas radically in the course of the research, Corrigan was interested in the relationship between delinquent behaviour and secondary schooling (pp. 2, 3, 5). The chapter titles give the flavour of the research: Why do kids play truant? Why do kids muck about in class? Why do boys choose dead-end jobs?

What do they get out of pop music and football? Why do kids get into trouble on the street? He outlines four methods of control used in the classroom.

The first model he styles 'attempts to win the hearts and minds of the working class' (pp. 66-7). This is the attempt to inculcate respect for figures of authority; 'that it is rude to speak unless spoken to; and that one should always be punctual'. The second model is the attempt to teach rules as guides to action. One boy's comment was: 'First they just tell us, and then they punish us to teach us it, since we don't listen much' (p. 68). The third method adds punishment after each infraction of the rule, a method of threat which worked for a minority of the boys. For most of the boys a fourth method was required: constant surveillance (Foucault again!) Corrigan comments:

> Rule-enforcement and rule-breaking become a totally creative process linked to the different sorts of power involved in the situation. The power and imagination of the controlled are pitted against the power and imagination of those controlling. It is this method that the boys accepted as the method that controlled them and controlled their friends' actions. (p. 69)

The enormous gulf in understanding which exists between the working-class pupils and the values of the school as system is brought out sharply in the chapter on the activities in the street.

> There seems to be no feeling of 'legitimisation' given to the police interference in the boys' actions, no feeling of a 'fair cop'. This reflects very strongly the model of control in the school, where there is no real recognition of the moral or legal rights of the teacher to interfere. Similarly with the police, the only way in which their rights of interference are recognised is through their *power* and that is recognised, like the teacher's, *only* in physical presence. (p. 137)

Turning to the USA and the primary level of schooling we have the example of *Ghetto School* described by Gerald Levy. Situated between a black ghetto and a Puerto Rican ghetto the school was built in 1954. At the time of the author's participant observation as a 'floater' teacher there were some 800 children, 75 per cent black and 25 per cent Puerto Rican with a 50-50 mix in the lower grades.

There were some 40 teachers (p. 25). This study was informed by the need to understand the political process by which 'ghetto teachers and administrators . . . mediate the discrepancy between their image of education and the educational tasks they see themselves performing' (p. xiv). The climate within which the study was pursued is well summed up in the following paragraph:

> Midway's [the pseudonym for the school] teachers are always rehashing school boycotts, wildcat strikes, incidents with black militants, flare-ups with the P[arent] T[eacher] A[ssociation], incidents of brutality with children, and teachers being attacked by children and parents — incidents that somehow never reached the press. Almost daily they read about and see televised accounts of conflicts between other ghetto schools and their communities similar to conflicts occurring in Midway School. They wonder when their school will become the focus of this crisis in ghetto education. (p. 25)

Indeed, the school suffers from considerable damage to property and the children's reading scores are on average two years behind the norm and are next to lowest in the district (p. 24). The issue of control becomes paramount:

> Most substitutes and floater teachers and one-third of the regular teachers cannot control their classes. In many of these classes, children refuse to do any work, fight with each other, leave the room, run through the halls, and harass the other classrooms. By the third grade, for many teachers the *only* issue is control. The children are hit, bribed, and manipulated in any way that will secure the class. The children respond by doubling their efforts to defeat the teacher. (p. 86)

This study is interesting in detailing the bureaucratic approach to these problems, a major feature of which is pretending they don't exist (p. 112, 130). The role of the Head lies in relaying endless directives from the Board of Education down to teachers and sometimes directly over the broadcast system to the children, and relaying endless statistics back upwards about how many are taking what with which teacher (pp. 110-12). Claims on federal and state budgets, and insurance and other questions of accountability require that keeping attendance records is a main task. Levy describes the failure of the Head to communicate with the teachers or apply consistent standards and accuses the administration of 'giving up the educational vision' and retreating to a 'garrison mentality' in which manning the various positions and 'securing the school' is almost all that can be accomplished (pp. 114-19).

One book which looks at two different kinds of schools comparatively is *Making the Difference* by R.W. Connell and three other Australians. Summing up a project which was entitled 'School, home, and work' the book is a mixture of the interplay of these 'larger social structures' with 'individual lives, hopes, fears, and sometimes passions' (p. 9). The researchers used in-depth interviewing of 14-year-old students and their parents and where possible their teachers. Students were obtained from seven independent (private) schools (50 students) and five state (comprehensive secondary) schools (50 students), and were chosen to represent contrasting positions in a scheme of social stratification modified from Wright.[10] Schools were located in both Sydney and Adelaide.

While there is a wealth of interesting material in this book to discuss I wish to select one narrow question here: the difference between the good independent school and all too many of the state schools. One teacher who had experienced both expressed it this way:

> I *enjoy* the work here, and I feel that as a professional I *enjoy* teaching. I found that in the state schools — *some* of the state schools I was in — I wasn't teaching. I was just trying to discipline apathetic students who didn't want to go, whose parents didn't care, and so I was — I looked after them. I almost baby-sat some classes, some of the lower streams . . . But here the response is *superb* and as a teacher I thoroughly enjoy it. (p. 103)

Of course, not all classes in private schools are 'superb' and particularly for particular students. Hence, as the authors sum up one private school student's comments: 'the unending guerilla-war aspect of class-room life'. Still, there is a difference to be theorised, and it is Australian teachers' perception that '"getting on top", and staying there' is much more difficult than it used to be, especially in the state system. Both students and teachers are abandoning it for that reason — rightly or wrongly.

With that brief excursion into what a variety of investigators have exposed to view of their pieces of the late capitalist world it is time to try and see how the pieces might be fitted together. All accounts testify to a wide gap between what is being taught, whether by hidden or open curriculum, and what is being learnt. All accounts speak of frustration and stress, of disappointments and failure, and of the enormous waste of time. Whether measured in Marx's terms (*CAP*, 3, 959), or in those of strict capitalist efficiency much schooling is a waste of time!

There are two types of questions to ask: those concerning understanding the problem; and those concerning possible solutions. On the first I remain uncertain whether, and if so, to what extent, schools are more unruly places than they have been in the past, or that working-class schools are generally worse than many catering for other strata in society. The insolent anti-intellectualism and wilful lack of interest of students in some schools in the suburbs inhabited by 'the new petty bourgeoisie' can be very hard to handle.

It seems clear that there will always be an element of compulsion in any schooling of the young and in all situations where attendance is compulsory. The degree to which this must give rise to conflict and the forms in which that is worked out is one question. Bourdieu's catchy phrase, symbolic violence (1977, 5) is probably not helpful, however true the extension about imposition of a cultural arbitrary. Violence implies too great an abuse to cover all cases of teaching though one has regretfully to agree that the term has been all too often appropriate.

One of the concepts mentioned a number of times in these studies is that of a 'good' school (e.g. Willis, p. 4). All too often that is seen only in terms of discipline, of whether the pupils are properly turned out, clean, tidy and well behaved. It may extend to no fighting, or neat work on display to parents and visitors. All too seldom is it extended to more specific learnings. But that question overlaps with the next section on curricula. Perhaps a 'good' school should be understood along the lines of Willis's analysis, in the way in which the school values match or do not match the values of the population from which its pupils are drawn. What is clearly needed is a two-fold classification along a more satisfactory social class/ethnic grouping than these studies provide and some qualitative measure of the degree of hostility/lack of 'control'. Here the concept of 'differentiation' used by Willis would be useful: that process of reinterpretation of the taught school culture through comparison with that of the class or group from which the students come (Willis, 62-85). But what about a school and its catchment population both sharing values judged bad by the great majority of the rest of the population? What about a racist or fascist community and school? In the present state of both marxist and liberal theory we have no clear answers to such questions and most of us prefer not to face them.

The Question of Standards

Standards is not a term which writers on the left like to employ in discussing education. They appear to regard its use as giving ground to the right, which enjoys brandishing the term and posing as standard-bearers of what in a former period of reaction was called 'Western Christian civilization'. Sarup, whose book begins with British Prime Minister James Callaghan's initiation of a 'Great Debate' on educational standards in 1976, never really allows himself to get to grips with the problem in spite of various mentions (1982, 1). The subject is usually handled obliquely, or more dangerously, by side-swipes at the Black Papers or other calls for a return to 'excellence'. It was, therefore, encouraging to see Rachel Sharp, in a recent number of the Australian *Radical Education Dossier*, saying:

> There is nothing inherently conservative about being concerned at the breakdown of discipline in many schools, nor about the appeal for standards, or respect for authority. What makes this discourse conservative is its silence about the underlying processes which are causing dissatisfaction. (Sharp, 1984)[11]

Of course, the whole radical movement in education, in France, in the USA, or wherever, had been about standards, about the rejection of old standards. But it had also in large part rejected the concept of standards. Paul Goodman caught one aspect of this when he wrote that for his students 'all functions could be reduced to interpersonal relations and power', that for them 'there was no knowledge, but only the sociology of knowledge' (cit. Silberman, 1971, 27).

A major problem is to be clear about just what the problems

are. Teachers are prejudiced by subjective impressions of their own and those of their colleagues and probably have a tendency to be more impressed and concerned by problems of failure than by successes. With impossible demands made on them they are in no better a position than other groups to evaluate the denunciations of school failure which periodically wash over them. General denunciations of 'graduate staff with honours degrees in English' allegedly in need of instruction in 'how to put sentences together and spell' and 'illiterate school leavers' (Cox and Dyson, 1968, 6) mingle with hard, but selected data.[12] Energy which might have been used more profitably has to be spent on defensive actions, in trying to sort out conflicting and misleading claims.

Claims that standards have decreased are probably untrue when like is compared with like. One has to recognise the great increase in young people staying on longer in secondary school and the large influx of both young and older people into all forms of tertiary college. Such claims also ignore changed expectations, very hard to impossible to measure. Nevertheless, there *is* illiteracy, considerable semi-literacy and a general level of innumeracy which the left ought to recognise makes any struggle for genuine socialism more difficult.

One expression of widespread concern with standards is the increasing number of children being sent to private schools. This varies from country to country according to the particular situation, but seems to be a rather general phenomenon.[13] Again, this is a complex question on which only tentative generalisations should be made, but it is one which would repay comparative study. Involved would seem to be a mixture of concern for moral behaviour (including such questions as drug peddling), discipline in the sense of order in classrooms and an atmosphere conducive to study, as well as for measured outcomes in literacy, mathematics, or particular subjects like music or fine arts. Whether parents are getting what they seek and expect is another question. Private schools vary widely and a school uniform and impressive report form can be deceptive where parents are unprepared to look deeper.

Problems raised by the increase in private schooling are difficult. Arguments on costs of subsidies often ignore the real cost of providing places in the public, state school system.[14] Teacher trade unionists should be concerned about the working conditions of teachers in the private schools, many of which demand unreasonable work loads, and where there are few safeguards regarding termination of employment. In perhaps a majority of private schools questions like this will prevent attention being given to the kind of debates needed to take the issue of standards back to those recurring questions raised and lost in the radical movement of the late sixties.

The attempt to follow Marx in asking in whose interest academic standards were has in the past produced conservative answers. Lenin, like a majority of the academically trained leaders of the Russian Social Democratic Party, advocated youth learning 'what human knowledge has accumulated . . . the sum of knowledge of which Communism itself is a consequence' (Lenin, 2, 663). Entwistle has shown how conservative of academic standards Antonio Gramsci was. Lenin's comment in the same speech (to the Youth League, 1920) that of the knowledge imparted in the old Russian schools 'nine-tenths . . . [was] useless and one-tenth distorted' (664) never seems to have produced that profound questioning which irrupted in quite different circles only in the sixties in Western Europe and North America.[15] In asking again in whose interest is the present clamour about standards one must not be mislead into simple answers. There is no doubt that behind many of the British Black Papers there is a desire to use traditional tracked systems to separate and favour those who find academic learning attractive and relatively easy and to direct the majority of youth into vocational training leading to factory-fodder type jobs. Only there will not be such jobs on the scale required, any more than there were jobs for all the well-qualified products of the new universities and tertiary colleges in the past decade. So we have standards used, as in Australia and the USA, as an excuse to blame the victims of unemployment. But having said all that it still remains to sort out the evidence and clarify the argument so as to establish standards of literacy, numeracy and other areas of knowledge which will be in the interest of working people and the achievement of genuine socialism.

An old and ongoing problem is the distinction to be made between spreading a selection of knowledge throughout the population and raising standards and creating new knowledge. These have traditionally been seen as distinct operations, the latter particularly associated with the concept of the university. Marx's vision of a classless society suggests that such a sharp distinction, like the related distinction between expert and layperson, should not continue for ever. But it is also tied up with the problem of age which I have discussed in the section on learning. Initially it might be advantageous were there to be a distinction between a general schooling providing a broad sampling of skills and knowledge areas followed by a specialised, more vocational training. This has certainly been one of the arguments for comprehensive schools in various European countries, though never a major one. Such a policy would require showing that the advantages outweighed any disadvantage which might be suffered by those who presently gain from that system of certification through selection examinations for the universities and other vocational tracks.

A second question links problems of learning with the establishment of broadly accepted standards. Contrary to those who wish simply to concentrate on an elite, those concerned with establishing a fundamentally different kind of future society need to be concerned with *raising* general standards. This runs into all kinds of now familiar problems, but Anne Junor said it well when she wrote: 'It is simply patronising to romanticise popular culture or say that kids' preoccupations should constitute a "relevant curriculum"' (1982, 5). We can only keep trying until we get it right, remembering there will be many different 'rights'. But in establishing the content and standards considerably more effort than in the past will have to be devoted to a variety of teaching-learning methods which will enable people from different starting points to arrive at the same standards. While something may be learnt from work which has been done under the title of remedial education it is more likely that completely new approaches will have to be worked out. In this connection it is worth mentioning developments at the tertiary level of schooling where many students now come from families without tertiary school experience and from minorities or immigrant communities. Practice in the USA is different from that in Australia, typically involving large centres rather isolated from the other faculties, making use of hardware and learning packages, where Australian efforts are on a smaller scale, closely linked with learning in the major faculty where the student functions (Clanchy in Bock and Gassin, 1982). One finding arising from this work of direct relevance to the question of standards is that concerning culture-specific rules of discourse, particularly as expressed in writing essays and answering examination questions. Clyne points to differences in such matters as 'degree of linearity, verbality and formalism and to the rhythm of discourse' (Bock and Gassin, p. 101).

One very obvious way in which standards are affected by the capitalist nature of the economy is in the access to information and materials. While it has clearly made information technically available in rich, exciting profusion — one has only to think of photocopying, television and now computers — at the same time, since capitalism is a commodity-exchange society motivated by profit, it both limits and denies access. Educators pay quite insufficient attention to this contradiction. While much cannot be changed without a total change in the political-economic system there are plenty of improvements which have been, and could be made within a capitalist economy if educators faced the realities more consciously and with greater imagination. One or two examples must suffice to show what I mean.

At the level of research and tertiary school teaching J.D. Bernal long ago drew attention to the unsatisfactory nature of natural science journals, particularly those produced by learned societies, as providers of required information. Subscribers had on the one hand articles they were not interested in and, on the other hand, did not receive articles from other periodicals in which they were interested. His solution was that instead of packaging articles in particular periodicals there should be a central distribution centre which should package articles according to readers' topic selections. There are, of course, problems other than vested financial interests in such a solution. It rules out vicarious reading which so often is a source of broadening one's interests, but there are no doubt ways in which that could also be handled more efficiently than is done by present methods.

An analogous problem is the production of teaching materials. The mode is the production of a textbook and all too often each publisher attempts to produce a competitive product. This results in a large number of similar books, each of which may be better in parts than its rivals without any one being wholly satisfactory. One alternative is the production of teaching materials in smaller, specialised parts which can be assembled by teachers and students according to the requirements of a particular course.[16]

Publishers may reply by drawing attention to the huge numbers of education topic packages and separate kits which they have produced in increasing numbers. But examination of these shows them to be often highly inflexible and expensive. Rather than encouraging teacher and student initiative, in the way they are packaged they discourage it. Again, they illustrate a feature of capitalist competition which seems ineradicable. Commodities are produced to sell in the largest possible market and, therefore, designed to be 'catchalls' rather than tailored to particular needs. This also means that they must not offend anybody — resulting, e.g., in evolution not being mentioned in certain biology textbooks (Fawns, 1981)!

Another limitation on access is that of language. With the recognition that previously ignored parts of the world have ideas to contribute, and with increasing production of knowledge in already recognised languages, the 'knowledge explosion' has already made being well informed very difficult. More, rather than less, attention to the teaching-learning of languages is only part of the answer. The other part is more translations. Unfortunately in many fields the English language publishers are reticent to publish translations. Germany, by contrast, has a tradition of such work, as has Japan. This raises the problems connected with English as clearly the winner in the international language stakes. All these questions affect standards. How can one claim high standards if one's work is parochial, if one has no knowledge of what is being done in other countries and cultures? Yet that is inevitable given the limitations posed by the present language situation. If one does read another language can the university library afford to stock more than a handful of books, much less periodicals, in that language? What about access for people out of reach of university libraries? How does one learn what is being published in other countries? Language is, of course, only one of the factors making for separation between academic cultures, but an exploration of its ramifications helps us to be clearer on what would be needed to really raise standards to what the few and fortunate, working in the well-endowed centres of the world, have the possibilities to accomplish.

This brings us again to a consideration of costs and copyright, both of which combine to limit access severely. This is very apparent in recently founded universities whose libraries would like to stock back sets of periodicals, or make use of modern methods of reproduction to place on their shelves works now out of print. The problem for lower level schools is naturally much worse. This leads to that contrast between the poverty of materials available in most classrooms and the wealth of what the children see on television, which is one factor making it very difficult for schools to be places of interest or excitement.[17]

Finally, questions of academic standards are part of the ongoing debate over academic freedom, a subject which I mention elsewhere. But at this point it is relevant to refer to some remarks by Amelie Rorty at a conference on the subject in 1972. She draws attention to the problems which innovators and original thinkers have in getting their ideas accepted. She notes: 'The fate of the scientific innovator is the same as that of the political reformer or dissident: they are all judged by the theories they are attacking' (Pincoffs, 103). She goes on to say that:

placing the burden of proof on change and transformation generally initially cripples all but the most rhetorically mellifluous or sophisticatedly ambiguous theories. Not only the weight of opinion, but also the whole machinery of existing institutions and the economics of research, make the conditions for receptivity to fundamental novelty unfavorable. (Pincoffs, 104)

These, then, are some of the ways in which capitalism impinges strongly on questions of standards. Much more attention needs to be given to them if educators are to achieve even the standards which liberal ideology sets itself.

Notes

1. In my experience teaching in an English tertiary college (polytechnic) there were certainly numbers of youth of 15+ for whom work was not attractive either in school or outside it.

2. The fallacy of equal opportunities is (1) that so long as jobs are significantly different in status and reward and good ones are few one can only postpone the bitter selection, and (2) the job and family situation reacts back through attitudes and motivation to ensure that opportunities, even at a very young age, cannot be equal.

3. Various aspects of state control in Western European countries are mentioned in Mallinson, including the instructive instance of the Netherlands where 'all who legally seek to run their own schools may do so' (106-7). For German FR state-private school regulations see *Woerterbuch der Paedagogik*, 1, 143-5 and 3, 214-15.

4. Examples of executive action are given in *Rank and File*, the group's publication, and also in *Radical Education*. The 1971 NUT Conference resolution is given in full in 'Heads Rule, OK?', *Teaching London Kids*, 18, 24-5. It would seem to be time for some comparative studies of teacher unionism from a marxist point of view.

5. Moodie and Eustace express the usual fear of delegate, as distinct from (mis)representative, democracy on p. 202 when they write: 'Both these fears were reinforced by the students' political style, with its emphasis on *mandating and*

reporting back, and (as it seemed to staff) its refusal to trust the students' own committee members, let alone any others.' Yet, as I have repeated elsewhere, it is only by developing delegate democracy that the required education about issues and interest in them can be developed and sustained.

6. See also *Radical Education* (4, autumn 1975, 28 and 5, winter 1976, 26).

7. Ollman has helped document this process in Ollman and Vernoff, *The Left Academy: Marxist Scholarship on American Campuses* (1982).

8. Already today there is a need for some form of honorary fellowships to allow those denied a job in tertiary schools opportunities to continue participating usefully in intellectual life. This would not simply benefit the individuals but would also be of not inconsiderable value to society. There are many ways in which this could be done without additional funding.

9. For an interesting discussion of the situation in Britain see Moodie and Eustace, pp. 207-16. They note the relatively recent proliferation of ranks.

10. Connell uses a confused concept of social class which lessens this and other work in which he has employed it. Especially confusing is the definition of ruling class, a much-used term, as those with 'access to power and privilege, and ... dependence on and contribution to an order of things which sustain it' (p. 146). I am not questioning the validity of using many of the group distinctions made here, but rather the need to analyse the relations between such groups and class in Marx's strict sense, where the ruling class would be quite other.

11. Anne Junor makes a similar call for more thought on these questions in 'Deconstructing Discipline' in the same periodical (1982).

12. Professor Giamatti of Yale, in an extract included in the 1977 *Black Paper* cited the *New York Times* as reporting that between 1964 and 1974 'verbal and maths scores on the scholastic achievement tests (SATs) have been steadily declining, and that the average test scores for 1975 high school graduates declined by 10 points on the verbal portion, and by 8 points on the maths portion since 1974. This was the largest single drop in the past 12 years ...' (Black Paper 1977, 48). One looks back at the Educational Testing Service material cited by Silberman (18). Has there been a decline?

13. Edmund King (1965) noted that about 15 per cent of children in the USA were in private schools, a majority in parochial (religious, mainly Roman Catholic) schools (61-2). The increase of RC enrolments between 1940 and 1960 was 219 per cent compared withonly 142 per cent for all schools. In France in the same period there were some 20 per cent of children in private pre-schools to secondary schools and public debate is in terms of religious versus secular schooling (Fraser, 1971, 23, Chapter 5). In Germany, where private schooling has never been a tradition, there has nevertheless been a recent rise in enrolments, from 3 per cent of children in 1971 to 4.5 per cent in 1980 (Max-Planck-Institut, 1984, 49, cf. 47-50).

14. For Australia see *Radical Education Dossier* 18 (1982) and for the UK *Radical Education* 11 (1978).

15. There were, of course, considerable changes in curricula during the twenties in Russia, a decade of experiment and openness in education much influenced by developments elsewhere in the world (Price, 1977).

16. My attention was drawn to this by Dr Jim Croll (London) who has produced course materials for engineering students on this principle.

17. It would be technically possible to provide schools with videotapes from broadcast programmes cheaply and freely but commercial interests intrude. Where taping of programmes has been allowed under copyright laws this has sometimes been for only a limited time, perhaps one year, and then tapes have had to be destroyed. The fact that many people have risked making copies of material in circumstances whose legal authority was untested may have blunted efforts to improve the legal situation.

PART FOUR: CASE STUDIES

TEACHERS AND LEARNERS (1)

In this and the next chapter a few further examples of agents of social education will be examined. The family, so often studied, but still insufficiently critically, is something into which all but a few are born and spend long and formative years. A majority of people are exposed to religious teaching of some kind, whether in the family, the school, or through their own volition by joining a religious organisation later in life. The peace movement has been chosen as an example of an agent of education of a very different kind. Until recently it could certainly have been regarded as a minority movement to which only the dedicated few belonged. Its message was also, until recently, seen by many to be 'idealistic' if not otherwise doubtful. Yet it inspires dedication among a highly motivated membership and sets out to teach members and non-members alike. How should we assess it? Each of these different agents requires more thorough study than can be given in a short book, much less a short section. But I hope to show both that they *must* be studied if social learning is to be understood, and how Marx's method and vision might influence one's approach to their study.

Education and the Family

Every writer on socialisation or the education of children acknowledges that the family plays an important role. Those influenced by Freud and psychoanalysis specially stress the early years and, therefore, put particular emphasis on relations between child and parents, particularly the mother. But *the* family is either a short-hand or an illusion which until recently too few writers were prepared to look at in its historical concrete forms. In part this was because of the pervasiveness of what Michele Barrett refers to as the *Ideology of Familialism* (1980, 206) which continues to be fostered by state, church and the advertising and mass media industries today. Psychologists and educators can speak of 'bad families' and 'broken homes', but always as the exception and normally considered to be found mainly among the unschooled and poor. To question fundamentally, the family is, in late capitalism, tantamount to heresy.

Marx and Engels looked critically at the family as a historically determined institution in which the form and relations between its members varied with time and social class. Marx already in *The German Ideology* drew attention to the relation between the family and property and spoke of the 'wife and children [being] the slaves of the husband' (*CW*, 5, 46, cf. 180-1). He and Engels criticised particularly the bourgeois family of their day for its hypocrisy and, in *The Communist Manifesto*, looked to the abolition of capitalism to abolish also 'the community of women springing from that system, i.e. of prostitution both public and private' (*CW*, 6, 502). The last point, 'private prostitution', is a protest at the inequality of the male-female relationship which recurred throughout their writings.

If education is taken as the social learnings and teachings which occur then the family, and particularly the ideology of familialism, must be seen as important, not simply for children, but also for adults. The family as it is provides the real concrete experience, cosseting or shattering illusions, comforting or making uncomfortable the men, women and children who comprise it. The ideology of familialism affects those who have broken with the family, the adolescents within still shaping their futures in their minds, and those few who have for one reason or another not taken the usual path of marriage. It holds up the norm against which others are to be judged abnormal. It is therefore important to consider the nature of the family and the ideology of familialism carefully.

The term family is used to cover a variety of different structures. Anthropologists distinguish the nuclear family (father, mother and the children), the joint family (paternal grandparents, father, mother, married sons and their children), the stem family (paternal grandparents, father, mother, one married son and children only). Where the grandparents are missing but the brothers and their wives and children remain together it is called a fraternal joint family. These families are assumed to form a single household, though whether there is literally one cooking fire depends on place and time. Much of the literature assumes an evolution from joint forms of family to the nuclear type, regarded by many as specially typical of capitalism. Marxists and anti-marxists alike argue heatedly over Engels' *Origin of the Family* which relied heavily on the work of Lewis Henry Morgan (1818-81).[1] Confusion is caused by not distinguishing between families of different classes. While many upper-class families in various countries have been joint or stem those of the lower classes have probably always been nuclear.

Another dimension to family is those kin with whom the nuclear family is in regular touch while not residing together. The importance of daughter-mother contact is widely attested to, but there are also links with sisters, brothers, aunts, uncles and others. In some cases family members are separated by great distances (Australia-Greece) but maintain regular, meaningful contact by letter and occasional visits. Such contacts must be regarded as educational, though the learning-teaching content is hardly likely to be revealed to academic study.

For education the question of co-residence is obviously important, whether of family (kin) or not. The composition of the household and its relation to the wider society has educational implications for all its members, though most attention has been given to the children. Class is significant here, too, for there are still families employing servants who live in, even if, in many cases, they are called *au pair*.[2]

One other definitional point needs to be made. Feminist literature abounds with the term *patriarchy*. Engels used the term for that stage in the evolution of the family when 'in order to make certain of the wife's fidelity and therefore the paternity of the children, she is delivered over unconditionally into the power of the husband' (*OF*, 122). Barrett discusses recent uses in feminist writings. Kate Millet uses it as 'an over-arching category of male dominance'. Shulamith Firestone adds a biological dimension. Christine Delphy sees patriarchal exploitation cutting across class exploitation. She sees marriage as a labour contract with the husband appropriating the unpaid labour of his wife in a 'domestic mode of production'. Patriarchy, not capitalism, is then for women the main enemy. Barrett ends her survey (1980, 10-19) by suggesting:

> It seems admissable in some contexts to refer to patriarchal ideology, describing specific aspects of male-female relations in capitalism, but as a noun the term 'patriarchy' presents insuperable difficulties to an analysis that attempts to relate women's oppression to the relations of production of capitalism. (1980, 19)

With that I concur.[3]

Fulminations from the extreme right combine with impressions in and around the tertiary school campuses of the late sixties and seventies to suggest that perhaps the nuclear family is under threat, that the family structure has really changed. Divorce, birth control and abortion, not to mention gay liberation, were all seen as contributing to a new pattern. Betty Friedan (1981, 100-1) sets out what she calls 'startling, hitherto publicly undiscussed facts' in a way which adds to that impression. Yet regrouping shows that 62 per cent of US family-households contain man and wife and only 6.7 per cent are single- (female) parent families (figures for 1980). In England and Wales the proportion of people who were married rose between 1901 and 1971 and then fell as a result of the 1969 Divorce Reform Act. In 1979 50.3 per cent of people were married and 43.6 per cent single (three-quarters of whom were children) (Mount, 1982, 249-50, 258-9). The major effect of easier divorce appears to have been to allow a change of partners, divorced persons preferring to remarry than to remain single.[4]

While the changes appear to be more in people's minds than in reality that, too, is significant, though the outcomes are likely to be again 'what nobody wants'. Betty Friedan, in her 'second stage', calls for a new kind of family in which women's 'needs for love and comfort and caring support, as well as the needs of children and men' are met (1981, 102). She was right — not all feminists agree. But the weight of opinion wishing to allow for change was sufficient to cause the 1973 American Home Economics Association Convention to define families in the following manner:

Two or more persons who share resources, share responsibility for decisions, share values and goals, and have commitments to one another over time. The family is that climate that one 'comes home to' and it is this network of sharing and commitments that most accurately describes the family unit, regardless of blood, legal ties, adoption or marriage. (Diamond, 1983, 8)

It would be nice if this were true.

Studies of Learning in the Family

The literature on this topic is very large. My own sampling has been confined to that from Australia and the USA. Henderson (1981) gives an idea of the range and scope of studies. Chapter titles include 'Home Environment and Intellectual Performance'; 'Children and Divorce'; 'Social Learning Theory and the Development of Prosocial Behaviour'; 'Parental and Peer Influences on Moral Development'; 'Maternal Behaviour'; and 'The Family in Context'. Much of the work stems from student failure at school and attempts to trace its cause, or from studies of delinquent behaviour. Interpretations of obvious correlations of 'family background of individuals and the intellectual, occupational, and economic attainments of those individuals as adults' have been of three types (Henderson, 3). Dominant in the 1960s was the belief that a particular family environment produced mental ability, i.e. mental ability which is genetically inherited. Against this others believe that intellectual skills which enable children to do well in school are learnt in the home. Parents may stimulate intellectual development, or they may simply pass on values, skills and concepts favourable to school learning. Henderson puts both options:

> Presumably, the more parents have been exposed to the culture of the school, the more they transmit it to their children, although it is also possible that brighter parents go further in school and also pass their ability on to their children via processes of hereditary transmission. (1981, 23)

Recent thinking sees the family as a system in which all members interact with each other to produce effects, and not simply as one where only parents produce effects on children. It has, therefore, been suggested that 'bright children cause the adults in their environments to respond to them in a stimulating fashion' (Henderson, 23).

To the non-specialist looking at this research a number of problems stand out. There is the problem of the number and particular nature of the families studied, many coming from the 'poor' or 'lower classes'. The testing instruments, while suitable for creating academic data, often admittedly leave much to be desired when it comes to understanding family learnings. Most methods depend on debatable statistics for their validity.[5] Then there are all the problems associated with middle-class academics attempting to communicate with and understand what is clearly and admittedly a highly closed and private system. Henderson notes how the 'socialization and schooling experiences' of 'a professional class of researchers . . . undoubtedly influenced their hypotheses concerning what experiential variables were worthy of attention' (1981, 27). Arthur Pearl, writing from a phenomenological point of view in the same volume makes the point in a different context: 'One reason young people appear to behave so unreasonably is that those who judge them operate with very different phenomenological orientations than do the persons they judge' (Henderson, 294). Such 'orientations' have no doubt influenced the way in which research is conducted into the effect of family break-up and divorce on children, until recently seen in very negative terms.[6] Finally, there is the problem that many of the studies concentrate on 'psychological effects and emotional management of the experience' and ignore other levels of experience. Smiley *et al.* claim that in studies of divorce the social and economic consequences have received insufficient attention in comparison with the psychological (1983, 2).

At another level there has been attention to social and economic factors. Numbers of studies situate families in some kind of social class or status analysis. But when predicting mental test performance is the aim 'quality of the home environment' or 'family processes' are found to be more important than 'socioeconomic status' (Henderson, 1981, 17; Ochiltree and Amato, n.d., 12).

A thorough analysis of learning within the family would have to consider both what knowledge, values and attitudes were present and the mediations through personal interrelations which enabled these to be accepted or rejected by the children or other family members. One thinks immediately of families where there have been traditions of medicine, music, or the doing of 'good works' and public service. It is relatively easy to see such phenomena, but quite a different matter to separate out mechanisms of learning involved. It is also harder to see cases where knowledge, etc. do not manifest themselves so obviously. In all too many cases available knowledge, together with attitudes and beliefs, is unsuitable for the circumstances in which the young persons find themselves. What is then acquired may be the 'learned helplessness' to which Ochiltree and Amato refer (n.d., 4, citing M.B. Smith, 1969; Abramson, Garber and Seligman, 1980).

Learned helplessness may not simply affect children in the family. This question is the main argument of the Women's Liberation movement against the family. Elizabeth Janeway describes how the subordination of the wife becomes internalised to shape attitudes and behaviour. She compares this with other 'subordinate groups', citing Norman Podhoretz, author of *Making It*, who wrote: 'It is hard for the poor to make demands, for they know the demands will not be met and they learn to avoid the added bitterness of unnecessary disappointment by settling for whatever the world in its arbitrary way pleases to let them have ' (Janeway, 1977, 117-18).

For many families this may be a major learning, reinforced by the public world outside. It may also affect the men. Michele Barrett, in a sensitive discussion of just who benefits from the present family-household system, notes that men, in the role of family breadwinners, are often forced to be 'politically docile' so as not to lose their jobs (1980, 217).

Learning to be Masculine and Feminine

In this section I want to examine one of the fundamental learnings which begins in the family but is influenced by many other agents outside it. Its fundamental nature was recognised in a famous passage in *The Economic and Philosophic Manuscripts* where Marx wrote: 'the relation of man to woman is the *most natural* relation of human being to human being. It therefore reveals the extent to which man's *natural* behaviour has become human' (*CW*, 3, 296).[7] Born male or female, the qualities associated with these fundamental biological differences are stamped in from birth by almost every aspect of our experience. Men occupy the leading positions in politics, the economy, the major professions including teaching, the arts and sciences and the entertainments business. Any exceptions to this are seen as anomalies. While it has become the rule rather than the exception for women to work outside the home for an increasing part of their post-school life this is mainly in sections of the labour market reserved for them. Secretarial and office work, teaching (in the lower-status and lower-paid ranks), nursing and the caring professions are seen as feminine preserves.[8] Many of these jobs are classified as less skilled compared with men's jobs and thus escape legislation on equal pay for equal work (Coote and Campbell, 1982, Chapter 2). Finally on the question of work, women, whether they go out to work or stay at home, bear the brunt of the housework and looking after the children, not to mention their husbands. Such work, involving the management of household affairs, is both highly skilled and a considerable strain. Contrary to popular myth the introduction of modern household equipment, from vacuum cleaners to electronically controlled washing machines, has not led to button-pressing leisure. Gadgetry has simply replaced servants or other family members. Careful estimates of time spent range from 25 hours per week for an employed wife with no children to 67 hours per week for a housewife with one very young child (Ferree in Diamond, 1983, 150).

The role of men in the home, while challenged by women, seems basically to have changed little. Coote and Campbell report a Gallup Poll conducted for *Woman's Own* in the UK in 1979 (February) which recorded very low levels of participation in child care or other help by husbands (1982, 83). The Newsons who studied a sample of 709 Nottingham (England) families report that the amount of help depended on the father's hours of work. It increased as the father was home during the child's waking period (Newson, 1965, 214, cf. 137). Regarding their findings as a big change from 'thirty years ago' (1933), they attribute it to a lack of servants in the middle classes and isolation from the larger family in the working class (1965, 140-1). But to see the problem simply in terms of help or time spent on housework and child care by husband and wife is only a start. The non-sharing of responsibility for home management is also only part of the 'double burden' which women in employment shoulder. Genuine solutions must return to some of the concerns of enlightened women, and men, of an earlier age in Europe and the Americas (Hayden, 1982).

It is against the realities of the public world of work and the private sphere of the home that the common stereotypes of masculine males and feminine females must be seen. These stereotypes belong to what Stoller of the California Gender Identity Center called gender:

> *Gender* is a term that has psychological or cultural rather than biological connotations. If the proper terms for sex are 'male' and 'female', the corresponding terms for gender are 'masculine' and 'feminine'; these latter may be quite independent of [biological] sex. (cit. Millet, 1972, 30)

The major stereotypic distinction is between aggressive masculine and passive feminine! Masculine includes physical and intellectual strength, emphasis on competition and achievement and qualities of self-assurance and self-reliance. Feminine in the stereotypic mode denotes, on the contrary, physical and intellectual weakness, subjection and obedience, and an emphasis on the nurturing, mothering role. That not all males are, have been or should be masculine in this mode, or females likewise feminine, is not the point — though it is a point which perhaps helps some of us to struggle against such gender typing.[9] The point is that males and females are still being taught to behave in these modes, not least by the advertising industry.[10]

Let us look for a moment at some classic education materials. *The Greater Learning for Women (Onna Daigaku)*, written by a virtuous wife in 1672, is still influential in Japan today. It begins: 'Seeing that it is a girl's destiny, on reaching womanhood, to go to a new home, and live in submission to her father-in-law and mother-in-law . . .'

In what follows a girl is advised:

> from her earliest youth, a girl should observe the line of demarcation separating women from men . . . a woman must form no friendship and no intimacy, except when ordered to do so by her parents . . .
> however humble and needy may be her husband's position, she must find no fault with him . . . once married, she must never leave her husband's house . . .
> It is the chief duty of a girl living in the parental house to practice filial piety toward her father and mother . . .
> The great lifelong duty of a woman is obedience. In her dealings with her husband, both the expression of her countenance and the style of her address should be courteous, humble, and conciliatory, never peevish and intractable, never rude and arrogant . . .
> In the morning she must rise early, and at night go late to rest. Instead of sleeping in the middle of the day, she must be intent on the duties of her household, and must not weary of weaving, sewing, and spinning . . . (Passin, 1965, 173-6)

In Europe Rousseau is still regarded as worthy of study by student teachers. Yet he wrote:

The man should be strong and active; the woman should be weak and passive; the one must have both the power and the will; it is enough that the other should offer little resistance. When this principle is admitted, it follows that woman is specially made for man's delight ...

If woman is made to please and to be in subjection to man, she ought to make herself pleasing in his eyes and not provoke him to anger; her strength is in her charms, by their means she should compel him to discover and use his strength. The surest way of arousing this strength is to make it necessary by resistance. Thus pride comes to the help of desire and each exalts in the other's victory. This is the origin of attack and defence, of the boldness of the one sex and the timidity of the other, and even of the shame and modesty with which nature has armed the weak for the conquest of the strong. (Rousseau, 1969, 322)[11]

Gender is highly valued in the education of the English upper classes. The masculine mode has been spelt out in military codes 'on the playing fields of Eton'. Bertrand Russell described how: 'physical fitness, stoicism and a sense of mission were carefully nurtured . . . kindliness sacrificed for toughness, imagination for firmness, intellect for certainty; and sympathy was rejected because it might interfere with the governing of inferior races' (cit. Mangan, 1981, 136). The working-class lads described by Willis espouse a masculinity which in its aggressive sexism is often currently labelled *machismo.*

The characteristic style of speech and movement, even in the absence of females, always holds something of the masculine spectacle. The ability to take the initiative, to make others laugh, to do unexpected or amusing things, to naturally take the active complement to the appreciative passive, these are all profoundly masculine attributes of the culture, and permanent goals for individuals in it. Not only this but a more concrete hallmark of being a member of the culture is to have either sexual experience or *at least aspirations which are exploitative and hypocritical.* Girls are pursued, sometimes roughly, for their sexual favours, often dropped and labelled 'loose' when they are given. (1977, 146)

I will now turn to some treatments of the topic by psychologists. A major problem here is that the majority are males, often formulating their ideas from studies of males only. But while their science may, therefore, be less than perfect it is nevertheless important to note what they say and ponder its significance in practice. But first, Kate Millet:

> Because of our social circumstances, male and female are really two cultures and their life experiences are utterly different — and this is crucial. Implicit in all the gender identity development which takes place through childhood is the sum total of the parents', the peers', and the culture's notions of what is appropriate to each gender by way of temperament, character, interests, status, worth, gesture and expression. Every moment of the child's life is a clue to how he or she must think and behave to attain or satisfy the demands which gender places upon one. In adolescence, the merciless task of conforming grows to crisis proportions, generally cooling and settling in maturity. (1972, 31)

Among the attempts of disentanglement have been those of Freud and the subsequent psychoanalysts who have focused on children's relations with their parents and identification with one or the other; those who have sought explanation by a process of imitation through the reward and punishment of sex-related actions; and, more recently, those who have sought to set sex-role development in the more general cognitive development through states as proposed by Piaget.

Kohlberg is one of the last, who describes his approach as cognitive in the sense that:

> it is rooted in the child's concepts of physical things . . .
> it stresses the active nature of the child's thought as he [!] organises his role perceptions and role learnings around his basic conceptions of his body and his world. We shall stress . . .
> the importance of the observational learning of social roles . . .
> it is selective and internally organized by relational schemata rather than directly reflecting associations of events in the outer world. (Kohlberg in Maccoby, 1967, 82-3)

Stressing that 'the child is a valuing and value-seeking organism' (Maccoby, 111) Kohlberg suggests 'five mechanisms by which the development of sex-role concepts leads directly to the development of masculine-feminine values';

1. The tendency to schematize interests and respond to new interests that are consistent with old ones.
2. The tendency to make value judgements consistent with a self-conceptual identity.
3. The tendency for prestige, competence, or goodness values to be closely and intrinsically associated with sex-role stereotypes, e.g., the association of masculinity with values of strength and power.
4. The tendency to view basic conformity to one's own role as moral, as part of conformity to a general socio-moral order.
5. The tendency to imitate or model persons who are valued because of prestige and competence, and who are perceived as like the self. (in Maccoby, 111)

Kohlberg assumes that 'neither socializing pressures nor direct motive teaching is a necessary part' of the cognitive learning process.

Identification as boy or girl, male or female, appears to take time to establish firmly, but once estalished is something about which few if any have doubt. Kohlberg claims that in his experiments this self-identification is firmly established by the age of five to six years (in Maccoby, 95). He cites evidence to suggest that this depends on wider social experience than simply the mother and father roles so stressed by psychoanalysis (in Maccoby, 97-102). This is not to say that in adolescence doubts about 'sex-role identity' do not, in some cases, occur. It is important to note the lack of any evidence of a clear relationship between masculinity-femininity and homosexuality-heterosexuality or an active or passive erotic role (Maccoby, 92).

Another mechanism which Kohlberg suggests may particularly affect young children is their tendency to what Piaget termed 'egocentrism'. This failure to imagine other points of view and values than their own predisposes them to evaluate their own sex and its cultural patterns more highly than that of the opposite sex (in Maccoby, 113-15). Kohlberg recognises that 'in part, this same-sex valuing reflects the encouragement of sex-appropriate behaviour by socializing agents' (114), but does not indicate how we might distinguish between the two processes.

In the seventies a number of investigators returned to placing the emphasis on the biological level in determining both sex and gender. Lloyd cites Bardwick (1971), Garai and Scheinfeld (1968) and Hutt (1972). Bardwick writes: 'I have nonetheless taken the apparently eccentric position that the body makes direct contributions to the psyche of the individual' (Lloyd and Archer, 1976, 11). She goes on to admit, however to making 'conceptual leaps'! Corinne Hutt writes: 'In much development and social psychological writing too little cognizance is taken of the structure and function of the brain' (Lloyd and Archer, 10). She appears to assume a significant difference between males and females, presumably connected with different hormone functioning. Lloyd notes 'a suprising degree of consensus' among these writers in what they regard as biologically determined differences between males and females. These include:

> greater size and musculature of the male but the faster physical development and greater biological resistance both to infection and genetic defect in females. Males are always described as more active, impulsive, aggressive and object-oriented while females are oriented to people, consistent and reactive. Males excel in verbal comprehension and reasoning, mathematics, spatial perception and abstract thinking but female performance in terms of verbal fluency, spelling, manual dexterity, clerical skills and rote memory is notably better. As might be expected, males are more competitive and achievement oriented while females are nurturant and dependent. (Lloyd and Archer, 17)

Lloyd goes on to note that 'the most recent and comprehensive summary' of these questions, that by Maccoby and Jacklin (1974) 'only finds evidence to support some of these conclusions' (1976, 17). But they claim significant, if slight, differences between males and females in aggression, and in verbal, mathematical and spatial skills (1976, 6).

Lloyd and Dorothy Ullian are among those who have attempted to bring together the biological and the social in what the former refers to as an 'interactionist model' (Lloyd and Archer, 12). But while Lloyd seems to be concerned with such problems as the effect of hormone balance on temperament and intellect Ullian has something else in mind. She speaks of how children 'view differences' or make 'sex-role judgements'. In delineating a series of six developmental stages she characterises the first two as having a 'biological orientation' because children questioned recognised sex differences in size, strength, length of hair (!), and voice characteristics (Lloyd and Archer, 33).

It is not surprising, in view of the serious problems of methodology which writers like Lloyd are now beginning to discuss, that none of this really helps us to understand the process of learning to be masculine and feminine. The very conceptualising of gender, of sex roles, in psychology, anthropology and sociology is unsatisfactory, with overlap between the disciplines and at the same time differences within each one singly (Lloyd and Archer, 3). Further, evidence is accumulating to show the influence of social norms in gender conceptualising and also in the way many scientists conduct their studies (Lloyd in Lloyd and Archer). It is also becoming clear that work on these questions, and also probably on wider issues of psychology and social theory, are affected adversely by the predominantly male reporting of work. In coming to some more definitive understanding of the relation between the biological and social, the marxist conception of integrative levels, or levels of development, could do a lot of good. Finally, there would seem to be doubts as to the value of the kind of experiments — toy preference, doll play (Kohlberg in Maccoby, 109) — used with children for understanding the socially significant adult role differences. More important for our understanding would seem to be studies of youth and adult relations which attempt to distinguish the different qualities stereotypically grouped as masculine and feminine and which specifically looked for variety and change.

Whatever doubts we may have about our understanding of the patterning of gender and differences between country, class, or between the private and the public sphere, there can be no doubt of the importance of the movements for Women's Liberation of the past two decades. It is increasingly recognised that sex discrimination is no longer tolerable and that questions which were once taken for granted must now be critically examined. Measures to ensure 'equal opportunity' or 'positive action in favour of women', as in the case of proposals supported at the 1981 British Trades Union Congress; consciousness-raising groups; refuges for battered women and rape crisis centres; these and other measures testify to a new awareness (Coote and Campbell, 1982, 235-8; cf. Richards, 1980, 137-43). There is evidence of changing attitudes too. A study of US families at the University of Michigan — 1,000

Detroit women questioned over an 18-year period — found changes in attitudes towards women being active in the community while their children were growing up (44 per cent of women in 1962; 64 per cent of women in 1980 and 73 per cent of their children in favour), and towards major family decision-making by the man (66 per cent of mature women in 1962; 28 per cent of mature women, but 32 per cent of 18-year-old daughters and 50 per cent of sons in favour of 1980) (Friedan, 1981, 235-6). Less tangible perhaps, and certainly in need of better documentation, are the cases of changes of lifestyle reported by Betty Friedan (Chapters 4 and 5). Male executives opting out of the rat-race and for the small town and helping with the babies and the shopping is good news, but it maybe wishful thinking to see it as 'the edge of a momentous change in their very identity as men' (Friedan, 125). One danger in all this is that changes will be cosmetic and women's rights assimilated to strengthen the capitalist system of inequalities. If that happens neither women nor men will be truly liberated.

The Women's Movement has been a major educator over the past two decades. In addition to producing a considerable litera-ture with a wide readership among both women and men it has organised numerous consciousness-raising groups and study sessions, and other meetings and discussions throughout the major countries of late capitalism. Books have explored women's history. Sheila Rowbotham's *Hidden from History* and *Women, Resistance and Revolution*, or A. Summers' *Damned Whores or God's Police* deal with more recent periods. Merlin Stone's *The Paradise Papers* goes far back. It begins with the claim that 'originally, God was a woman' and examines the archaeological, mythological and histor-ical evidence which supports it. Engels' *Origin of the Family, Private Property and the State* had placed the subjection of women together with the sharpening division of labour and the rise of class-divided societies (1972, 41, 233). Leacock, in her intro-duction, points to the need for further empirical work and at the same time notes the importance of 'the secondary diffusion of commodity production and colonial domination' for its effect on relations between the sexes (Engels, 1972, 42).

The concept of matriarchy, which plays a big role in some argu-ments for a 'return' of power to women, has been usefully clarified in recent writing. Leacock noted: 'it soon became clear that matri-archy, in the sense of power held by women over men comparable to that later held by men over women, had never existed' (Engels,

1972, 35). Rather, as she argues from African and North American Indian evidence particularly: 'what such data reveal is *the dispersed nature of decision-making in pre-class societies* — the key to understanding how such societies functioned as "collectives"' (Leacock, 1981, 20). She argues that: 'the analysis of women's status in egalitarian society is inseparable from the analysis of egalitarian social-economic structure as a whole' (1981, 133). In the hunter-gathering societies she refers to as *band societies* she argues that:

> the relations of power and property characteristic of our own obscures the qualitatively different relations that obtained when ties of economic dependency linked the individual directly with the group as a whole, when public and private spheres were not dichotomized, and when decisions were made by and large by those who would be carrying them out. I shall attempt to show that a historical approach and an avoidance of ethno-centric phraseology in the study of such societies reveals that their egalitarianism applied *as fully to women as to men.* (1981 133, emphasis added)

While these studies are concerned with the actual position of men and women in pre-class and early class societies another approach has been to consider the material conditions which may have promoted those qualities associated with masculine and feminine gender. Needham, developing suggestions made by André Haudricourt and de Hetrelon, points to differences between societies in which people's work has been concerned largely with animals (pastoralism) or plants (agriculture). Needham notes that 'the shepherd and the cowherd beat their beasts, and take up an active attitude of command over their flocks and herds' (Needham, 2, 576). Similarly: 'maritime usages strongly reinforce this command-psychology'.

But agriculture is different: 'often the less he interferes with the growth of his crops the better. Until harvest he does not touch them. They follow their Dao, which leads to his benefit' (Needham, 2, 576. I have not corrected the sexist language employed!) Needham discusses this question in relation to differing conceptions of both human law and laws of nature held in Europe and China. It would seem worthwhile to explore them in relation to those educational processes by which we learn to be masculine and feminine. What effect a deeper understanding of the historical role of women and possible origins and under-pinnings of 'masculine' and 'feminine' qualities might have on the learnings of present and future generations is hard to say. Experience suggests that it could only be minimal compared with the weight of current practice. But it would give confidence that things were not always the same and might therefore support hope, that necessary ingredient of change. A deeper understanding of the origins of male dominance might also suggest strategies by which future equality might be hastened.

Turning to the future and what ought to be rather than what was and is, the aim of abolishing exploitative and dominance-submission relations between the sexes was clearly spelled out and in Marx's and Engel's vision of communism. Needham cites the American entomologist, Ernst Bergmann, whose essays:

> urge that the liquidation of masculine aggressiveness is one of the most important limiting factors for the success of that co-operative and collectivist society towards which mankind is inevitably moving as the scope and potentialities of the highest social organisations continue to increase. (Needham, 2, 60)

One must, alas, qualify that 'inevitable'! Even in that propagandist document, *The Communist Manifesto* (1848), Marx and Engels foresaw the possible alternative of 'the common ruin of the con-tending classes', though they did not visualise it as nuclear extinc-tion (*CW*, 6, 482). But to return to the Women's Movement, sections of it are outspoken on the need to 'destroy *masculinity*' and 'transform men as human beings' (Coote and Campbell, 1982, 29). Coote and Campbell see women as 'struggling to change society' and 'patterns of behaviour'. They specifically note, as women:

> enter into spheres of activity that are dominated by men, we find we need to transform these too, if we are to survive without becoming surrogate men. We are struggling to change the values and priorities of men alongside us, as well as the way they conduct themselves — in short, to change the world. (1982, 238)

While the standpoint here is working class and socialist, the same need is being grasped by people with very different standpoints.

Betty Friedan cites the sociologist, William J. Goode who, in a lecture entitled 'The Male Sex Role: An Insider's View', argued that

> in today's complex society the top posts in government and business are not best filled by the stereotypical male but by people, male and female, sensitive to others' needs, adept at obtaining cooperation — in short, with the intuitions and social skills and nurturing qualities once considered feminine. (Friedan, 1981, 156-7)

Betty Friedan also describes relevant thinking about leadership in the American business world, developed by Peter Schwartz of Stanford Research Institute International, and supported by such organisations as the Bell Telephone Company, the Diebold Corporation, and the Yale School of Management. Schwartz contrasts two styles of leadership, an alpha-style and a beta-style. The former, 'in our society considered more masculine . . . relies on hierarchical relationships of authority and looks for "deterministic engineered solutions to specific problems"'. The beta-style: '"generally perceived as feminine", is based on a synthesizing, intuitive, qualitative thinking and a "contextual", "relational" power style'. Schwartz points out that no claims were being made that such styles 'are innate to one sex or another', but that 'sex role expectations have been found to polarize these behaviours'. Top executives have become interested because: 'as the research showed, (beta-style leadership) gets the job done more effectively and quickly, and is, in fact increasingly necessary for business survival' (Friedan, 1981, 244-5). Again, the need is to take these understandings further and not allow them to be used to consolidate capitalism.

To close this section I will briefly consider some of the ways in which schools perpetuate the inequalities of women and men and, in spite of recent initiatives, teach gender stereotypes.[12] As mentioned earlier, there are the inequalities in staff positions, men occupying a grossly disproportionate number of senior and permanent positions in all levels of schools (Spender, 1982, 45; Castle and Jones, Reilly, Over and McKenzie and Burns, all in Burns and Sheehan, 1984). At the level of research in tertiary schools women are discriminated against in several ways. Most who do research do it for men, often with little or no acknowledgement (Spender, 1982, 48-9, cf. 84). Much research in education is about males (Spender, 46). In the primary and secondary schools there is the question of under achievement, especially in subjects like mathematics and the natural sciences, and the availability of such subjects as woodwork, metalwork, or cookery and housecraft to the two sexes. There have been counter-attacks, including such schemes as that started in 1979 by the Manchester (England) Poly-technic called 'Girls into Science and Technology' (*Teaching London Kids*, 19, 5-7; Coote and Campbell, 182, 173). The dif-ferential treatment by teachers is now well documented, if less widely understood. Boys monopolise teachers' attention whichever the sex of the teacher and denigrate the work of girl students (Coote and Campbell, 175-6; Spender, 54-85). The unfairness of co-operative schooling has been acknowledged by its leading British advocate, R.R. Dale, but is widely supported by authorities (Spender, 118-27). The portrayal of women, even their absence from many textbooks (e.g. science) has received growing attention but not all reforms have been much of an improvement.[13] Finally, in the area of careers advice girls also lose out (Spender, 97-117).

These then are gender distinctions which are learnt in con-temporary capitalism. That they long pre-date capitalism is clear, though the forms may have been different. That they can persist into post-capitalist societies is shown by experience of the USSR. What is clear is that a genuine socialist alternative cannot be con-structed so long as they persist.

Religious Organisations

The phenomen of religion as ideology was briefly discussed in the section on Marx above. Here I am concerned to identify religious agents of education significant for social change, either positively or negatively. Like the family and like social class, for a majority of people, religion is something one is born into and it takes effort to break out and join another or deny religion in some way. In addition, there is the backing of tradition and the state for membership of one or another form of Christianity, sanctified in various state symbols and rituals, some of which also penetrate the school system. With the exception of Japan, late capitalist societies are all Christian by tradition. Only recently has migration and what might be called a crisis of consciousness, mainly among youth, broken this near-monopoly, introducing Islam, and forms of Buddhism and other Asian religions into the capitalist metropoles.

In considering any organisation as religious one is faced with problems of definition. Moberg suggests that 'most social scientists would agree' that the quality 'religious' must include one or more of the following:

(1) Belief in supernatural power, force, or beings, accompanied by attempts to get and remain in a relationship believed to be favourable;

(2) Belief in values thought to transcend immediate social situations and hence to be worthy of allegiance, together with the organizations and symbolic activities for promoting these values;

(3) Systematized beliefs and values used to explain the mysterious and the unknown or to answer teleological questions; these become organized into a social institution in which emotional attitudes dominate. (Moberg, 1964, 3)

With belief so central to religions one might have hoped that the many studies of the psychology of religion and the process of religious conversion would have thrown light on what is a fundamental problem of learning: what makes us believe something. But surveys of the literature offer little beyond the most general platitudes (e.g. Moberg, 421-44). Many writers stress that conversion is a process of the individual joining the group, taking on a group identification. Moberg suggests that in most cases no 'new teachings' or beliefs are required in the majority of cases of conversion, but rather a 're-commitment to loyalties, doctrines, or standards already possessed' (426). However, it would seem probable that when new beliefs are involved these are normally internalised in a process of identification with the group or individuals in it. That is certainly ᵗhe conclusion of Lofland's study of a small, activist 'Doomsday cult'. He comments: 'The development or presence of some positive, emotive, interpersonal response seems necessary to bridge the gap between first exposure to the message and coming to accept its truth' (Lofland, 1966, 51-2). However, Lofland is dealing with behaviour rather than particular beliefs and worrying doubts remain.

Turning from the process of belief to its content and the various groups and organisations which teach that content raises the question of theology and marxism. The dialogue of the sixties between communist parties and the churches is a background requiring exploration in a deeper study. Dorothee Soelle sees this dialogue as having given marxists renewed understanding of the double nature of religion. On the one hand it acts as a veil over the realities of capitalist exploitation. On the other, it is a force for liberation. Christians learnt from the dialogue 'to take material existence more seriously' (1984, 20-6). These themes are met in the different context of liberation theology, a Third World phenomenon with effects on religious movements in the USA and other metropoles, and to some extent in religious feminism, another important contemporary phenomenon.[14]

In a number of *Telos* devoted to 'Religion and Politics' (58, 1983-4) the editor distinguished 'religion as a subjective, pre-rational and pre-political dimension' from religion as an 'objectified institutional manifestation' (1983-4, 2). But here it is precisely the effects of the institutions to which I wish to draw attention. The questions I would like to have answered include: what are the moral-political teachings of the institution or group?; how do these teachings reach the individuals affected?; how are they understood by the individuals?; how does the religious teaching affect beliefs, and behaviour?; how does the religious organisation or group rate as an influence compared with other educational agents?; to what extent do the organisation's teachings promote or hinder the development of democratic and socialist beliefs and practices in those affected? As will be clear from other sections of this book, I am not confident that academic study can provide really useful answers to the most important of these questions. Only moral-political practice can do that.

A Problem of Numbers

There is a problem of numbers in more than one sense. It is impossible to define with any certainty membership of various religious organisations. In some cases figures appear in national censuses where individuals have been asked their religious affiliation. In others the figures are supplied by the organisation concerned. In neither case is it easy to distinguish what for education is a key question: to what degree a person is an active or practising member of a religious organisation? Where does one place the person who was born into a church, married in church and buried in church, but who otherwise rarely or never attended? Equally,

how does one detect the social attender for whom the church provides a venue for social contact only and who pays little or no
attention to the beliefs and values of our definition above? These
are well-known problems and they are not confined to religious
organisations. But that is no reason for not reminding ourselves of
them.

A second problem of numbers is that of the huge number of
organisations. It takes a book of over a thousand pages simply to
list and briefly describe the 1,200 churches to be found in the USA
in 1978 (Melton). In Australia the figure is nearer 500. How is the
educator to handle this problem, to make sense of such diversity?
To begin with, some classification may help. Melton himself
divides them into 93 major groups ranging from 'the Western
Roman tradition' to 'the Hawaiian Family Churches'. For educational purposes such a classification might be combined with
categories such as degree of involvement required (and
obtained?); and relation between religious and social theory and
practice. It need hardly be said that a classification is required for
each country, and, if one were to attempt to estimate significance,
for smaller areas within countries, depending on the local situation.

It is apparent that the USA is different from the countries of
Europe and from Japan in having such large numbers of different
religious organisations. It is said to be different in its 'degree of
involvement', which Luckmann regards as 'a fairly recent upward
movement rather than a decrease from a yet higher previous level'
(in Robertson, 1969, 148). But on the basis of studies made to
date this would seem not to be a very useful generalisation. Many
of these studies have been of a sociographic nature, comparing
church membership in urban with rural areas, or relating it to
social class or ethnic grouping. Those studies I have read on Japan
fall into this category. Morioka especially shows the way in which
current religious patterns in Japan are shaped by the shift in population from rural to urban areas, a shift directly connected, of
course, with the peculiarity of Japanese capitalism (Morioka,
1975, cf. Sieffert, 1968).

For Europe and the USA the bulk of studies seems to have
been on the traditional 'mainstream' religions: Roman
Catholicism, the major Protestant denominations and Judaism.
Luckmann notes two interesting trends. In the USA there has been
a process of 'doctrinal levelling' which has reduced the differences
between these major groups, not on a theological level, but in their

adoption of many of the business methods and structures associated with modern capitalism. Luckmann describes it as 'bureauc-
ratization along rational businesslike lines' (in Robertson, 147). He
adds: 'today secular ideas of the American Dream pervade church
religion' (149). One wonders whether this might have played a
part in the drift away from these churches on the part of the young
and stimulated them to join quite different groups. However,
Sieffert also notes strong disaffection, especially with 'established
religions' in Japan and a similar 'multiplication of "new religions"', though the historical development is somewhat different (128-9).

Some Pointers

I have chosen the following examples to suggest the range of educational experiences and influences which require consideration.
First there are the mass, traditional churches into which many are
born and which are accepted by many as part of the society in
which they live. We shall see in another section how these churches
today often present their members with moral-political challenges
which if accepted would cause them to question fundamentally the
nature of present capitalism and especially the suicidal armaments
of policies of governments. However, the structure of these
churches, whether Roman Catholic, Anglican, or mainstream
Jewish remains hierarchical and unconducive to learning the practice
of grassroots democracy. Rather, it reinforces other teaching of
hierarchy and expert-lay differences and therefore reinforces
acceptance of the status quo. Aiding this is the way in which such
churches take part in the symbol and ritual of patriotism, though
the 'normality' of membership may mean that little significance is
attached to these by the learners, who may easily hold conflicting
attitudes and beliefs regarding them.

Concern with social welfare programmes and what many on the
left have tended to dismiss as do-gooding is a practice of many
churches. In Victoria, Australia, the Brotherhood of St Laurence
concerns itself with poverty, with the aged, and with such mundane
tasks as the regular collection of waste paper to help pay for its
charity. It teaches through practice in all these areas and its
message spreads much wider than those who take part. Probably
the best-known church in the welfare field is the Salvation Army.
Founded in London in 1865 by a Methodist minister, William
Booth, it has spread around the world and also given rise to a

number of other churches.[15] At the other end of the scale is the Bible Holiness Movement, a small, mainly US church, interesting in that it is interracial and specifically forbids members to join the John Birch Society and labour unions which require secret oaths. It engages in drug rehabilitation, alcohol counselling and helping runaway youth (Melton, 215-16). The question in all this is the social analysis within which the various good works are performed. To what extend does a church or religious organisation question the fundamental nature of capitalist society, or even recognise clearly that it is capitalist?

Within the past 15 years the major religious traditions of the United States, Catholic, Protestant, Evangelical, Jewish and Mormon, have seen the development of a feminist consciousness. This has expressed itself variously, but clearly. In 1969 some 35 people, mainly Catholics from Holland, Belgium, France, Switzerland, Germany and the USA met at the Grail Centre in the Netherlands to discuss 'The Co-operation of Men and Women in Church and Society'. This was followed by an informal caucus of women at the general assembly of the National Council of Churches, discussing more recognition and participation of women in the Protestant churches. In 1970 the Boston Theological Institute hosted a conference on 'The Role of Women in Theological Education'. Women entered seminaries in greater numbers. Important theological books and articles by women were published. The demand for women to be ordained received especial media cover and controversy. Conferences on women's ordination were held in 1975 and 1978. All this has brought women on to seminary faculties and into team ministries. It has produced new forms of theological education, e.g. the new Women's Theological Center in Boston. But it has also sparked off a conservative backlash and the immediate future is uncertain.

More recently founded churches occupying a considerable part of a member's time must be presumed to exert a greater educational influence, though it is uncertain how far their influence extends and in what ways. One of these is the Divine Light Mission which began in India in 1960 and, since his father's death in 1966, has been led by Guru Maharaj Ji, then only 8 years old. In 1971 it entered the USA where it spread rapidly to involve, by 1977, it was said, between ten and twelve thousand activists. In addition to publishing two periodicals, *And It Is Divine* and *Divine Times*, it has produced several colour films and albums of stereo records through its subsidiary, Shri Hans Productions (Cameron, 1973, 37). Shri Hans Humanitarian Services operates a clinic in New York and runs a farm retreat on Rhode Island. The Mission also runs a number of sale outlets which according to Cameron take 'from the rich and give to the poor' (38).

Another conspicuous group is the International Society of Krishna Consciousness, or the Hare Krishna people. This has been actively propagated since the late fifties when the former business-man, A.C. Bhaktivedanta Swami Prabhupada (1896-1977), already a member of the Krishna Consciousness movement, entered a monastic order known as Sanyasa. In 1965 he went to the USA and by 1977 the Society claimed 2,500 activists (monks, priests and ministerial students) and a laity in the order of 250,000 (Melton, 372). In America a monthly, *Back to Godhead*, is published.

Of strong, if in most cases short-lived, educational significance have been the various communities established over the centuries. While the practice has roots in East and West, in both Christianity in Euro-America and in Buddhism and Daoism in Asia, our interest must be in survivors and newly created communities today.[16] In such ventures the numbers involved are also usually very small. Melton, who devotes a chapter to the topic, deals specifically only with communities which he regards as based on religion. Among the twelve communities Melton lists as being founded after 1960 two illustrate the diversity. A number of Mennonite Christian-inspired communities are associated with the Reba Place Fellowship, a group which began in 1966 as an off-campus ministry of Goshen College, Indiana. Membership involved 'renuncia-tion of property; love as an alternative to anger, violence and war; faith-fulness in marriage as the context for sex; a servanthood stance in all human relationsips, and a communal organization of personal affairs' (Melton, 43). Emphasising peace and social service, one of the groups is part-financed by construction work. In 1973 the membership totalled some 200 spread between three sites. A dif-ferent kind of community is The Farm, started by Stephen Gaskin in October 1970, after a cross-country 'caravan', involving 500 counter-culturists. Their religion is mystical, drawing on Mahayana Buddhism, and using marijuana for meditation and other purposes — something for which Stephen Gaskin and three others were imprisoned in 1971. In 1976 the Farm near Summertown, Tennessee, contained about 1,000 members and there were ten other communes loosely associated with it elsewhere (Melton, 47).

Finally mention should be made of religious groups which have arisen around or out of recent social issues, in part perhaps through the failure of the larger churches to handle these issues helpfully. A number of these groups arose on the US west coast in the aftermath of the flower people and hippie movements, in the early seventies. Collectively known as the Jesus People, some, like the New Covenant Apostolic Order, had a strong social problems approach. A second grouping is around the issue of homosexuality. In spite of attempts by groups within many of the major churches to accept homosexuals (Melton, 455) the over-whelming majority have not responded and a number of gay churches have been formed.

Fundamentalism and the Schools

One of the widely publicised phenomena of the seventies was the renewal of the attack on certain aspects of science teaching in the schools, especially in the USA. This took a different form from the attacks of the twenties which resulted in the prohibition of the teaching of biological evolution in a number of American states — Mississippi, 1926; Arkansas, 1928; Texas, 1929 (Nelkin, 31). The thrust of the seventies was for the teaching of creation theories alongside evolutionary ones. Much of the organising effort for creationist views comes from a small handful of organisations. The American Scientific Affiliation was formed in 1941 and has grown from a membership of 5 to some 3,000. While believing that evolutionary ideas lead to moral laxity the membership is divided on policies (Nelkin, 77-8). The Creation Research Society was formed in 1963 in order to 'publish research evidence supporting the thesis that the material universe, including plants, animals, and man are the result of direct creative acts by a personal God' (cit. Nelkin, 78). Their quarterly journal is said to have a circulation of 2,000. The organisation fragmented in 1970, giving rise to the Creation Science Research Center which also aimed at research and publishing. This organisation is interesting for its use of one of capitalism's favourite devices, the direct-mail list which it employed in the early seventies. It also used a connection with the Southern California branch of the Bible Science Association which has a radio programme. The combined mailing list of these two organisations is said to total some 200,000 and to include schools, other churches and textbook committees as well as individuals (Nelkin, 79-80). Finally I will mention the Institute for Creation Research which after 1972 became the dominant of these organisations. This is connected with Christian Heritage College whose site in a former monastery in San Diego, California it shares. The College has both undergraduate and graduate programmes in 'The Study of Christian Evidence and Scientific Creationism'. The activities of the Institute include radio programmes; holding conferences, workshops and summer institutes; publishing a monthly *Acts and Facts* with a circulation of 60,000, and numerous books (55 up to 1980) (Nelkin, 80-2). One of the significant things about such organisations is that they are supported by, and in some cases staffed by, active scientists. Unsurprisingly in view of their narrow schooling, these frequently come from the fields of physics, chemistry and engineering. A slightly different organisation is Educational Research Analysts formed by the two prominent Texas censors of textbooks, Mr and Mrs Mel Gabler (Nelkin, 63-5).

While these 'knowledge creating' organisations are the spearhead of the recent attack on the natural and some of the social sciences, their denunciation of materialism, atheism, and various practices which they see as immoral finds support among many of the fundamentalist churches. Many of these claim greatly increased memberships during the sixties and seventies, memberships which they have probably gained from a contemporary decline in the numbers in other, less conservative and demanding churches. Among those with gains of between 11.8 and 22.0 per cent[17] were the Assemblies of God, the Southern Baptist Convention, the United Pentecostal Church, the Seventh-Day Adventists, Jehovah's Witnesses (USA) and the Missouri Synod of the Lutheran Church (Nelkin, 59-61).

It was out of one of these churches that a new style of school for children of primary and secondary age was begun in the late seventies (Hunter, 1982). This united a strange mixture of old-style religion and modern capitalist technicism. Started by a Baptist minister, Donald Howard, and his wife in Garland, Texas, the movement has spread to 37 countries. In the USA these schools, named the Accelerated Christian Education Schools, or ACE schools, claimed 210,000 students in 3,000 schools in 1980. In Australia, 110 schools were established between 1977 and 1982. These schools use curriculum materials carefully packaged in the USA. According to ACE's statement of faith and practice, they are produced on the foundation of faith and the purchase agreement forbids any 'written corrections in the curriculum to conform with variations in doctrine'. Hunter notes the infallibility accorded the Bible ('equally in all parts and without error in its origins', as the statement of faith puts it); the acceptance of 'modest dress'; and avoidance of such organisations as the World Council of Churches (161). The technicism of late capitalism expresses itself mainly in the programmed-learning style of the curricula materials, the isolating of learners in individual study carrels and the emphasis on self-markable tests with behavioural objectives. To these is added the more biblical-age support of corporal punishment, said to be for 'moral violations' rather than 'procedural' ones. Backed by Proverbs 29.15, 'the rod and reproof give wisdom', this policy was further supported by one school's set of procedures: 'To rule out spanking is to omit a key ingredient in discipline! It brings repentance and thus allows the child to clear his conscience' (Hunter, 165). One interesting criticism of these schools has been that while the religious rights of the parents may be protected those of the children, and their right 'to join the mainstream of society', is being denied (Hunter, 166).

Fundamentalism need not be 'Right'

Gil Dawes, a former missionary in Latin America, describes the experiences which brought a United Methodist congregation in Camanche, Iowa, to a remarkable pitch of religious and social consciousness (1984, 81-91). Sunday sermons, during which the congregation was encouraged to read the Bible as well as hear it, carefully set text in context, both in Biblical times and today. A well-attended, weekly Wednesday night study group studied the text for the coming Sunday, again with a stress on historical background. This was followed by a hour on sharing information and opinion on current events considered important. After Sunday worship a coffee hour for 40 to 50 people catered for those who could not attend on Wednesdays. Gradually, but not easily, consciousness was raised so that the congregation took part in such activities as demonstrations against the Vietnam War, supported Native Americans at Wounded Knee, and hosted Angela Davis when she came to support a union.

After ten years work there Gil Dawes moved on to another parish. The congregation found the new pastor's policy of 'unity above all' not to their taste and left the church to become a sub-group of the Methodist Federation for Social Action. Dawes expresses pleasure at having demonstrated that fundamental Christianity need not become 'the mythological base for an American fascism', and that liberation theology can take root in America's Bible Belt.

Notes

1. Kate Millet (1969) and Michele Barrett (1980) discuss Engels from different but sympathetic points of view. Ferdinand Mount (1982), a strong and interesting defender of the nuclear family, is very unsympathetic. Mount's arguments require a careful attention to sources and methods which would reward the serious reader. But one feels he missed the point with Marx and Engels, as exemplified by the following quotation: 'For the charm of Marxism is that it liberates you from nature — and from the duties and restrictions of the family' (45).

2. Barrett introduces the work of Jean-Louis Flandrin who examines French usage of the term family in the sixteenth, seventeenth and eighteenth centuries and distinguishes kinship and co-residence (1980, 200-1).

3. Mount gives evidence for what he calls 'an alternative pattern of marriage — a pattern of equality between husband and wife', citing legal history for England (1982, 229-33).

4. Figures for England and Wales show 58,445 remarriages of both parties in 1979 out of a total of 368,853 marriages (Mount, 258).

5. One blatantly dubious procedure is reported in work on children's competence. Children's ability in everyday skills such as bed making or using a washing machine was scored by giving children a checklist and asking them whether they knew how to do something and if so how frequently they did it (never, often, etc.) (Ochiltree and Amato, 1983, 9-10, 18).

6. A review article on the negative effects in Herzog and Sudie (1968). Recent, more positive findings, have been reported in Dunlop and Burns (1983). I am indebted to Dr Derek Toomey for these and other materials on the family.

7. This quotation was criticised by a friend in the Women's Movement as an example of 'the intrinsic attitude of superiority in men'. She pointed out that a relation is reciprocal whereas Marx speaks only of 'man *to* woman'. An equal relationship requires the preposition with. To my mind this is to underrate Marx's position and to expect a sensitivity to sexism in language which is rare even today.

8. About 51 per cent of women in the USA worked outside the home in 1980 (Friedan, 1981, 203). In the UK 10.4m women were in employment compared with 15.6m men in 1980, but while the figure for men was static that for women had risen by some 45 per cent between 1931 and 1970 (Coote and Campbell, 1982, 49). In Japan, while it is normal for the unmarried women now to work they normally retire on marriage or childbirth (Livingston *et al.*, 1973, 478).

9. Eleanor Leacock's *Myths of Male Dominance* is one such aid. On p. 6 she writes about working against racial discrimination and getting to know 'black women who in their persons denied the stereotyped alternatives that the media constantly pose to women in our society; either to be strong, initiating, and assured, or to be "feminine", considerate, and mothering. As heirs to their culture history, most black women I came to know combined characteristics that male

supremacist ideologies assert to be mutually exclusive.

10. Kate Millet analyses literature from D.H. Lawrence to Norman Mailer in her *Sexual Politics*. Mount's argument that these writers cannot be taken as guides to 'the emotional realities of marriage in their societies' is not the point (1982, 228). Literature constantly reinforces the gender stereotypes.

11. I am indebted to Nancy Shelly for reminding me of such passages. One should also consult his recommendations for the education of Sophy!

12. Again I must apologise for selecting from only UK and Australian materials. There is a need for a survey which takes in French, German and Japanese experience at least.

13. Coote and Campbell criticise the revision of the famous 'Peter and Jane' reading scheme (1982, 174). Dixon, *Catching them Young*; the Children's Rights Workshop, *Sexism in Schools* and a series in the *New Statesman* (14 Nov. 80, pp. 16-20; 21 Nov. 80, pp. 16-18; 28 Nov. 80, pp. 28-30; 5 Dec. 80, pp. 28, 29; 12 Dec. 80, pp. 19-20; 19/26 Dec. 80, pp. 46-7) all deal with gender. Spender gives other references (1982, 93).

14. It is significant that all three left magazines, *New Left Review*, *Telos* and *Monthly Review* choose to treat of religion in 1984, the latter two with special issues on the topic. *MR* has a valuable bibliographic article giving items on liberation and black theology (138-41). While *Telos* and *MR* look to unity in social practice, Peter Fuller's article on 'The Historical Jesus' in *NLR* is an exploration of the bases for theological belief. In view of Fuller's final paragraph the aptness of the editor's comment ('In a world where fundamentalist Christianity can still play a ferociously reactionary role the criticism of religion remains an important and too often neglected task for materialists') seems questionable.

15. For membership and activities worldwide see *The Salvation Army Year Book*, published by the Salvationist Publishing and Supplies, Ltd, London.

16. Dolores Hayden has some interesting things of contemporary relevance to say in *The Grand Domestic Revolution*, a book which also has much food for thought about the educative effect of our material environment.

17. Total membership of these churches rose from 13,374,240 to 19,220,002, which is a gain of 43.7 per cent, cf. Table 4.1 in Nelkin, p. 61.

Trade Unions

As Draper points out, trade unions are a touchstone, a 'litmus-test' for a socialist, distinguishing those who, like Marx, hold 'a socialist theory about the primary role of *class organisation as such*' (Draper, 2, 83). They are, as Engels phrased it, 'the real class organisation of the proletariat, in which it carries on its daily struggles with capital, in which it trains itself' (*COR*, 336; cit. Draper, 2, 88). Already in *The Condition of the Working Class in England*, that first socialist work to take a sympathetic view of the trade unions, Engels had referred to them as 'schools'; 'the military school of the working-men' and 'schools of war' (*CW*, 4,512, cit. Draper, 2, 97). Marx also attached great importance to trade unions and strikes as means by which the working class learnt. In one example he spoke of 'conflicts between masters and men' as an 'indispensable means of holding up the spirit of the labouring classes', 'of preventing them from becoming apathetic, thoughtless, more or less well-fed instruments of production', and hinted at the 'moral and political consequences' of 'strikes and combinations' (*CW*, 12, 169; cit. Draper, 2, 96). It is in this tradition that we should pay careful attention to the trade union movement today.[1]

A thorough examination of the educational role of trade unions would have to examine both the members and the effect of unions on non-members. This would have to include a study of the image of unions created in the mass media, an image which studies have already shown to be ideological (Glasgow University Media Group, 1976). It would consider education and the union leadership separately from education and the ordinary members. And it would tease out the different aspects of education: the creation and distribution of knowledge; the teaching that the union engages in consciously, as distinct from what it provides as a 'hidden curriculum'; and the learnings which occur. An important question for socialists is the degree to which the structures and functioning of the unions is limited to bread and butter questions and to what extent these contribute to the development of a socialist consciousness. Here I can only touch on these questions to suggest their importance and point the way.

Numbers

It is important to recognise there is a qualitative as well as the obvious quantitative aspect to the numbers of trade unionists. In educational terms it is important to know how many of *what kind of people* are involved. The differences between the old craft unions and the new unions of Engels' and Eleanor Marx's time were educationally significant, and the union membership of Mallet's 'new working class' is differently significant again. This is easy to assert and many will easily nod agreement. But marxist educators have yet to establish this in meaningful detail.

Numbers are important in many ways. Most obviously, if one is not a member, or is a member and does not participate, one has no chance of learning from the experience of membership and participation; though one may learn something rather different through knowledge at a distance. Numbers are important also as a proportion of potential membership. The idea has, perhaps, been the universally closed shop, every worker a union member. I say perhaps because that was certainly not so for the craft unionists who rejected organising the unskilled, jut as today many unionists ignore the unemployed, women or, often, migrant workers. Such attitudes, I suspect, have profound educational significance.

First some suggestive figures, suggestive because I lack the resources to do better. Beginning with Britain, membership in some of the important unions has been as follows:

Union	Membership (thousands)	
	1981	1961
Transport and General Workers (TGWU)	1,887	1,302
Amalgamated Union of Engineering Workers (AUEW)	1,100	973
General and Municipal Workers (GMWU)	916	796
National and Local Government Officers' Association (NALGO)	782	285
National Union of Public Employees (NUPE)	699	200
Association of Scientific, Technical and Managerial Staff (ASTMS), formerly (ASSET)	491	25
Union of Shop, Distributive and Allied Workers (USDAW)	450	355
Electrical, Electronic, Telecommunication and Plumbing Union (EETPU), formerly (ETU)	405	243
Union of Construction Allied Trades and Technicians (UCATT), formerly (ASW)	312	192
National Union of Mineworkers (NUM)	257	586

Source: Sampson, p. 63.

Many of these giants have grown both by amalgamation and recruitment. Other formerly important unions have lost strength through dwindling employment and competition from other unions. An example of these is the National Union of Railwaymen, founded in 1871 as the Amalgamated Society of Railway Servants! Its membership of some 170,000 is half what it was 20 years ago. It is in competition with the Amalgamated Society of Locomotive Engineers and Fireman (ASLEF), with 27,000 members, as well as the Transport Salaried Staff Association.[2] Against these must be set the new unions, those of the white-collar professionals and semi-professionals. The Confederation of Health Service Employees (COHSE) has 216,000 members; the National Union of Teachers 232,000; and the National Union of Public Employees (NUPE) 700,000. Anthony Sampson draws attention to the contrast between the generally conservative politics of their membership and the much more left public image of their leaders, particularly Clive Jenkins of ASTMS. Of the latter Sampson alleges: '[P]rovided Jenkins got them more money, they were content to let him play his own part on the national stage' (70). This is the view from above, from an author-journalist. It would be illuminating to see the picture also from below.

The picture of very large organisations, if often with dwindling memberships, is repeated in the other countries of late capitalism. In the Federal Republic of Germany some 8 million workers are organised in 17 unions linked in the Deutsche Gewerkschaftsbund (DGB). The Metal Workers Union enrolled over 2 million members in 1971; the Public Service Union enrolled 993,879; Textile Workers were 287,388; while the smallest membership was in Art Workers, 34,778 (Castles, 1984, 150; Jaeggi, 1973, 101). In the USA, where in 1978 20,459,000 workers, or 23.6 per cent of non-agricultural employment, were reported members of unions, the largest unions were (in 1980): Teamsters (1,891,000); Automobile Workers (1,357,000); Food and Commercial (1,300,000); Steelworkers (1,238,000); and the State and County (AFSCME) (1,098,000) (US Department of Commerce, 1982).

While sheer numbers — union size — has important educational implications, particularly as it affects organisational structure and possibilities for membership participation, with the lessons which this allows, it is also important to see membership as a percentage of those eligible for it. This is itself an educational question. In the USA Richard Edwards notes that from a peak membership year of 1953 union membership as a proportion of the workforce has declined from over 25 per cent to 20 per cent. In manufacturing it has declined from over 50 per cent in 1956 to about 45 per cent in the mid-seventies (202). Employer anti-unionism drives appear to have been highly successful, and the 'Sunbelt' and 'Silicon Valley' have low membership rates (Davis, 1982).

Ethnic membership of the unions is an important question throughout the countries of late capitalism. In the USA the attitude of the unions especially to the black minority, but also more recently to the Hispanic-Americans, has long been an issue. In Western Europe, where in recent decades there has been huge migration, the question has increasingly become important. Castles *et al.* report that by 1977 the DGB unions had enrolled 611,000 foreign members, 'one-third of all foreign workers (1984, 152). Over half of these belonged to the Metal Workers' Union. Other unions with high foreign membership were the Chemical Workers' Union and the Clothing and Textile Workers' Union. But these relatively high participation rates were not, apparently, matched by a high rate of active participation or confidence that the unions really represented the foreign workers' interests (153-6). In Australia no records are kept by unions of the country of birth of members, but estimates by officials range from about 30 per cent for occupations like carpentry and clerical work and rising to 70-80 per cent in the Clothing Trades and Vehicle Builders' Unions (Hearn, 1976, 113).

Any serious study of education and trade unions would have to pay careful attention to the work of shop stewards, that class of union representatives standing closest to the membership. More wil be said on them below.[3] Their numbers are hard to come by. In Britain two estimates for 1960 varied between 90,000 and 200,000. In 1971 the Commission on Industrial Relations suggested a figure of between 250,000 and 300,000 (Topham, 1975, 12-13 who also gives figures for individuals unions, 14). For Germany data is scarcer. Castles *et al.* report figures of 119,851 in the metal industry in 1973, of which 5,633 were foreign (153).

Organisational Structure

The unions began in England as craft unions and only later embraced the unskilled and other sections of the working population. In other countries organisation has been along industry lines, all those working in a particular enterprise belonging to the same union. This immediately has educational significance, the craft approach encouraging pride in particular skills and attitudes. Miners are an outstanding example. But one would expect craft organisations to be divisive and parochial. Against this one would have to weigh traditions of union solidarity extending beyond national boundaries, traditions of which many of the craft unions have been justly proud.

At higher levels the unions have long been linked together. On a local level this may take the form of trades councils. At the national level there may be one body, like the British Trades Union Congress, or unions may be divided by political or religious affiliation as in France and Italy. On a world level there is division between the World Federation of Trade Unions which includes members unions from the USSR and Eastern Europe, and the International Confederation of Free Trade Unions. The latter was set up in 1949 in opposition to the former body. It embraced 70 trade union organisations in 53 countries with an aggregate membership of 50 million. It has been active in the so-called developing countries. It would be interesting to know to what extent these major, more remote divisions have an impact on the consciousness of union members. Their role as active creators and distributors of knowledge also merits investigation. Unions publish various journals and other materials at the national and international levels.

Within the individual unions attention needs to be focused on the ways in which members are either drawn into or excluded from various forms of participation. At a high level of abstraction it can be said that structures parallel those of the general electoral process and thus reinforce ordinary members' feelings of powerlessness and detachment from active control over their own lives. This may be reinforced where membership contributions are collective and passed on to the union in bulk by management, the 'check-off' system, and not, as formerly, collected personally by a union representative. Thus personal contact, with its possibilities for exchange of information and views, is further reduced and the union becomes the more impersonal (cf. Topham, 34).

One institution which one might have expected to be highly educational is the union branch meeting. In a negative sense it certainly is, for increasingly members have learnt not to attend. One would like to think that the account given by Richard Pfeffer is not representative. He summons evidence to suggest it may be.[4] He describes a typical union meeting he attended. It lasted some two and a half to three hours, beginning with 'a mechanical salute to the flag'. This was followed by about an hour of minutes' reading and reports of routine business and letters. This was followed by reports from committees. Only well after half time did anyone from the floor have a chance to speak, in a period entitled 'For Good and Welfare' (116-21). Pfeffer points out that important grievances brought up at this point in the meeting by members were then dealt with by committees whose procrastination killed any interest or enthusiasm for the union they might have aroused (225-6).[5]

Pfeffer's account of his experiences is interesting also for his description of how he was foiled in his attempt to become a union representative (193-214). It is full of examples of negative teaching-learning and one would like to think it was exceptional. Certainly there are plenty of accounts of shop stewards standing up for their members, but the general charge that full-time officials, by the nature of their involvement with employers and the capitalist state become isolated and incorporated, seems all too fully proven.[6] That this is a lesson not lost on members is equally clear.

Any examination of union organisation in the context of their educational role must look outside the unions at their connections with other bodies. These may be the political parties with which some are affiliated or otherwise connected. Others are religious bodies which influence them. But more directly the unions' functions bring them into continual contact with employers' organisations and the government. Murray Edelman goes as far as to say that: 'Major unions in both advanced and developing countries serve as an integrating link, helping to furnish political and organisational support for government, union and business bureaucracies, and at the same time providing symbolic reassurances for the workers and the mass public' (1971, 142). He stresses how, without conscious conspiracy, the union officials 'reassure their members that their interests are being protected' and by concentration on immediate issues channel discontent away from more revolutionary demands. (145) Certainly, there is considerable evidence that this is so.

Strikes

It was of strikes that Engels spoke when he referred to 'schools of war'. Certainly these are the ultimate in participation, testing the membership in loyalty, resolution and organisational skills. It is no wonder that strikes have always elicited the sharpest condemnation of the capitalists and their spokespeople, even when they have themselves provoked a strike for their own purposes.

Again, any estimate of the educative effect of strikes must consider both the numbers involved and other people affected nearly or distantly by it. Then again, strikes are different in their intensity, duration, and the degree to which they have been the result of pressure from below or above. Some idea of crude, comparative numbers is given by the following figures (for 1955-61).

Country	Participants (yearly average)	Work days lost (yearly average)	Days lost per participant
Germany	137,000	637,000	4.7
France	1,523,000	2,196,000	1.5
Great Britain	762,000	4,154,000	5.4
Japan	1,255,000	5,102,000	4.1
Italy	1,761,000	6,202,000	3.5
Australia 1956	414,000	1,121,400	2.62
1960	592,100	725,100	1.20

Source: Dahrendorf, p. 182. Australian data from Plowman in Ford, *et al.*, 1980.

More important is consideration of just who is striking and why. As an example of the dangers of overall figures like those above let us take some figures for Australia. Between 1913 and 1953, 71 per cent of all stoppages were in mining and quarrying, particularly in coal. These amounted to 48 per cent of man days lost. Seven per cent of stoppages were in the maritime trades which accounted for a further 13 per cent of man days lost. A further 11 per cent of stoppages were in the metal trades. Between 1953 and 1967 there was a large decline in coal industry strikes, perhaps because of large pockets of unemployment in the coalfields. On the cause of strikes, or rather, the issue negotiated: strikes over wages rose from 7 per cent in 1953 to 25 per cent in 1967. But one must remember that it is often easier to negotiate over wages than over the real grievances of workers.

Trade Unions and Education

In this section I want to suggest some of the ways in which trade unions have been directly or indirectly involved in conscious knowledge production and distribution. This is a rich history, full of lessons for us and only now being more fully explored. My aim is to set out a framework within which we can most fruitfully study the question. Regrettably, examples will be mainly drawn from Britain for which I am best informed.

From a marxian standpoint educational activities should be divided into three categories: education for socialism; education for improving the workers' conditions under capitalism; and education which serves the interests of capitalism. Of course, not all activities can be neatly divided into these categories but the effort to analyse them in these terms would prove illuminating. Another dimension of analysis is in terms of who is educated: members or non-members; officials or rank and file.

First of all let me mention briefly an activity which cuts across these categories. That is the way in which trade unions and their national bodies have acted as pressure groups for the provision and improvement of the general school system. Brian Simon documents this very thoroughly for Britain (1960, 1965, 1974). Typical of such action was the British Trades Union Congress support, in 1922, for the policy of the Labour Party, *Secondary Education for All* (Simon, 1974, 60). A more current example is the demand for 'Advancement through schooling' (Aufstieg durch Bildung) put forward by the German Gewerkschaftsbund. This body, in its 'Education–Political Concepts of the DGB' (1972), put forward a plan for comprehensive schooling from primary through to adult education (Boehm, 203). Such actions are clearly designed to improve the conditions of the working class within the capitalist system. Some, especially those concerned with technical skill training, must be regarded as serving the interests of capitalism and even harming the interests of workers. I will return to these in another section.

Britain has a long and revealing history of co-operation between the trade unions and teachers in the tertiary education institutions. I say revealing because it shows the double role played by schooling: support for socialism, and opposition to it. The history of Ruskin College and of the Workers' Educational Association demonstrate nicely the complexities of the struggle (Simon, 1965). The work of the Plebs League (f. 1909) and the National Council of Labour Colleges is also illuminating. Today such co-operation between academics and trade unions is carried on by new bodies. One of the interesting ones is the Centre for Alternative Industrial and Technological Systems (CAITS) which was set up in February 1978, in the course of the work of the Lucas Aerospace Combine Committee's work (Wainwright and Elliott, 168-71). Based at the North East London Polytechnic, this organisation has both produced and distributed knowledge, publishing books, pamphlets, information kits, and a quarterly bulletin, *CAITS Quarterly*.[7]

Another important group linked with the trade unions is the Work Hazards Group of the British Society for Social Responsibility in Science (BSSRS). This Group publishes the monthly *Hazards Bulletin* which contains reports of research, news items on dangerous practices in particular industries and firms and trade union efforts to combat them, book reviews and useful addresses. Local groups have brought scientists together with trade unionists to work on particular hazards, such as asbestos, noise or vibration.

The trade unions both sponsor students attending formal courses with the formal school system and themselves hold numerous schools and courses. In the UK the Trades Union Congress, through regional education advisory committees, can arrange for courses drawing on university adult education departments, local education authority technical colleges or the Workers' Educational Association for help in tutoring and administration (Corer and Stuttard, 1975, 14-19).

A Recapitulation

My argument is that the trade unions are organisations embracing huge numbers of people, some voluntarily and others involuntarily, which in a variety of ways influence their thinking. Where membership is voluntary and active, particularly during strikes and other forms of struggle, learnings of various kinds take place which are positive. These may be about the operations of their particular industry or firm, its level of profits, markets, management. They may be about alternatives which offer in the immediate or more distant future. They most certainly will be about the way in which the union itself operates, whether the union officials support or oppose the demands of the workers and their shop stewards. For those really active in the struggle much will be learnt about organisation: lobbying; writing leaflets; communicating with a variety of people including the mass media. At other times and where membership is compulsory the learnings may be of mainly a negative kind. People's feeling of powerlessness and remoteness from those taking the decisions which affect their life may be reinforced. There are important learnings for the maintenance of capitalism. The trend to big unions and nationwide negotiated agreements, Bob Hawke's 'accord', all contribute to this. It is here where the Lucas Shop Stewards' Combine gives hope that there are antidotes to this trend.

In addition to this teaching-learning process I argue that trade unions, or bodies working closely with them, are important creators and disseminators of knowledge. Research into the workings of the national economy, whole industries or particular firms, produces knowledge needed for the daily struggles. Such research at the same time often reveals the fundamental weakness of capitalism and ways in which things could be different. Again the Lucas Combine is one of the most important examples in recent trade union history, but it is far from being alone.

The Peace Movement

On two counts must the Peace Movement be judged deeply educational: on the content with which it deals; and on the numbers and variety of people who as participants or observers hear its message. While it consists of many strands and deals with many issues the supreme issue which unites it is the threat of nuclear annihilation which experts now agree would result from quite a small portion of the nuclear stockpile being exploded. That would leave humankind, aggressor and victim alike, with no future. There could be no vision of socialism, real or otherwise. Marx's and Engels' alternative of 'the common ruin of the contending classes' would come true in a way that in their day was unthinkable, and should be unthinkable today.

In this examination of the Peace Movement the term will be used broadly to include some organisations which teach about peace issues but which are not committed in the same way as the majority of groups and organisations normally understood by the term. Since it is such a very diverse collection of organisations and looser groupings it is perhaps even more difficult than in the case of, say, the trade unions, to estimate the membership, the number of people directly involved in the teaching-learning experience. In certain cases there is an enrolled membership. In the cases of institutions like the Churches not all members can be regarded as part of the Peace Movement even where the Church officially speaks out on peace. In other cases there is no registered membership, yet people participate in some way which is obviously educational — the Aldermaston Marches, the Greenham Common demonstrations. As with the other educational agencies I discuss there is no question of a single lesson being learnt, or taught. Learnings will be both positive, in line with the intentions of the teachers, and negative, depending on the individuals concerned and the particularities of the experience. I would only claim that for some these learnings are profound, often much more profound and valuable than those acquired in the formal schooling situation. In part this is because they concern issues of deep moral significance which when perceived affect people deeply on an emotional as well as intellectual level. Is it for this reason that recently there have been attempts in several countries to take these issues into the schools?

Organisations and Issues

The Peace Movement has roots going far back into the past. They range from Christian pacifism to the widespread mutinies of soldiers sickened by the senseless killing of the First World War, or the military intervention against the new, revolutionary regime in Russia in 1919. One root which today's socialist parties and labour movement seldom like to recall is the Basle Congress of the Second International. All the parties present, including the British Labour Party, passed a resolution affirming it was, in the case of war:

> their duty to intervene in favour of its speedy termination and with all their powers to utilise the political and economic crisis created by the war to arouse the people and thereby to hasten the downfall of capitalist class rule. (Morton, 1948, 530)

Party leaders, with the exception of a handful like Rosa Luxemburg and Karl Liebknecht in Germany, Connolly in Ireland and John McLean in Scotland chose to forget this resolution as soon as the First World War was declared. But I mention all this only to suggest the variety of today's movement is not new, and that there is a history to learn.

John Cox (1981, pp. 189-235) gives a survey of the variety of organisations in Britain today, tracing their growth since the Cold War period of 1945-55 when peace was a dirty word and supportes of the British Peace Committee were attacked as 'communists' and dupes of the Soviet Union. This was the time of the Stockholm Peace Appeal (1950) which demanded 'uncond- itional prohibition of the atomic weapon as a weapon of aggression and mass annihilation of people', an Appeal which obtained over 750,000 signatures in Britain alone. CND (the Campaign for Nuc- lear Disarmament) was formed seven years later, in 1957, 'to reduce the nuclear peril and to stop the armaments race'. It was CND which organised the Aldermaston to London Easter marches, so well attended between 1958 and 1962 when they were led by such colourful figures as Bertrand Russell, Canon L.J. Collins, Michael Foot and J.B. Priestley. In 1978 it was CND which took the initiative in calling the Camden Assembly where some 700 delegates passed an important declaration on disarmament which it sent to the United Nations at a Special Session on Disarmament (Cox, 236-7). In addition to these organisations there have been organisations with more limited aims, like the Vietnam Solidarity Campaign; organisations specialising in civil disobedience tactics, like the Committee of 100; and there are numerous smaller groups enrolling members of particular professions, medical workers, lawyers or teachers. Most of these groups are affiliated to the National Peace Council (NPC) which acts as a co-ordinating body.

The Women's Peace Camp on Greenham Common in England was set up in the autumn of 1981 following a ten-day, 125 mile march from Cardiff which failed to achieve a television debate requested on the stationing of cruise missiles in Britain (Cook and Kirk, 1983). It was the first of some dozen such long-term peace camps to be established outside important military bases in the UK. The Chemical and Biological Warfare Research Centre at Porton Down and the Royal Ordnance factory at Burghfield were among sites chosen (Cook and Kirk, 32-3). Greenham Common was sig- nificant for the numbers of women taking part. On 12 December 1982, when the whole base was encircled, some 30,000 women took part, including groups from Sweden, Holland, West Germany and Ireland (32). But it was also significant for the style of the actions. Great effort was made to arrive at conscious, intelligent, non-violent action through a process of consensus and teaching- learning. Preparation was thorough and flexible, aiming at all times to bring out the humanity of participants and opponents (72-8;

84). Communication through a system of chain letters ensured the personal touch in a mechanized and impersonal 'age of communication' (105-6). A noteworthy feature of the action was the way in which arrests were handled. Participants had been thoroughly briefed about the law and some women acted throughout as legal observers (111). At the trials those arrested and their (women) lawyers conducted a series of legal arguments about the right and duty of citizens to prevent their government and that of the USA from breaking the terms of the Genocide Act 1969 (115-19).

The Christian churches have played a part in the Peace Movement in various ways. They have supported individuals, as in the case of the Sisters of Saint Joseph for Peace who seconded Sister Deirdre Duffy to work full-time for disarmament (1977) (Cox, 226). Official organs of the churches have made important statements on the queston of peace, such as that of the 1979 Autumn Assembly of the British Council of Churches (Cox, 227), or of the pastoral letter of the National Conference of US Bishops on War and Peace, 'The Challenge of Peace: God's Promise and Our Response' (1983) (*Peace Studies*, 2.5, July 1983, pp. 3-8). The Society of Friends (Quakers) has a long history of work for peace. Then there are special organisations like Pax Christi with national sections in Western Europe, Britain, the USA and Australia. A Roman Catholic oriented organisation, in Australia it has attemped to be ecumenical.[8]

The US Catholic bishops' letter of 1983 contains some important judgements, among them the following:

> Offensive war of any kind is not morally justifiable and Catholic teaching on war begins with a presumption against war.
>
> Although defensive war is sometimes morally permissable, no defensive war which violates either the just war prohibition against non-combatant immunity or requirement of proportionality of response can be morally legitimate.
>
> 'We do not perceive any situation in which the deliberate initiation of nuclear war, on however restricted a scale, can be morally justified.'
>
> 'Limited nuclear war is a very dubious tactic morally and no use of nuclear weapons against population centres or other predominantly civilian targets is morally legitimate.
>
> 'The arms race is one of the greatest curses on the human race' and an 'act of aggression against the poor'.

There is a legitimate tradition of Christian pacifism which finds a place in Catholic thought and practice and which gives an important witness to elements of the Gospel.

However, they shrank from condemning the policy of deterrence, contenting themselves with following Pope John Paul II:

The policy of deterrence is morally acceptable if seen 'as a step on the way toward a progressive disarmament' but it is not adequate as a long-term basis for peace. (M. and T. Coady, 1983)

There is no doubt of the importance of this document as a piece of moral teaching. It has received wide publicity on national media and will be studied in peace groups around the world.

In Japan, which suffered the supreme atrocities of the nuclear bombing of Hiroshima (6 August 1945) and Nagasaki (9 August 1945), the movement against nuclear weapons took shape after the incident of the fishing boat, Lucky Dragon, which strayed into the radioactive dust from the US Bikini Island test of 1954. In September 1955 the Japan Council Against Atomic and Hydrogen Bombs (Gensuikyo) was formed. It included political, religious, intellectual and labour leaders and victims of the atomic bombs. Later the movement divided. In 1961 the Democratic Socialist Party joined with the Liberal Democratic Party to form the National Council for Peace and Against Nuclear Weapons (Kakkin Kaigi). Then in 1965 the Japan Socialist Party established the Japan Congress Against Atomic and Hydrogen Bombs (Gensuikin). In spite of these divisions a high level of activity has been maintained around protesting the Security Treaty, American military bases, the construction of local atomic plants and proposals to revise article 9 of the constitution which concerns renunciation of war. In 1978 20 million signatures were collected and presented to the UN Special Session on Disarmament, calling for complete disarmament (Kodansha Encyclopedia, 1, 114-15).

Activities as Education

The most obviously educative activity of the Peace Movement is the flood of publications which it has encouraged, some officially sponsored and others produced by individuals inspired by the movement. These range from leaflets, through pamphlets to weighty tomes like that by John Gofman on *Radiation and Human*

Health. The educational effect of leaflets can only be in drawing attention to issues, perhaps sensitising some people or adding to their motivation for further study. The problem with books is they have to be read! It is a sad fact of contemporary capitalism that the motivation to tackle something like Gofman's 908 pages, despite his careful writing to make it accessible to patients as well as medical personnel, concerned citizens as well as journalists, is seldom strong enough and even highly schooled people continue to operate in a state of ignorance.[9] Nevertheless, the knowledge is increasingly being provided and people are studying it. John Cox estimates a readership of 200,000 for *Overkill* and *On the Warpath* (for schools) in 1976 and 1977 (Cox, 230). More certainly, the range and quality is improving as the movement gains strength and more expert knowledge is made available.

The next most obviously educative activity is probably the holding of study and discussion groups. Examples of these are myriad in spite of a general social climate in which such activities have declined in popularity. This is obviously a minority activity and, as many activists complain, it is almost entirely 'talking to the converted'. But that does not detract from the educational value of such activities for those concerned. What other medium provides opportunity for people to discuss and learn about issues so pertinent to their future and that of their children? Where else can they become informed on issues of world politics, the biology of nuclear radiation, the effects of the arms industry on the national economy? Above all, these factual questions are studied in an atmosphere where moral concern is regarded as healthy and the value-free objectivity of the academic world is regarded not simply as false, but as a perversion of humanity.

The Peace Movement also holds numerous meetings, many with informed and specially qualified speakers. These are equally as informative as many a university lecture and the audience is probably as attentive and may be more highly motivated. The teaching quality of such events is more easily ascertainable than the learnings, which are highly individual and depend on informational input fitting into a receptive frame.

Demonstrations and rallies are part of the educative process, in part for their effect on emotions and in contributing to motivation, and also because they are occasions on which people are introduced to various publications. These are on sale in circumstances which encourage buying and in a concentration which draws

attention to what is either unavailable in ordinary commercial outlets, or invisible in the wealth of competing interests.

Peace Research

A tremendous amount of research has been carried out during the
period after the Second World War which has contributed to arguments for peace. Not all of it would be labelled peace research in
the strict sense of being motivated by any desire to contribute to
peace. Much of the research into the victims at Hiroshima and
Nagasaki was no doubt motivated by quite other considerations.
Nevertheless, the point here is that there is a considerable fund of
research to draw on which, motivations apart, is used in the arguments about the possibility of genuine peace in the world. One
particularly significant piece of such research is that reported in the
Swedish journal *Ambio* in 1982. Crutzen and Birks, in an article
on 'The Atmosphere after Nuclear War', reported on the effect of
soot in the atmosphere, showing how through darkening it could
prevent plant growth and seriously disrupt food supplies throughout the world (Pittock, 1983).

Peace research has become part of the formal education system
in several countries. It is significant that the entry for Konflict- und
Friedensforschung (Conflict and Peace-research) in the recently
published *Politsch-Paedagogisches Handworterbuch* (Gutjahr-
Loeser and Hornung, 1980) occupies five pages and a biblio-
graphical entry of six (German) monographs. Five German centres
for such research[11] are listed in the 1984/5 *Fischer Oeko
Almanach* (Michelson, 1984, 384), which also contains factual
articles on disarmament, the ecological effect of militarisation and
abandoning the arms race (353-83). Other institutions which
might be mentioned are the International Peace Research Association, the International Peace Research Institute, Oslo, where the
Bulletin of Peace Proposals is edited, and the School of Peace
Studies in the University of Bradford (England).

Within the field of Peace Research peace is defined variously.
For some it is an absence of war, a question of disarmament, or
particularly the prohibition of nuclear weapons. For others the
word peace implies a much wider range of ideas: various forms of
inequality which are referred to (unhelpfully?) as 'structural
violence', or individual training in non-violent problem solving.
Gutjahr-Loeser and Hornung list major research questions as:
studies of conflict and crises at the level of the individual, group

and state; socio-economic, security and armaments policies in East-West and North-South potential conflicts; the relation between social structure and foreign policy behaviour; questions of armament production, export and control (e.g. SALT and MBFR); problems of peaceful change; and education as a means of bringing about peace (181).

Peace Education

Both Boehm and Rombach, in their entries for Friedenserziehung refer back to Komensky (Comenius, 1592-1670), J.H. Pestalozzi (1746-1827) and M. Montessori (1870-1952) as educators who, albeit in a way which overrated the influence of schooling, saw peace as having its place among the aims of education. Today it is recommended in the constitutions of several of the Federal German states (Bundeslaender) that peace education finds its place in the schools. This should not be as a separate subject, but rather incorporated into such subjects as political education and religion (Boehm, 188). Boehm notes the close connection between peace education and peace research. He goes on to say that it must address humankind as a whole: on the cognitive, ethical, emotional and spiritual levels. It must be concerned with the wider, political aspects: wars, military conflicts, liberation struggles, acts of terrorism and repressive struggles for markets and scarce resources. It must also deal with narrower issues: crime, and violence within the family.

Nigel Young, writing from the School of Peace Studies in the University of Bradford, has a similar perspective. He sees peace studies as having, by the 1970s, evolved to combine research with education (teaching) and an action component. He notes criticism of the negative definition of peace (as concern with preventing wars, especially a third world war, and inter-state policy) as being potentially conservative and even repressive. Such critics put the stress increasingly on concepts of liberation and social justice (Young, 1981, 123-35). Against such a view there is danger that peace education will remain at the level of safe platitudes on which all can agree, but which lead to nothing.

One problem which does not seem to have been mentioned in the literature on peace education is the negative effect of incorporation in the academic schooling process itself. This can operate at two levels. Writing on peace becomes subject to the rules of the publish or perish game. Authors will be tempted to pull punches, remain on safe levels of abstraction and to coin jargon in attempts to stamp their creations as original commodities. On another level, learners will see peace as just another topic in the compulsory curriculum, something *they* want *us* to learn, and not something vital and enlightening. But these are dangers which can only be struggled with. They cannot be avoided.

Sport and Education

Two memories stand out in my mind as testimony to the grip of sport on diverse classes and nationalities. The first is of being accosted by a well-dressed man in a street in the City of London who simply asked: 'Have you got the score?' The second is of a visiting delegation of university presidents from the People's Republic of China at an Australian university in whose science programmes they were interested. They were solemnly seated in front of a colour television set to watch the Melbourne Cup and then given envelopes containing their 'winnings'. What the explanation of that grip is and what teaching-learning processes are involved remains far from clear although the question has been the subject of public comment for many centuries.[12] Clearly connected with religion, politics and as television demonstrates to us daily, capitalist business interests, it is surprising that more marxists, and particularly marxists interested in education, have not seen it as a subject for study.

Sport here is used to cover a very broad range of activities. Careful study would require consideration of which activity had special significance for particular social groups. For that some classification of activities would be necessary, such as that which divides games into three classes: (1) those requiring essentially physical skill; (2) those depending on rational choices and strategy; and (3) games of chance (Roberts and Sutton-Smith in Loy and Kenyon, 1969, 116-17). Competition is an obvious feature of sport, a feature which has been praised and criticised by different people. Gofman draws attention to the importance of 'sanctioned display', listing such qualities as dexterity, strength, knowledge, intelligence, courage and self-control (cit. Loy in Loy and Kenyon, 66). Such display is the basis for spectacle, a characteristic feature of commercial sport. Loy draws attention to sport as a social institution. He sees it organised on four levels. At the primary level people meet in face-to-face contact, e.g. in a sports team. At the technical level the group is still small enough for people to know each other but coaches and others play administrative roles. At the managerial level members may still know one or more administrators personally, as in one of the larger professional ball clubs. But at the corporate level such personal relations are replaced by the impersonal, bureaucratic relationships of modern business. This is the level of national and international sports organisations (in Loy and Kenyon, 67-8).

Any consideration of possible educational effects must take into account the nature of people's involvement in the particular sport. This requires analysis as to degree and kind. Degree involves frequency, duration and intensity. Loy divides kind into producers and consumers. Producers may be players, or facilitators of play such as club owners, coaches and other officials. In addition there are 'tertiary producers' who act as cheerleaders, band members or who do other service work. Consumers can also be divided according to whether they attend sports functions personally, follow them through the mass media, or relate to them in some other way (in Loy and Kenyon, 69-70). Superficial consideration would suggest that players and non-players would be exposed to some very different teachings (obviously those concerned with skills and fitness) and would share others. It is also a common criticism to sneer at spectators. But Baker claims that 'several recent studies' show that 'people who attend athletic events also read more books, attend more concerts and plays, visit more museums, and participate more regularly in politics than do nonspectators' (1982, 337). Another trap is to make facile distinctions between professional and amateur sport when study reveals the overlapping of these categories in a highly complex manner. More useful here is the distinction between professionalism and commercialism, the former concerning the individual player and the latter the organisation surrounding the team (Tyrrell in Cashman and McKernan, 1980, 88).

What has been said so far applies very generally. The sports which come to mind as socially significant are the various forms of football, cricket, baseball, basketball and athletics. But attention must also be given to sports education as a special and to a large degree separate organisation. This has been actively promoted since at least the late 1700s when Johann Basedow founded a school in Dessau, Germany, where many sports and physical activities were undertaken (Lockhart and Slusher, 1975, 15). For a long period considered as physical training, as 'education *of* the physical', it was in the 1930s spoken of as 'an education *through* the physical' (Williams in Lockhart and Slusher, 1). Much later attempts were made to co-ordinate teaching around the theme of movement, and more recently again to link it with health, recreation and ecology (Lockhart and Slusher, 339-54, 383-91). In part genuine responses to new thinking, these changes also reflect what Charles McCloy called the 'inferiority complex' of many physical educators (Lockhart and Slusher, 5). Like other branches of education they felt the need to justify themselves in the university by strengthening their 'theoretical' foundation. For the USA at least the financial attraction of some sports activities has been a more telling argument.

Typical of the kinds of claims made in the USA are the following, made in 1958 (Brace in Lockhart and Slusher, 243). They are prefaced by the assertion that they 'should have been received by those who have gone through our school programs'. 'Should' or 'can result' are the key phrases which, typically, are not examined. The 'values' include knowledge of 'one's health status', 'one's physical abilities', and of games and recreations and how to learn necessary skills for them. It also mentions attributes like confidence and interest. But most important if difficult to substantiate, it includes the following moral-political learnings:

(1) concepts of fair play, and respect and consideration for the shortcomings or achievements of opponents;
(2) respect for authority as embodied in the team captain, game official, coach, or school principal.

The second is presumably linked with the final claim, to provide 'experience in leadership of fellow students' through minor official positions. Just what 'an understanding of our heritage in sports and [their] place in American culture' is intended to mean is not clear but it is open to interpretations of teaching patriotism, a value widely believed to be teachable through sport.

The article which follows Brace's in the collection, that by Obertueffer and referring to the 1960s, has doubts about what values are actually taught. He speaks of someone saying 'nice guys finish last', and of competition gone mad, leading to cheating, greed and bribery. He calls for research into how movement education can teach the ethics of 'respect for personality', which he sees as the essence of 'the democratic way'. But typically a teacher, he prejudges the results and asserts that it can (Lockhart and Slusher, 246-53).

A case study was made of the use of sport as moral-political teaching in the English and some Scottish, public schools. This has been nicely described in its complexities by J.A. Mangan (1981). He describes how 'the ideology of athleticism' was first used in a few schools to rescue them from a period of decay in discipline and falling numbers in the mid-1800s. It was, writes Mangan, 'the utilisation of games as a form of *social control*' (28). By the end of the century the ideology had been widely adopted, and it was not 'widely ridiculed, savaged and moribund' until the late 1960s (218). The ideology:

> embraced a complex of ideas and feelings deliberately and carefully created through ritual and symbol; ... on occasion, a form of 'pseudo-reasoning', a deliberate rationalisation for ambitions such as status and power; and . . . it constituted value-judgements masquerading as facts to reinforce commitment. (6)

The ideology was taught by a daily ritual of house and school matches in cricket and football, compulsory and rigorous. These were supplemented by school songs which one ex-Harrow schoolboy described as follows:

> Harrow songs make for something greater than entertainment. They are redolent with the public school spirit, a clarion call to strenuous endeavour, an injunction to work and play with faith and courage, to fight against the odds ... to sacrifice self, if need be, to the common end. (180)

There was, writes Mangan, a 'touching dogmatism and moral fervour' which reminds the present writer of the hymns to Mao Zedong in the recent Chinese Cultural Revolution. Certainly both kinds of songs, different in political content as they were, were sung with equal fervour. In the tighter social class milieu of England of the period, particularly that of the First World War, they may have had much more lasting effect.

The values of these rituals were an anti-intellectual muscularity (106); an asexual masculinity ('that curious paradox', as Mangan calls it (190); and a chauvinism which complemented the tasks of empire for which so many from these schools were called on to perform. The cluster of sport, militarism, religion and empire are nicely illustrated in this quotation of Baden-Powell:

> Don't be disgraced like the young Romans, who lost the Empire of their forefathers by being wishy-washy slackers without any go or patriotism in them. Play up. Each man in his place and play the game. Your forefathers worked hard, fought hard and died hard to make the Empire for you. Don't let them look down from heaven and see you loafing about with your hands in your pockets, doing nothing to keep it up. (203)

It may be hard today to realise how seriously even the remark about hands in pockets was taken. But an examination of the ritual and rhetoric of today's sports and games shows them to be taken equally seriously, and not always for very different moral-political reasons. Daniels draws attention to the long history of relationship between sport, physical education and the military. He cites training through sport during the Second World War, and its use for maintaining morale and fitness. Finally he notes that today 'sports and exercise is considered a primary factor in national security' (Loy and Kenyon, 1969, 20). Caldwell, looking at sports in Australia, sees them as a 'substitute for war', a means of expressing 'unrestrained emotion and passion in public'. He suggests that more young Australians, and not a few older ones, are 'doing their own thing', (water) skiing, gliding or surfing rather than playing team games (Jaques and Pavia, 1976, 145-7). Generalisation is difficult and, as usual, what is learnt is not necessarily what is taught. Athlete trainer Percy Cerutty found life 'highly competitive' and thought the honest position to take was to treat a competitor as 'the enemy'. Champion miler Herb Elliott agreed with him and would not shake hands with opponents before a race, much less wish them luck. World champion Ron Clarke, however, was criticised for lacking 'the killer instinct' (Jaques and Pavia, 12-13). Gary Whannel argues that competition can encourage 'cooperation, friendship, mutual support and genuine human aspiration'. That, as he claims, it is also 'fun' only poses further questions (1983, 108).

To those concerned about the creation of a peaceful world in which human beings co-operate for the general good the question of what values sports teach is a serious one. One of the arguments for the modern series of Olympic Games, attributed to its founder, the French Baron Pierre de Coubertin, is that they promote 'the principles of fair play and good sportsmanship, thus creating international friendship and goodwill' (Lockhart and Slusher, 19; cf. Baker, 1982, 192-7). Examination of the realities, particularly the various national press and television coverage in the decades after the Second World War must make one wonder. But the message is complex. Rowe and Lawrence suggest the Olympics create 'the opportunity for audiences to be made aware of, for example, black power as much as any supposed white supremacy, of women's capability and achievement as much as their supposed physical inferiority' (1984, 27).

The professionalisation and commercialisation of sport, increasingly incorporating it into the capitalist mode of production, is a fact which many deplore, but the degree to which it is educationally significant is very hard to tell. Critcher traces changes in style of professional footballers in England in the course of football developing as a capitalist enterprise. He distinguishes four styles: traditional/located represents the values of a 'traditional respectable working-class culture'; transitional/mobile, where players begin to assume 'middle-class life styles'; incorporated/embourgeoised, where they become small-scale entrepreneurs; and superstars/dislocated, where under the blaze of media publicity players are drawn into the film and television star world of the *nouveau riche* (1979, 164). Players learn behaviour off and on the field, the latter as styles of play are adapted to what business judges the consumer to demand. At the same time, footballers are heroes and to some extent models for many young males.

Critcher raises another point which has implications far wider than football when he describes how particularly television presents and interprets games for the viewing public. Focusing attention on a limited part of the field only, not allowing the viewers to see the whole or choose for themselves where to look, the media impose their view of the game on them. Critcher comments:

Far from understanding or defending the traditional role of the 'supporter', they have sought to educate him out of it into the world of technical sophistication and managed melodrama which they fondly believe to be an accurate and desirable presentation of the game. (1979, 175)

This is part of the general thrust of late capitalism towards the authority of experts, deskilling ordinary people and 'managing public opinion'. It may be countered to the degree that people participate as players and live spectators, but the trend seems to be away from that so far as team games are concerned. In part this is a question of the economics of facility provision, itself a function of capitalism.

Critcher's account of football begins with a discussion of how its values, masculinity, aggression, physical emphasis and regional identity, relate to English working-class values (1979, 161). It is not clear whether one can identify other class values in such sports as polo, tennis or golf. In any case, the latter two are examples of where in different countries games are differently class distributed. There is also a distinction to be made between a sport being played by different classes, but in socially segregated circumstances and where the classes are brought together in the same game. Baker ignores such questions when he writes of 'the social barriers [being] broken through sports' and 'class barriers [having] fallen' in the USA (1982, 283). Some sports clearly distinguish between the rich who watch and own-employ and the employees who perform. Much horse racing is a clear example, though one must also look at local gymkhanas where there may be more of a social mixing. Whether mixing of social classes on the sports field contributes to class consciousness or to a blurring of the differences and social peace is another of the hard questions on which there are probably many answers. So far as political leaders are concerned there is no doubt that many find an image of being 'a good sport' a useful one (Hartung in Cashman and McKernan, 1980, 194-215).

One other aspect of sport which affects what at least some see as education must be mentioned. That is particularly the connection, real and imagined, between sport and gambling, and to a lesser degree, drinking. Baker sketches the long tradition of suspicion and open hostility which various Protestant sects have displayed to 'traditional sports and pastimes' in a chapter entitled 'Frowning Puritans' (1982, 72-84). Early opposition was about promoting 'idleness', or diverting people from observance of the Sabbath. Currently there are confused attitudes and not a little lack of hard data on the connection between illegal starting price bookmaking and organised crime in New South Wales (McCoy in Cashman and McKernan, 1980, 34-67). The degree to which the sport itself can be fairly blamed for encouraging gambling or other condemned adjuncts does not seem to be often considered. In addition, there have been class as well as religious distinctions made about the morality and accessibility of both gambling and drinking. The lessons which people have drawn from such distinctions have certainly surfaced in the long history of starting price bookmaking.

As something which occupies so many people for such a large amount of time, and one clearly mainly entered into voluntarily, sport would clearly repay much further study. As in all the areas here considered, one cannot expect to gain any certainties about learnings, but clarification of what is and is not taught might enable us to make sounder decisions when it comes to social policy.

Notes

1. The question of the relation of Marx and Engels to the trade union movement is thoroughly dealt with in Draper, 2, Chapters 4 and 5 and special note B. The last deals with an incident which is misleadingly cited in Mallet, p. 189, and in Rubel and Manale, p. 249.

2. Much of the detail in this section is from Sampson, Chapter 4. He draws attention to another aspect of union competition. Extension of the railways which would appear to have been in the general interest was defeated by lobbying by the Transport and General Workers Union, representing the interests of lorry drivers against those of railwaymen *and* the general public (p. 64). This is no doubt one of many examples where capitalism sets up conflicts of interest between workers; conflicts which would disappear with a different, socialist, society.

3. The shop steward is known by different names according to union and trade. In printing the term is father or mother of the chapel, in the iron and steel industry the works representative. The role is that of non full-time workplace representative elected by his or her workmates.

4. To back up his own account Pfeffer cites extensively from six books about work in America chosen to represent different points of view. Two he describes as 'conventional' are Richard Balzer's *Clockwork* and the Report to the US Department of Health, Education and Welfare, *Work in America*. One he places 'at the other end of the political-intellectual spectrum': Harry Braverman's *Labor and Monopoly Capital*. The others are: Studs Terkel's *Working*; Richard Sennett's and Jonathan Cobb's *The Hidden Injuries of Class*; and Barbara Garson's *All the Livelong Day* (Pfeffer, 236-7, and Chapter 16, 'Unions, Policemen for the Bosses').

5. E. Davis (1977, 356) notes a similar state of affairs for the Amalgamated Metal Workers and Shipwrights' Union in Australia. In 1976 the voting figures for the Victorian State Conference suggest an average of about six attending branch meetings when membership might be as many as two thousand.

6. Already Marx had occasion to protest at the way in which the English trade union officials allowed themselves to be bought up by the capitalist class and the government (Draper, 2, 130). As Draper comments, it is not simply a matter of 'rewards and blandishments', of being publicly praised as 'responsible', but that 'as *ex*-workers they cease to live the same life as their fellow workers, even with the

best of intentions, to a small or great degree'. Life for the big union official can, as Sampson notes, include 'a house in Regent's Park, a cabin cruiser, and endless cocktail parties' (70)!

7. This bulletin is interesting for the entry it gives to information about the various trade union combines which have been formed since that at Lucas Aerospace. These include that at Metal Box, the Renold Group and ICL, and there is a Joint Forum of Combine Committees active in educational work (*CAITS Quarterly*, 14, 1984, p.2).

8. A survey of the churches and the Peace Movement in Australia is given in *Peace Studies*, November, 1984.

9. This is, of course, the general problem often complained about in terms of the 'knowledge explosion'. It cannot be solved in an interest-divided society in which the production and distribution of disinformation is a major industry. The complexity of the problem requires special study.

10. These are: Berghof Stiftung fur Konfliktforschung, Berlin; Forschungsinstitut fuer Friedenspolitik, Starnberg; Hessische Stiftung Freidens- und Kofliktforschung, Frankfurt am Main; Institut fuer Friedensforschung und Sicherheitspolitik an der Universitat Hamburg; and the Verein fuer Friedenspaedagogik, Tubingen.

11. Ironically the women were being charged under an Act of 1361, while defending their actions using the Genocide Act of 1969. They argued that the actions of the British government were illegal in that they are planning for genocide by agreeing to have cruise missiles in their country. The Act they cite states under Article 2:

> In the present Convention, genocide means any of the following acts committed with intent to destroy, in whole or in part, a national, ethnical, racial or religious group, as such:
> (a) Killing members of the group;
> (b) Causing serious bodily or mental harm to members of the group;
> (c) Deliberately inflicting on the group conditions of life calculated to bring about its physical destruction in whole or in part;
> (d) Imposing measures intended to prevent births within the group;
> (e) Forcibly transferring children of the group to another group. (Cook and Kirk, 1983, 115-16)

12. William Baker describes how Romans tried to ban Greek games for fear they would corrupt Roman youth and the church and various monarchs tried to forbid popular sports and pastimes in medieval Europe (1982, 31, 53, etc.)

12 CONCLUSION

The major argument of this book has been that efforts to construct a 'marxist analysis of education' centred on schools and schooling is mistaken. There may be a 'marxist theory of schooling' which sets the school within the wider society, or looks at it with the concepts of dialectics in mind. But this will still fail to understand the central problem of education, which surely is where human beings learn the lessons which determine their being and their becoming. Clearly, for most of us this is located outside the school, making the school less than teachers, parents and others would like it — and often wishfully think it — to be.

A second argument has been that both social scientists and educators need to be clearer about the distinction between the individual, psychological level and the social, sociological. Individual learning is unpredictable and probably beyond the reach of sceintific determination. What can be determined is the content of the teachings to which individuals are exposed and the context within which they take place. In addition, it is highly uncertain what the relation is between beliefs and attitudes and a person's behaviour. The latter is circumscribed by practical possibilities which often do not allow for certain beliefs and attitudes to be expressed. This situation is itself probably a determinant of the person's belief system. Moreover, the same behaviour occurs on the basis of different ideas and beliefs, and the same beliefs result in different behaviour. This makes nonsense of those social doctrines which put the emphasis on conversion prior to and as the means to social change. Social change is a question of practice to which people with very different beliefs and attitudes must contribute. Marx's vision of a rational co-operative future society poses a tendency towards increasing rationality, not rationality as a prerequisite as some socialists suppose. This is Marx's conception of the possibility of moving from the realm of necessity into a realm of freedom, a conception which I have tried to show in its complexity.

Two difficult theoretical problems which arose in connection with education as knowledge were the process of abstraction and the concept of levels of organisation of matter. It seems clear that the kinds of abstraction used in mathematics and physics are

279

unsuitable for most other forms of knowledge, yet have been reiified and upheld as the model for us all to emulate. The resulting threat to human survival is forcing more people to recognise the source of the problem, but as yet there seems to be no theory to guide the abstraction process. People speak of different levels of abstraction, but there is no guidance as to what this means and, therefore, how it should be applied in different fields of enquiry.

The second problem, that of levels of organisation of matter, has been illustrated in the discussion of the individual and the social levels. Failure to make this distinction is the basis of most of what is called 'reductionism'. There is a need to distinguish levels of organisation from different spheres or interacting systems within the same level in the social world. Such a distinction would finally dispose of that bothersome metaphor, basis and superstructure, which still clouds rather than illuminates certain marxist writings.

Finally, the point of this study has been to suggest that marxists, along with thinkers of other persuasions, have attributed both too much and too little to education. They have seen schools as too central and teaching too easily resulting in corresponding learning. Putting teaching and learning in the full social context and making careful and concrete assessment of who is teaching what, and who is learning what and where, precludes the easy generalisations we would like to make. It may seem to put in doubt education as a theoretical process. But that is to misread the question. That many ideas are *post facto* rationalisations, or that individual beliefs are only indirectly related to actions does not mean that we should abandon our study of education, but rather redirect it. Study of the teachings of various social agents suggests that they are good at what might be called executive skills, but weak on legislative ones. They teach people to understand regulations, to appreciate the social implications of technology which threatens us, to organise. But at the same time they do little to breakdown the hierarchies, the barriers between ordinary people and experts. They teach people to follow more often than to lead. If we are to solve our major problems, the threat of extinction through nuclear war or slow radiation poison, and an economic system that puts the pursuit of profit in place of the social good, this must be changed. Ways must be found of teaching co-operation in the formulation of policies and the direction of action, and this must become the goal of education.

SELECT BIBLIOGRAPHY

Abramson, L.Y., Garber, J. and Seligman, M. 'Learned Helplessness in Humans: An Attributional Analysis' in Garber and Seligman (1980), pp. 3-31.

Adorno, T.W. *et al. The Positivist Dispute in German Sociology* (trans. G. Adey and D. Erisby, Heinemann, London, 1976)

Adorno, T.W., Frenkel-Brunswick, E., Levinson, D.J. and Norton, W.W. *The Authoritarian Personality* (W.W. Norton, New York, 1969)

Althusser, L. *For Marx* (Penguin Books, Harmondsworth, 1969)

———— and Balibar, E. *Reading 'Capital'* (New Left Books, London, 1970)

Amin, S. *Accumulation on a World Scale: A Critique of the Theory of Underdevelopment* (Monthly Review Press, New York, 1974)

Anderson, P. *Considerations on Western Marxism* (New Left Books, London, 1976, verso edition 1979)

———— *Arguments within English Marxism* (New Left Books, London, 1980)

Anderson, R.S. *Education in Japan* (US Department of Health, Education and Welfare, Washington, 1975)

Apple, M.W. *Ideology and Curriculum* (Routledge and Kegan Paul, London, 1979)

———— (ed.) *Cultural and Economic Reproduction in Education: Essays on Class, Ideology and the State* (Routledge and Kegan Paul, London, 1982)

Archambault, R.D. *Philosophical Analysis and Education* (Routledge and Kegan Paul, London, 1965)

Archer, M.S. *Social Origins of Educational Systems* (Sage, London, 1979)

Aron, R. *Main Currents in Sociological Thought, 2* (Penguin Books, Harmondsworth, 1967)

Ausubel, D.P. *The Psychology of Meaningful Verbal Learning* (Grune and Stratton, New York, 1963)

Avineri, S. *The Social and Political Thought of Karl Marx* (Cambridge University Press, 1970)

Bad News, see Glasgow University Media Group

Bahro, R. *The Alternative in Eastern Europe*, trans. D. Fernbach (New Left Books, London, 1978)

Baker, W.J. *Sports in the Western World* (Rowan and Littlefield, Totowa, NJ, 1982)

Bannock, G., Baxter, R.E. and Rees, R. *The Penguin Dictionary of Economics*, 2nd edn (Penguin Books, Harmondsworth, 1978)

Baran, P.A. and Sweezy, P.M. 'Monopoly Capital: An Essay on the American Economic and Social Order', *Monthly Review Press* (New York, 1966)

Barratt Brown, M. *After Imperialism* (Merlin Press, London, 1970)

Barrett, M. *Women's Oppression Today: Problems in Marxist Feminist Analysis* (Verso, London, 1980)

Barrister, A. *Justice in England* (Victor Gollancz, London, 1938)

Baudelot, C. and Establet, R. *L'Ecole capitalist en France* (Maspero, Paris, 1972)

———— and Malemort, J. *La Petite Bourgeoisie en France* (Maspero, Paris, 1975)

Beck, C.M., Crittenden, A.S. and Sullivan, E.V. (eds) *Moral Education: Interdisciplinary Approaches* (University Press, Toronto, 1971)

Becker, E., Herkommer, S. and Bergmann, J. *Erziehung zur Anpassung?* (Wochenschau Verlag, Schwalbach bei Frankfurt am Main, 1970)

Beer, W. *Lernen im Widerstand: politisches Lernen und politische Sozialisation in*

Burgerinitiativen, (Verlag Association, Hamburg, 1978)

Bell, D. *The Cultural Contradictions of Capitalism,* 2nd edn (Heinemann, London, 1976)

Ben-David, J. and Zloczower, A. 'Universities and Academic Systems in Modern Societies', *Archive of European Sociology,* 3 (1962), pp. 45-84

Benn, T. *Arguments for Socialism,* Chris Mullin (ed.) (Penguin, Harmondsworth, 1980)

Berg, I. *Education and Jobs: The Great Training Robbery* (Penguin, Harmondsworth, 1973)

Bernal, J.D. *World without War* (Routledge and Kegan Paul, London, 1958)
_____ *Science in History,* 4 vols (Penguin Books, Harmondsworth, 1965)

Bernfeld, S. *Sisyphos oder die Grenzen der Erziehung* (1925) (Suhrkamp, Frankfurt am Main, 1981)

Bernstein, B. *Class, Codes and Control,* 3 vols (Routledge and Kegan Paul, London, 1971)

Bessant, B. and Spaul, A. *Politics of Schooling* (Pitman, Carlton, Vic., 1976)

Blackburn, R. (ed.) *Ideology in Social Science* (Fontana/Collins, London 1972)

Blaug, M. (ed.) *Economics of Education,* 2 vols (Penguin Books, Harmondsworth, 1970)

Bluestone, B. and Harrison, B. *The Deindustrialisation of America: Plant Closings, Community Abandonment, and the Dismantling of Basic Industry* (Basic Books, New York, 1982)

Bock, H. and Gassin, J. (eds) Papers from the Conference, 'Communication at University: Purpose, Process and Product' (La Trobe University, Melbourne, 1982)

Boehm, W. *Woerterbuch der Paedagogik* (Kroener Verlag, Stuttgart, 1982)

Bourdieu, P. 'Cultural Reproduction and Social Reproduction' in Brown, R. *Knowledge Education and Cultural Change* (1973)
_____ and Passeron, J-C. *Reproduction: In Education, Society and Class* (Sage, London, 1979)
_____ 'Contradictions and Reproduction in Educational Theory' in Dale *et al. Education and the State,* Vol. 1, (1981), pp. 45-59

Bowles, S. and Gintis, H. *Schooling in Capitalist America* (Routledge and Kegan Paul, London, 1976)
_____ 'Reply to Sherry Gorelick', *Monthly Review,* 30, 6 November (1978), pp. 59-64

Brake, M. and Bailey, R. *Radical Social Work and Practice* (Edward Arnold, London, 1980)

Branson, J. and Miller, D.B. *Class, Sex and Education in Capitalist Society,* (Sorrett Publishing, Malvern, 1979)

Braverman, H. *Labor and Monopoly Capital: The Degradation of Work in the Twentieth Century* (Monthly Review Press, New York, 1974)

Brockway, F. *Britain's First Socialists: The Levellers, Agitators and Diggers of the English Revolution* (Quartet Books, London, 1980)

Brown, G. and Desforges, C. *Piaget's Theory: A Psychological Critique* (Routledge and Kegan Paul, London, 1979)

Brown, R. (ed.) *Knowledge, Education and Cultural Change,* (Tavistock Publication, London, 1973)

Brueckner, P. *Zur Sozial-psychologie des Kapitalismus* (Europaeische Verlagsanstalt, Frankfurt am Main, 1972)

Bunge, M. *Causality* (Meridian Books, New York, 1963)

Bunn, R.F. 'Treatment of Hitler's Rise to Power in West German School Textbooks', *Comparative Education Review,* 6, 1 June (1962) pp. 34-43

Bunyan T. *The History and Practice of the Political Police in Britain* (Quarter

Books, London, 1976)

Burback, R. and Flynn, P. *Agribusiness in the Americas* (Monthly Review Press, New York, 1980)

Burns, R. and Sheehan, B. (eds) Women and Education, Proceedings of the 12th Annual Conference of the Australian and New Zealand Comparative and International Education Society, Bundoora, La Trobe University, 27-9 November (1984)

Butcher, H., Collins, P., Glen, A. and Sills, P. *Community Groups in Action: Case Studies and Analysis* (Routledge and Kegan Paul, London, 1980)

Cameron, C. (ed.) *Who is Guru Maharaj Ji?* (Bantam Books, New York, 1973)

Cameron, K.N. 'The Fallacy of "the Superstructure"', *Monthly Review*, 31, 8 January (1980), pp. 27-36

Carlton, D. and Schaerf, C. *International Terrorism and World Society* (Croom Helm, London, 1975)

Cashman, R. and McKernan *Sport, Money, Morality and the Media* (New South Wales University Press, Kensington, 1980)

Castle, E.B. *Ancient Education and Today* (Penguin Books, Harmondsworth, 1961)

Castles, S. and Wuestenberg, W. *The Education of the Future: An Introduction to the Theory and Practice of Socialist Education* (Pluto Press, London, 1979)
_____ with Booth, H. and Wallace, T. *Here for Good: Western Europe's New Ethnic Minorities* (Pluto Press, London, 1984)

Center for Research and Education in American Liberties *Civic Education in a Crisis Age: An Alternative to Repression and Revolution* (Columbia University and Teachers' College, New York, 1970)

Chan Wing-tsit *A Source Book in Chinese Philosophy* (University Press, Princeton, 1963)

Chu Hsi and Lu Tsu-ch'ien, Reflections on Things at Hand, Chan Wing-tsit (trans.) (Columbia University Press, New York, 1967)

Chang, Chung-li *The Income of the Chinese Gentry* (University of Washington Press, Seattle, 1962)

Children's Rights Workshop (ed.) *Sexism in Children's Books, Facts, Figures and Guidelines* (Writers and Readers Publishing Co-operative, London, 1976)

Cipolla, C.M. (ed.) *The Fontana Economic History of Europe: Contemporary Economics*, 1 (Fontana-Collins, Glasgow, 1976)

Clarizio, H.F., Craig, R.C. and Mehrens, W. *Contemporary Issues in Educational Psychology*, 3rd edn (Allyn and Bacon, Boston, 1977)

Clarke, A.D.B. 'Predicting Human Development: Problems, Evidence, Implications', *Bulletin of British Psychological Society*, 31 (1978), pp. 249-58

Clawson, D. *Bureaucracy and the Labour Process, the Transformation of US Industry, 1860-1920* (Monthly Review Press, New York, 1980)

Clegg, S. and Dunkerley, D. *Organisation, Class and Control* (Routledge and Kegan Paul, London, 1980)

Coady, M. and T. 'The Bishops and the Bomb', *Arena*, 65 (1983), pp. 23-9

Cockburn, A. and Blackburn, R. *Student Power* (Penguin Books in association with New Left Review, London, 1969)

Cohen, G.A. *Karl Marx's Theory of History: A Defence* (Clarendon Press, Oxford, 1978)

Cohn, T. 'Social Justice and Social/Political Education: A Theoretical Exploration', *International Journal of Political Education*, 6 (1983), pp. 1-23

Cohn-Bendit, G. and D. *Obsolete Communist, the Left-wing Alternative* (Penguin Books, Harmondsworth, 1969)

Colletti, L. 'Marxism and the Dialectic', *New Left Review*, 93, October (1975), pp. 3-29

Connell, R.W. *The Child's Construction of Politics* (Melbourne University Press, 1975)

Connell, R.W., Ashenden, D.J., Kessler, S. and Dowsett, G.W. *Making the Difference: Schools, Families and Social Division* (Allen and Unwin, Sydney, 1982)

Connerton, P. (ed.) *Critical Sociology* (Penguin Books, Harmondsworth, 1976)

Cook, A. and Kirk, G. *Greenham Women Everywhere: Dreams, Ideas and Actions from the Women's Peace Movement* (Pluto Press, London, 1983)

Coote, A. and Campbell, B. *Sweet Freedom: The Struggle for Women's Liberation* (Pan Books Picador, London, 1982)

Corer, E. and Stuttard, G. (ed.) *Industrial Studies 1, The Key Skills* (Arrow Books in association with the Society of Industrial Tutors, London, 1975)

Cornforth, M. *In Defence of Philosophy against Positivism and Pragmatism* (Lawrence and Wishart, London, 1950)

Corrigan, P. *Schooling the Smash Street Kids* (Macmillan, London, 1979)

Cosin, B.R., Dale, I.R. *et al.* (eds) *School and Society: A Sociological Reader* (Routledge and Kegan Paul, London, 1977)

Cowen, G.A. *Karl Marx's Theory of History: A Defence* (Oxford University Press, 1978)

Cox, C.B. and Boyson, R. *Black Papers* (Temple Smith, London, 1977)

Cox, C.B. and Dyson, A.E. *Fight for Education: A Black Paper* (The Critical Quarterly, London, 1968)

Cox. J. *Overkill: The Story of Modern Weapons* (Penguin Books, Harmondsworth, 1981)

Coxon, H. 'The Freedom of Information Debate in Australia', *Government Publications Review*, 8A (1981), pp. 373-9

Cremin, L.A. *Public Education* (Basic Books, New York, 1976)

Critcher, C. 'Football Since the War' in Clarke, J., Critcher, C. and Johnson, R. *Working-class Culture* (Hutchinson, London, in association with the Centre for Contemporary Cultural Studies, University of Birmingham, 1979), pp. 161-84

Crittenden, B. 'Lawrence Kohlberg, Developmental Psychology and Moral Education' in D'Cruz, J.V. and Hannah, W. *Perceptions of Excellence* (The Polding Press, Melbourne, 1979)

Crough, G. and Wheelwright, T. *Australia: A Client State* (Penguin Books, Harmondsworth, 1982)

Curran, J., Burevitch, M. and Woollacott J. *Mass Communication and Society* (Edward Arnold/Open University Press, London, 1977)

Current Background, Hong Kong, US Consulate General, (serial)

D'Cruz, J.V. and Hannah, W. *Perceptions of Excellence* (The Polding Press, Melbourne, 1979)

Dahrendort, R. *Gesellschaft und Demokratie in Deutschland* (Deutsches Taschenbuch Verlag (dtv), Munchen, 1977)

Dale, R., Esland, G., Fergusson, R. and Macdonald, M. *Education and the State*, 2 vols (The Falmer Press/Open University, Lewes, 1981)

Dale, R., Esland, G. *et al.* (eds) *Schooling and Capitalism: A Sociological Reader* (Routledge and Kegan Paul, London, 1976)

Davis, E. 'Decision-making in the Amalgamated Metal Workers' and Shipwrights' Union' *The Journal of Industrial Relations*, December (1977), pp. 348-65

Davis, M. 'The AFL-CIO's Second Century', *New Left Review*, 136, December (1982)

Dawes, G. 'Liberation Theology in the Bible Belt', *Monthly Review*, July-August (1984), pp. 81-91

Debray, R. 'Revolution in the Revolution', trans. Bobbye Ortiz, *Monthly Review*, 19, 3, July-August (1967)

_____ *Teachers, Writers, Celebrities: The Intellectuals of Modern France*, trans. David Macey (Verso, London, 1981)

Dewey, J. *Democracy and Education* (Macmillan, New York, 1963)

Diamond, I. (ed.) *Families, Politics, Public Policy: A Feminist Dialogue on Women and the State* (Longman, New York, 1983)

Dimmaggio, P. and Useem, M. 'Cultural Property and Public Policy: Emerging Tensions in Government Support for the Arts', *Social Research*, 45, 2 (1978), pp. 356-89

Dixon, B. *Catching them Young, 1: Sex, Race and Class in Children's Fiction* (Pluto Press, London, 1977)

Dore, R. *The Diploma Disease: Education, Qualification and Development* (Allen and Unwin, London, 1976)

Dorfman, A. and Mattelart, A. *How to Read Donald Duck: Imperialist Ideology in the Disney Comic* (International General, New York, 1975)

Draper, H. *Writings on the Paris Commune* (Monthly Review Press, New York, 1971)

_____ *Karl Marx's Theory of Revolution*, Vols, 1 and 2 (Monthly Review Press, New York, 1977, 1978)

Dreeben, R. *On What Is Learnt in School* (Addison-Wesley, Cambridge, Mass., 1968)

Duhem, P. *The Aim and Structure of Physical Theory* (Atheneum, New York, 1962)

Dumas, W. and Lee, W.B. *Social Studies in West German Schools: Firsthand Perspectives for Educators* (University of Missourie Press, Columbia, 1968)

Dunlop, R. and Burns, A. 'Adolescents and Divorce: The Experience of Family Break-up', paper presented to the Australian Family Research Conference, Canberra, 23-25 November (1983)

Dyson, A.E. and Lovelock, J. *Education and Democracy* (Routledge and Kegan Paul, London, 1975)

Eagleton, T. *Criticism and Ideology: A Study in Marxist Literary Theory* (New Left Books, London, 1976)

Easton, D. and Dennis, J. *Children and the Political System* (McGraw Hill, New York, 1969)

Edelman, M. *Politics as Symbolic Action: Mass Arousal and Quiescence* (Markham Publishing Company, Chicago, 1971)

Edwards, R. *Contested Terrain: The Transformation of the Workplace in the Twentieth Century* (Basic Books, New York, 1979)

Eisele, J.C. 'Defining Education: A Problem for Educational History', *Educational Theory*, winter, 30.1 (1980), pp. 25-33

Elkind, D. and Flavell, J.H. *Studies in Cognitive Development* (Oxford University Press, New York, 1969)

Engels, F. *Dialectics of Nature* (Lawrence and Wishart, London, 1946)

_____ *Dialectics of Nature* (Foreign Languages Press, Moscow, 1954)

_____ *Anti-Duehring: Herr Eugen Duehring's Revolution in Science* (AD) 3rd edn (Foreign Languages Publishing House, Moscow, 1962)

_____ *The Origin of the Family, Private Property and the State*, introduction and notes by Eleanor Burke Leacock (International Publishers, New York, 1972)

Entwistle, H. *Antonio Gramsci: Conservative Schooling for Radical Politics* (Routledge and Kegan Paul, London, 1979)

Fawns, R.A. 'Ideology and Curriculum: The Legitimating Assumptions of "The Web of Life"', paper presented to the annual conference of the Australian Comparative and International Education Society, University of New England, November (1981), pp. 1-16

Fisher, E. *Marx in His Own Words* (Allen Lane, London, 1970)

Flavell, J.H. and Wohlwill, J.F. 'Formal and Functional Aspects of Cognitive Development' in D. Elkind and J.H. Flavell (eds), *Studies in Cognitive Development: Essays in Honor of Jean Piaget* (Oxford University Press, New York, 1969)

Fleming, C.M. *Teaching: A Psychological Analysis* (Methuen, London, 1958)

Ford, G.W., Hearn, J.M. and Lansbury, R.D. (eds), *Australian Labour Relations: Readings* (Macmillan, Melbourne, 1980)

Foster, C.R. 'Civic Education in the United States and the Federal Republic of Germany', *International Journal of Political Education*, 1 (1977), pp. 45-60

Foucault, M. *Surveiller et Punir: Naissance de la Prison* (Gallimard, Paris, 1975) trans. as: *Discipline and Punish* (Penguin Books, Harmondsworth, 1977)

Frankel, B. *Marxian Theories of the State: A Critique of Orthodoxy* (Arena Publications, Melbourne, 1978)

_____ *Beyond the State? Dominant Theories and Socialist Strategies* (Macmillan, London, 1983)

_____ 'Jurgen Habermas: The Relationship of Communication to Learning' in D'Cruz and Hannah (1979)

_____ 'Identifying Dominant Misconceptions of States', Thesis Eleven, 4 (1982), pp. 97-123

Fraser, W.R. *Reforms and Restraints in Modern French Education* (Routledge and Kegan Paul, London, 1971)

Freedman, R. *Marx on Economics* (Penguin Books, Harmondsworth, 1968)

Friedan, B. *The Second Stage* (Summit Books, New York, 1981)

Gandy D.R. *Marx and History: From Primitive Society to the Communist Future* (University of Texas Press, Austin, 1979)

Garber, J. and Seligman, M. *Human Helplessness: Theory and Applications* (Academic Press, New York, 1980)

Guakroger, S. Explanatory Structures; a Study of Concepts of Explanation in Early Physics and Philosopy (Humanities Press, NJ, 1978)

Gerth, H.H. and Wright Mills, C. *From Max Weber* (Routledge and Kegan Paul, London, 1970)

Giddens, A. *Studies in Social and Political Theory* (Basic Books, New York, 1977)

Giroux, H.A. *Ideology, Culture and the Process of Schooling* (Temple University Press, Philadelphia, 1981)

Glasgow University Media Group, *Bad News*, 2 vols (Routledge and Kegan Paul, London, 1976, 1980)

Gofman, J.W. *Radiation and Human Health* (Sierra Club Books, San Francisco, 1981)

Goodman, P. *Compulsory Miseducation* (Penguin Books, Harmondsworth, 1971)

Gorz, A. 'Technical Intelligence and the Capitalist Division of Labour', *Telos*, 12, summer (1972) pp. 27-41

_____ *Farewell to the Working Class: An Essay on Post-industrial Society* (Pluto Press, London, 1982; France, 1980)

Goslin, D.A. *Handbook of Socialization Theory and Research* (Rand McNally, Chicago, 1969)

Goulden, J.C. *The Money Givers* (Random House, New York, 1971)

Gouldner, A. *The Coming Crisis of Western Sociology* (Heinemann, London, 1971)

Greenstein, F. *Children and Politics* (Yale University Press, New Haven, 1965)

Gretton, J. and Jackson, M. *William Tyndale: Collapse of a School — or a System* (Allen and Unwin, London, 1976)

Groll, J. *Erziehung im gesellschaftlichen Reproduktionsprozess* (Suhrkamp, Frankfurt am Main, 1975)

Gurvitch, G. *The Social Framework of Knowledge*, trans. M.A. and K.A.

Thompson (Blackwell, Oxford, 1971)

Gutjahr-Loeser, P.J. and Hornung, K. *Politisch-Paedagogischer Handwoerterbuch* (Guenter Olzog Verlag, München, 1980)

Habermas, J. and Luhmann, N. *Theorie der Gesellschaft oder Sozialtechnologie* (Suhrkamp, Frankfurt am Main, 1971)

Habermas, J. *Knowledge and Human Interests* (Heinemann, London, 1972)
_____ *Communication and the Evolution of Society* (Heinemann, London, 1979)

Hagstrom, W.O. *The Scientific Community* (Basic Books, New York, 1965)

Hall, S. and Jefferson, T. *Resistance through Rituals: Youth Subcultures in Post-war Britain* (Hutchinson, London, 1976)

Halliday, J. and McCormack, G. *Japanese Imperialism Today* (Monthly Review Press, New York, 1973)

Halliday, J. *A Political History of Japanese Capitalism* (Pantheon Books, New York, 1975)

Harris, K. *Education and Knowledge: The Structured Misrepresentation of Reality* (Routledge and Kegan Paul, London, 1979)
_____ *Teachers and Classes: A Marxist Analysis* (Routledge and Kegan Paul, London, 1982)

Harris, R. and Paxman, J. *A Higher Form of Killing: The Secret Story of Gas and Germ Warfare* (Chatto and Windus, London, 1982)

Haxey, S. *Tory MP* (Victor Gollancz, London, 1939)

Hayden, D. *The Grand Domestic Revolution: A History of Feminist Designs for American Homes, Neighbourhoods and Cities* (MIT Press, Cambridge, Mass., 1982)

Hearn, J.M. 'Migrant Participation in Trade Union Leadership', *Journal of Industrial Relations*, June (1976), pp. 112-23

Hegel, G.W.F. *Science of Logic*, trans. W.H. Johnston and L.G. Struthers (Allen and Unwin, London, 1951)

Heimann, F.F. *The Future of Foundations* (Prentice Hall, Englewood Cliffs, NY, 1973)

Held, D. *Introduction to Critical Theory: Horkheimer to Habermas* (University of California Press, Berkeley, 1980)

Henderson, R.W. *Parent-Child Interaction: Theory, Research, and Prospects* (Academic Press, New York, 1981)

Hersh, S.M. *Chemical and Biological Warfare: The Hidden Arsenal* (Panther Books, London, 1968)

Hertzberg, H.W. *Social Studies Reform, 1880-1980* (Social Science Education Consortium, Inc., Boulder, Colorado, 1981)

Herzog, E. and Sudie, L.F. 'Fatherless Homes: A Review of Research', *Children*, September-October (1968), pp. 177-82
_____ 'Fatherless Heroes: A Review of the Research', *Children*, September (1968b)

Hess, R.D. and Torney, J.V. *The Development of Political Attitudes in Children* (Aldine Publishing Company, Chicago, 1967)

Hill, C. *The World Turned Upside Down: Radical Ideas During the English Revolution* (Penguin Books, Harmondsworth, 1980)

Hinkson, J. 'The Emergence of Education as Therapeutic Management of an Unconstrained Self', PhD thesis (School of Education, La Trobe University, Melbourne, 1977)

Hirst, P.H. 'Liberal Education and the Nature of Knowledge' in Archambault (1965)

Hogben, L. *Science in Authority* (Allen and Unwin, London, 1963)

Holmes, B. *Problems in Education: A Comparative Approach* (Routledge and Kegan Paul, London, 1965)

Horkheimer, M. and Adorno, T.W. *Dialectic of Enlightenment* (Allen Lane, London, 1973)

Hubeman, L. *Man's Worldly Goods* (Victor Gollancz, London, 1937)

Hunt, J. McV. *Intelligence and Experience* (The Ronald Press, New York, 1961)

Hunter, R. 'The Shock of the Old — the Militant Church and Education' in Liesch, J.R. (ed.), Comparative Perspectives on Futures in Education, Proceedings of the 10th Annual Conference of the Australian Comparative and International Education Society, Sydney, November (1982), pp. 155-72

Husen, T. 'An International Research Venture in Retrospect: The IEA Surveys', *Comparative Education Review*, 23, 3 October (1979) pp. 371-85

Inkeles, A. 'National Differences in Scholastic Performance', *Comparative Education Review*, 23, 3 October (1979), pp. 386-407

Institut Für Marxistische Studien und Forschungen (IMSF) *Ban on Professional Employment (Berufsverbote) in the FGR: A Juridical and Political Documentation* (Informationsbericht 22, Frankfurt am Main, 1975)

Irvine, J., Miles, I. and Evans, J. (eds) *Demystifying Social Statistics* (Pluto Press, London, 1979)

Isaacs, N., Lawrence, E. and Theakston, T.R. *Some Aspects of Piaget's Work* (National Froebel Institute, London, 1959)

Jackson, P.W. *Life in the Classroom* (Holt, Rinehart and Winston, New York, 1968)

Jaeggi, U. *Kapital und Arbeit in der Bundes-republic: Elemente einer gesampt-gesellschaftlichen Analyse* (Fischer Verlag, Frankfurt am Main, 1973)

Janeway, E. *Man's World, Woman's Place: A Study in Social Mythology* (Penguin Books, Harmondsworth, 1977)

Jacques, T.D. and Pavia, G.K. *Sport in Australia: Selected Readings in Physical Activity* (McGraw-Hill, Sydney, 1976)

Jensen, A.R. 'How Much Can We Boost IQ and Scholastic Achievement?' *Harvard Educational Review*, 39 (1969), pp. 1-123

Jones, G.S. 'Engels and the Genesis of Marxism', *New Left Review*, 106, November, December (1977)

Jones, H.G. *Planning and Productivity in Sweden* (Croom Helm, London, 1976)

Jungk, R. *Der Jahrtausendmensch* (Rowohlt, Reinbek bei Harnburg, 1976)

Junor, A. 'Deconstructing Discipline', *Radical Education Dossier*, 17 (1982), pp. 4-6

Kamenka, F. *The Ethical Foundations of Marxism* (Rouledge and Kegan Paul, London, 1972)

Kamin, L.J. *The Science and Politics of IQ* (Penguin Books, Harmondsworth, 1977)

Kaplan, C. and Schrecker, E. *Regulating the Intellectuals: Perspectives on Academic Freedom in the 1980s* (Praeger, New York, 1983)

King, E.J. *World Perspectives in Education* (Methuen, London, 1965)

Kitson, F. *Low Intensity Operations* (Faber and Faber, London, 1971)

Knorr, K.D., Krohn, R. and Whitley, R. *The Social Process of Scientific Investigation* (D. Reidel Publishing Company, Dordrecht, 1981)

Kodansha, *Encyclopedia of Japan* (Kodansha International, Tokyo, 1983)

Koestler, A. *The Act of Creation* (Hutchinson, London, 1964)

Kohlberg, L. 'Stages of Moral Development as a Basis for Moral Education', in Beck, Crittenden and Sullivan (1971a), pp. 23-92

_____ 'The Cognitive-developmental Approach to Moral Education', in Clarizio, Craig and Mehrens (1971b), pp. 53-71

Kolakowski, L. *Positivist Philosophy, from Hume to the Vienna Circle* (Penguin Books, Harmondsworth, 1972)

_____ Main Currents of Marxism, 3 vols, (Clarendon Press, Oxford, 1978)

Kolkowicz, R. *The Soviet Military and the Communist Party* (The University Press, Princeton, NJ, 1967)

Konrad, G. and Szelenyi, I. *The Intellectuals on the Road to Class Power*, trans. A. Arato and R.E. Allen (Harvester Press, Brighton, 1979)

Krimerman, L.I. The Nature and Scope of Social Science (Appleton-Century-Crofts, New York, 1969)

Krovoza, A., Oestmann, A.R. and Ottometer, K. (eds) *Zum Beispiel Peter Brueckner: Treue zum Staat und kritische Wissenschaft* (Europaeische Verlagsanstalt, Frankfurt am Main, 1981)

Krupskaya, N. *Pedagogicheskie Sochineniya v Desyati Tomakh*, 11 vols (Akadem Pedagogischeskich Nauk, Moskva, 1959)

Lahore, J. *Photocopying, a Guide to the 1980 Amendments to the Copyright Act* (Butterworths, Sydney, 1980)

Langford, P. 'Attitudes of the Left to Freud', unpublished, 1980

Langrish, J., Gibbons, M., Evans, W.G. and Jevons, F.R. *Wealth from Knowledge: Studies of Innovation in Industry* (Macmillan, London, 1972)

Lawton, D. *Class, Culture and the Curriculum* (Routledge and Kegan Paul, London, 1975)

_____ 'Towards a Worthwhile Curriculum', in Richards *Power and the Curriculum* (1978)

_____ *The Politics of the School Curriculum* (Rouledge and Kegan Paul, London, 1980)

Leacock, E.B. *Myths of Male Dominance* (Monthly Review Press, New York, 1981)

Lees, J.D. 'Open Government in the USA: Some Recent Statutory Developments', *Public Adminstration*, 57 (1979), pp. 333-48

Lenin, V.I. *The Essential Lenin in Two Volumes* (Lawrence and Wishart, London, 1947)

_____ *Collected Works*, Vol. 38 (Foreign Languages Publishing House, Moscow, 1963)

Lever, C. 'The Segmentation and Articulation of the Working Class: An Exploration of the Impact of Postwar Australian Immigration', PhD thesis (School of Social Studies, Flinders University, Adelaide, 1984)

Levine, A. *When Dreams and Heroes Died: A Portrait of Today's College Student* (Jossey-Bass, San Francisco, 1980)

Levinson, C. *Vodka-Cola* (Gordon and Cremonesi, London, 1978)

Levitas, M. *Marxist Perspectives in the Sociology of Education* (Routledge and Kegan Paul, London, 1974)

Levy, G.E. *Ghetto School: Class Warfare in an Elementary School* (Pegasus, New York, 1970)

Lippert, E., Schneider, P. and Zoll, R. 'The Influence of Military Service on Political and Social Attitudes: A Study of Socialisation in the German Bundeswehr', *International Journal of Political Education*, 1, 3 July (1978), pp. 225-40

Livingstone, J., Moore, J. and Oldfather, F. (eds) *The Japan Reader: Postwar Japan, 1945 to the Present* (Pantheon Books, New York, 1973)

Lloyd, B. and Archer, J. *Exploring Sex Differences* (Academic Press, London, 1976)

Lockhart, A.S. and Slusher, H.S. Contemporary Readings in Physical Education, 3rd edn (Wm. C. Brown, Dubuque, Iowa, 1975)

Loevinger, J. with the assistance of Blasi, A. *Ego Development* (Jossey-Bass, San Francisco, 1982)

Lofland, J. *Doomsday Cult: A Study of Conversion, Proselytization and Maintenance of Faith* (Prentice-Hall, Englewood Cliffs, NJ, 1966)

290   *Select Bibliography*

Loy, J.W. Jr and Kenyon, G.S. *Sport, Culture and Society: A Reader on the Sociology of Sport* (Macmillan, New York, 1969)

Maccoby, E.E. *The Development of Sex Differences* (Tavistock Publications, London, 1967)

Machlup, F. *The Production and Distribution of Knowledge in the United States* (University Press, Princeton, 1962)

_____ *Knowledge: Its Creation, Distribution, and Economic Significance: Vol. 1, Knowledge and Knowledge Production* (University Press, Princeton, 1980)

Mallet, S. *Essays on the New Working Class*, ed. and trans. Dick Howard and Dean Savage (Telos Press, St Louis, 1975)

Mallinson, V. *The Western European Idea in Education* (Pergamon Press, Oxford, 1980)

Mandel, E. *Marxist Economic Theory* (Merlin Press, London, 1968)

_____ *The Foundation of the Economic Thought of Karl Marx* (Monthly Review Press, New York, 1971)

_____ *Late Capitalism* (New Left Books, London, 1975)

Mangan, J.A. *Athleticism in the Victorian and Edwardian Public Schools* (The University Press, Cambridge, 1981)

Mao Zedong *Selected Works*, 5 vols (Foreign Languages Press, Beijing, 1965-77)

_____ *Four Essays in Philosophy* (Foreign Languages Press, Beijing, 1966)

Marceau, J. *Class and Status in France: Economic Change and Social Immobility 1945-1975* (Clarendon Press, Oxford, 1977)

Marcuse, H. *One-dimensional Man: The Ideology of Industrial Society* (Sphere Books, London, 1968)

Marx, K. *Grundrisse: Foundations of the Critique of Political Economy* (rough draft) [GRUND] (Penguin Books in association with New Left Review, Harmondsworth, 1973 [w. 1857-8])

_____ *Surveys from Exile* (SFE) (Penguin Books, Harmondsworth, 1973)

_____ *The First International and After* [FI] (Penguin Books in association with New Left Review, Harmondsworth, 1974)

_____ *Theories of Surplus Value*, 3 vols [TSV] (Foreign Languages Publishing House, Moscow [w. 1861-3])

_____ *Early Writings* [EW] (Penguin Books in association with New Left Review, Harmondsworth, 1975)

_____ *The General Council of the First International, 1864-66* [GCFI] (Foreign Languages Publishing House, Moscow, n.d.)

_____*Selected Works*, 2 vols (Lawrence and Wishart, London, 1943)

_____ and Engels, F. *Selected Correspondence, 1846-95* [COR] (Lawrence and Wishart, London, 1943)

_____ *On Britain* (Lawrence and Wishart, London, 1953)

_____ *Capital*, 3 vols [CAP] (Penguin Books in association with New Left Review, Harmondsworth, 1976, 1978, 1981 [w. 1867, 1885, 1894])

_____ *A Contribution to the Critique of Political Economy* [CCPE] (Abinash Chandra Saha, Calcutta, n.d. [w. 1859])

_____ *Collected Works* [CW] (Lawrence and Wishart, London, 1975)

Massey, D. and Catalano, A. *Capital and Land: Landownership by Capital in Great Britain* (Edward Arnold, London, 1978)

Mattelart, A. *Multinational Corporations and the Control of Culture: The Ideological Apparatuses of Imperialism* (Harvester Press, Brighton, 1979)

Matthews, M.R. *The Marxist Theory of Schooling: A Study of Epistemology and Education* (Harvester Press, Brighton, 1980)

Max-Planck Institut für Bildungsforschung, Arbeitsgruppe *Das Bildungswesen in der Bundesrepublik Deutschland* (Rowohlt, Hamburg, 1984)

McHale, J. *World Facts and Trends* (Collier Books, New York, 1972)

McLellan, D. *Marx Before Marxism* (Macmillan, London, 1970)
_____ *Karl Marx: His Life and Thoughts* (Macmillan, London, 1973)
McNeill, D.H. *The Pursuit of Power: Technology, Armed Force, and Society Since AD 1000* (The University Press, Chicago, 1982)
Melton, J.G. *The Encyclopedia of American Religions*, 2 vols (McGrath, Wilmington, 1978)
Mepham, J. and Ruben D-H *Issues in Marxist Philosophy*, 4 vols (Harvester Press, Brighton, 1979)
Merquior, J.G. *The Veil and the Mask: Essays on Culture and Ideology* (Routledge and Kegan Paul, London, 1979)
Meszaros, I. *Marx's Theory of Alienation* (Merlin Press, London, 1970)
_____ (ed.) *Aspects of History and Class Consciousness* (Routledge and Kegan Paul, London, 1971)
Michelsen, G. *Der Fischer Oeko Almanach, 84/85* (Fischer, Frankfurt am Main, 1984)
Miliband, R. *The State in Capitalist Society* (Quartet Books [The Open University] London, 1973)
Millet, K. *Sexual Politics* (Sphere Books, London, 1972)
Mills, C.W. *The Power Elite* (The University Press, Oxford, 1956)
Mitchell, G.D. *A Dictionary of Sociology* (Routledge and Kegan Paul, London, 1973)
Moberg, D.O. *The Church as a Social Institution* (Prentice-Hall, Englewood Cliffs, NJ, 1964)
Mollenhauer, K. *Theorien zum Erziehungsprozess* (Juventa, München, 1972)
Moodie, G.C. and Eustace, R. *Power and Authority in British Universities* (Allen and Unwin, London, 1974)
Morioka, K. *Religion in a Changing Japanese Society* (University of Tokyo Press, Tokyo, 1975)
Morton, A.L. *A People's History of England* (Lawrence and Wishart, London, 1948)
Mosher, R.L. *Moral Education: A First Generation of Research and Development* (Praeger, New York, 1980)
Mount, F. *The Subversive Family: an Alternative History of Love and Marriage* (Cape, London)
National Swedish Board of Education *The Teaching of Religious Knowledge in Swedish Schools*, by John Ronnas, 1 (8), 5, 6 (1970)
_____ *Curriculum for the Comprehensive School*, lgr 69, 07-01 (1978)
_____ *The Orientational Subjects*, lgr 69 (n. 2)
_____ *Civics*, lgr 69, 1 (4) (n.d.)
_____ *Religious Knowledge*, lgr 69, 1 (6) (n.d.)
Needham, J. *Time: The Refreshing River* (essays and addresses, 1932-42) (Allen and Unwin, London, 1944)
_____ *Science and Civilisation in China*, Vol. 2 (The University Press, Cambridge, 1956)
Nelkin, D. *The Creation Controversy: Science or Scripture in the Schools* (W.W. Norton, New York, 1982)
Newson, J. and E. *Patterns of Infant Care: In an Urban Community* (Penguin Books, Harmondsworth, 1965)
Nidditch, P.H. *Elementary Logic of Science and Mathematics* (University Tutorial Press, London, 1960)
Nielsen, W.A. *The Big Foundations* (Columbia University Press, New York, 1972)
Nunn, Sir P. *Education: Its Data and First Principles* (Edward Arnold, London, 1949)
O'Donnell, P. 'Lucien Seve, Althusser and the Contradictions of the PCF',

Critique, 15 (1981), pp. 7-29

Ochiltree, G. and Amato, P.R. 'Family Conflict and Child Competence' (a preliminary report), presented to the Australian Family Research Conference, Canberra, 23-25 November (1983)

―――― 'The Child's Use of Family Resources', manuscript (n.d.)

Ollman, B. and Vernoff, E. *The Left Academy: Marxist Scholarship on American Campuses* (McGraw-Hill Book Company, New York, 1982)

Oppenheim, A.N. *The Measurement of Children's Civic Attitudes in Different Nations* (Almqvist and Wiksell International, Stockholm, 1974)

Owen, R. and Sutcliffe, B. *Studies in the Theory of Imperialism* (Longman, London, 1972)

Parinetto, R.F. 'The Legend of Marx's Atheism', *Telos,* winter (1983-4), pp. 7-19

Passin, H. *Society and Education in Japan* (Teachers College Press, New York, 1965)

Pearson, N. *The State and the Visual Arts* (The Open University, Milton Keynes, 1982)

Pfeffer, R.M. *Working for Capitalism* (Columbia University Press, New York, 1979)

Phenix, P.H. *Realms of Meaning: A Philosophy of the Curriculum for General Education* (McGraw-Hill, New York, 1964)

Phillips, P. *Marx and Engels on Law and Laws* (Martin Robertson, Oxford, 1980)

Piaget, J. *The Moral Judgement of the Child* (The Free Press, New York, 1965)

Pincoffs, E.L. *The Concept of Academic Freedom* (University of Texas Press, Austin, 1975)

Pines, M. 'A Headstart in the Nursery (re. J. McVicker Hunt's work)', *Psychology Today,* September (1979), pp. 56-68

Pinkevitch, A.P. *The New Education in the Soviet Union,* trans. N. Perlmutter, G.S. Counts (ed.) (John Day, New York, 1929)

Pittock, B. *Nuclear Winter: Its Implications for Australia and New Zealand* (Victorian Association of Peace Studies dossier, Melbourne, 1983)

Ploman, E.W. and Hamilton, L.C. *Copyright: Intellectual Property in the Information Age* (Routledge and Kegan Paul, London, 1980)

Polemic *The Polemic on General Line of the International Communist Movement* (Foreign Languages Press, Beijing, 1965)

Postman, N. and Weingarten, C. *Teaching as a Subversive Activity* (Penguin Books, Harmondsworth, 1971)

Poulantzas, N. 'The Problem of the Capitalist State' (1972) in Blackburn, R. (1978)

―――― *Political Power and Social Class* (New Left Books and Sheed and Ward, London, 1973)

―――― *Classes in Contemporary Capitalism* (New Left Books, London, 1975)

Price, R.F. 'The Part-work Principle in Chinese Education,' *Current Scene,* Hong Kong, xi, no. 9, pp. 1-11 Sept. (1973)

―――― 'Labour and Education in Russia and China', *Comparative Education,* 10, no. 1 pp. 13-23 March (1974)

―――― *Marx and Education in Russia and China* (Croom Helm, London, 1977)

―――― *Education in Modern China,* formerly: *Education in Communist China* 1970 (Routledge and Kegan Paul, London, 1978)

Radice, H. *International Firms and Modern Imperialism* (Penguin Books, Harmondsworth, 1975)

Richards, C. (ed.) *Power and the Curriculum, Issues in Curriculum Studies* (Nafferton Books, Driffield, 1978)

Richards, J.R. *The Sceptical Feminist* (Penguin Books, Harmondsworth, 1980)

Ridley, C.P., Godwin, P.H.B. and Doolin, D.J. *The Making of a Model Citizen in Communist China* (The Hoover Institution Press, Stanford, 1971)

Rieff, P. *On Intellectuals: Theoretical Studies, Case Studies* (Doubleday, New York, 1969)

Rieselbach, L.N. and Blach, G.I. *Psychology and Politics: An Introductory Reader* (Holt, Rinehart and Winston, New York, 1969)

Ripple, R.E. (ed.) *Readings in Learning and Human Abilities*, 2nd edn (Harper and Row, New York, 1971)

Robertson, R. (ed.) *Sociology of Religion*, Penguin Modern Sociology Readings (Penguin Books, Harmondsworth, 1969)

Rombach, H. *Woerterbuch der Paedagogik*, 3 vols (Herder, Freiburg, 1977)

Rose, S. *The Conscious Brain*, revised edn (Penguin Books, Harmondsworth, 1976)

Rousseau, J.J. *Emile*, trans. B. Foxley (Dent, London, 1969)

Rowe, D. and Lawrence, G. 'The Olympics as Popular Culture', *Arena*, 69 (1984), pp. 26-30

Rubel, M. *Marx critique du marxisme* (Payot, Paris, 1974)

_____ and Manale, M. *Marx Without Myth, a Chronological Study of his Life and Works* (Basil Blackwell, Oxford, 1975)

Ruben, D-H. *Marxism and Materialism: A Study in Marxist Theory of Knowledge* (Harvester Press, Sussex, 1979)

Russell, B. *History of Western Philosophy* (Allen and Unwin, London, 1947)

Sampson, A. *The Arms Bazaar* (Hodder and Stoughton, London, 1977)

_____ *The Changing Anatomy of Britain* (Hodder and Stoughton, London, 1982)

Sarup, M. *Marxism and Education* (Routledge and Kegan Paul, London, 1978)

_____ *Education, State and Crisis: A Marxist Perspective* (Routledge and Kegan Paul, London, 1982)

Sawer, G. *The Australian and the Law* (Penguin Books, Harmondsworth, 1968)

Sayer, D. 'Marx's Method: Ideology, Science and Critique' in *Capital* (Harvester Press, Brighton, 1979)

Schram, S. *Mao Tse-tung Unrehearsed: Talks and Letters, 1956-71* (Penguin Books, Harmondsworth, 1974)

Schutz, A. and Luckmann, T. *The Structures of the Life-world* (Northwestern University Press, Evanston, 1973)

Science *Science and the Nation* (Penguin Books, Harmondsworth, 1947)

Scott, A. and Scott, R. 'Censorship and Political Education: The Queensland Experience', *International Journal of Political Education*, 3 (1980), pp. 49-66

Seve, L. *Man In Marxist Theory and the Psychology of Personality* (Harvester Press, Brighton, 1978)

Sharp, R. *Knowledge, Ideology and the Politics of Schooling: Towards a Marxist Analysis of Education* (Routledge and Kegan Paul, London, 1980)

Sharp, R. 'Reclaiming the Agenda: Socialist Directions', *Radical Education Dossier*, 22, autumn (1984), pp. 25-9

Shoup, L.H. and Minter, W. *Imperial Brain Trust: The Council on Foreign Relations and United States Foreign Policy* (Monthly Review Press, New York, 1977)

Shul'gin, V.N. *Marx and Engels in Their Pedagogical Statements*, in Russian (Workers' Enlightenment, Moscow, 1925)

Sieffert, R. *Les Religions du Japon* (Presses Universitaires de France, Paris, 1968)

Siegel, L.S. and Brainerd, C.J. *Alternatives to Piaget: Critical Essays on the Theory* (Vintage Books, New York, 1978)

Sigel, R.S. *Learning About Politics: A Reader in Political Socialization* (Random House, New York, 1970)

Silberman, C.E. *Crisis in the Classroom: The Remaking of American Education*

(Vintage Books, New York, 1971)

Simon, B. *Intelligence Testing and the Comprehensive School* (Lawrence and Wishart, London, 1953, also in Simon, 1971)

_____ *Education and the Labour Movement, 1870-1920* (Lawrence and Wishart, London, 1965)

_____ *Intelligence, Psychology and Education: A Marxist Critique* (Lawrence and Wishart, London, 1971)

_____ *The Politics of Educational Reform, 1920-40* (Lawrence and Wishart, London, 1974a)

_____ *The Two Nations and the Educational Structure, 1780-1870* (Lawrence and Wishart, London, 1974b)

Slater, P. *Origin and Significance of the Frankfurt School: A Marxist Perspective* (Routledge and Kegan Paul, London, 1977)

Smiley, G.W., Chamberlain, E.R. and Dagleish, L.I. 'Some Social, Economic and Relationship Effects for Families and Young Children', paper presented at the Australian Family Research Conference, Canberra, 23-25 November (1983)

Smith, L. and Jones, D. *Deprivation, Participation and Community Action* (Routledge and Kegan Paul, London, 1981)

Smith, M.B. *Social Psychology and Human Values* (Aldine, Chicago, 1969)

Smith, W.I. and Moore, J.W. *Programmed Learning: Theory and Research* (Van Nostrand, Princeton, 1962)

Soelle, D. 'The Christian-Marxist Dialogue of the 1960s', *Monthly Review*, July-August (1984), pp. 20-6

Sohn-Rethel, A. *Intellectual and Manual Labour: A Critique of Epistemology* (Macmillan, London, 1978a)

_____ *Warenform and Denkform: mit zwei Anhangen* (Suhrkamp, Frankfurt am Main, 1978b)

Spender, D. *Invisible Women: The Schooling Scandal* (Writers and Readers Publishing Co-operative, London, 1982)

Stace, W.T. *The Philosophy of Hegel* (Dover Publications, New York, 1955)

Stavrianos, L.S. *Global Rift: The Third World Comes of Age* (William Morrow, New York, 1981)

Ste Croix, G.E.M. *The Class Struggle in the Ancient Greek World: From the Archaic Age to the Arab Conquests* (Duckworth, London, 1981)

_____ 'Class in Marx's Conception of History, Ancient and Modern', *New Left Review*, 146 (1984), pp. 94-111

Stedman Jones, G. 'Engels and the Genesis of Marxism', *New Left Review*, Nov.-Dec., 106 (1977), pp. 79-104

Steed, H.W. *The Press* (Penguin Books, Harmondsworth, 1938)

Stenhouse, L. *An Introduction to Curriculum Research and Development* (Heinemann, London, 1975)

Strom, R.D. *Teachers and the Learning Process* (Prentice Hall, Engelwood Cliffs, New Jersey, 1971)

Students and Staff of Hornsey College of Art *The Hornsey Affair* (Penguin Books, Harmondsworth, 1967)

Sweezy, P.M. *The Theory of Capitalist Development: Principles of Marxian Political Economy* (Monthly Review Press, New York, 1956)

Taylor, C. *The Explanation of Behaviour* (Routledge and Kegan Paul, London, 1980)

Therborn, G. *Science, Class and Society* (New Left Books, London, 1976)

_____ *What does the Ruling Class Do When It Rules?* (New Left Books, London, 1978)

Thomas, P. *Karl Marx and the Anarchists* (Routledge and Kegan Paul, London, 1980)

Thompson, E.P. *The Making of the English Working Class* (Penguin Books, Harmondsworth, 1968)
_____ (ed.) *Warwick University Ltd: Industry, Management and the Universities* (Penguin Books, Harmondsworth, 1970)
_____ *The Poverty of Theory and Other Essays* (Merlin Press, London, 1978)
_____ *Writing by Candlelight* (Merlin Press, London, 1980a)
_____ *Protest and Survive* (Penguin Books, Harmondsworth, 1980b)
Thomson, G. *Studies in Ancient Greek Society: Vol. 2, The First Philosophers* (Lawrence and Wishart, London, 1955)
Timpanaro, S. *On Materalism* (New Left Books, London, 1975)
_____ 'Freudian Slips and Slips of the Freudians', *New Left Review*, 95, Jan.-Feb. (1976), pp. 45-54
_____ *The Freudian Slip* (New Left Books, London, 1976)
Topham, T. *The Organised Worker*, Trade Union Industrial Studies (Arrow Books, London, 1975)
Torney, J.V. 'The International Attitudes and Knowledge of Adolescents in Nine Countries: The IEA Civic Education Survey', *International Journal of Political Education*, 1, 1, September (1977), pp. 3-20
Torney, J.V., Oppenheim, A.N. and Farwen, R.F. *Civic Education in Ten Countries, an Empirical Study* (Almqvist and Wiksell, International, Stockholm, 1975)
Udom, V.E. *Economic Socialisation from an Educational Perspective* (The Institute of Constructive Capitalism, The University of Texas, Austin, 1982)
Ullrich, O. *Technik und Herrschaft* (Suhrkamp, Frankfurt am Main, 1979)
US Department of Commerce *Statistical Abstract of the United States, 1981* (Department of Commerce, Washington, 1982)
Van Ijzendoorn 'Moral and Political Education: A Case for Integration', *International Journal of Political Education*, 6 (1983), pp. 25-41
Varga, E. and Mendelsohn, L. *New Data for V.I. Lenin's Imperialism* (International Publishers, New York, 1940)
Wainwright, H. and Elliott, D. *The Lucas Plan: A New Trade Unionism in the Making* (Allison and Busby, London, 1982)
Walker, P. (ed.) *Between Labour and Capital* (South End Press, Boston, 1979)
Weatherford, R. *Philosophical Foundations of Probability Theory* (Routledge and Kegan Paul, London, 1982)
Weir, D. *Men and Work in Modern Britain* (Fontana, London, 1973)
West, C. 'Religion and the Left: An Introduction', *Monthly Review*, July-August (1984), pp. 9-19
Westergaard, J. and Resler, H. *Class in a Capitalist Society: A Study of Contemporary Britain* (Penguin Books, Harmondsworth, 1976)
Whannel, G. *Blowing the Whistle* (Pluto Press, London, 1983)
Whitaker, B. *The Foundations: An Anatomy of Philanthropic Societies* (Penguin Books, Harmondsworth, 1979)
Whitley, R. (ed.) *Social Processes of Scientific Development* (Routledge and Kegan Paul, London, 1974)
Whitty, G. and Young, M. (eds) *Explorations in the Politics of School Knowledge* (Nafferton Books, Driffield, 1976)
Whyte, W.H. *The Organisation Man* (Penguin Books, Harmondsworth, 1960)
Wilkinson, P. 'English Youth Movements, 1908-30', *Journal of Contemporary History*, 4, 2, April (1969), pp. 3-23
Williams, R. *Communications* (Barnes and Noble, New York, 1967)
_____ *Marxism and Literature* (The University Press, Oxford, 1977)
Willis, P.E. *Learning to Labour: How Working Class Kids Get Working Class Jobs* (Saxon House, Farnborough, 1977)

Wilson, M. *The Effective Management of Volunteer Programs* (Volunteer
    Management Associates, Boulder, Colorado, 1976)
Wintrop, N. (ed.) *Liberal Democratic Theory and Its Critics: An Introduction to
    Modern Political Theory* (Politics Discipline, Flinders University, Adelaide,
    1982)
Wolff, Janet *The Social Production of Art* (Macmillan, London, 1981)
Wood, E.M. 'The Separation of the Economic and the Political in Capitalism',
    New Left Review, 127, June (1981), pp. 66-95
Woodward, K. (ed.) *The Myths of Information: Technology and Postindustrial
    Culture* (Routledge and Kegan Paul, London, 1980)
Wright, E.O. *Class, Crisis and the State* (New Left Books, London, 1978)
Young, M.F.D. *Knowledge and Control: New Directions for the Sociology of
    Education* (Collier/Macmillan, London, 1971)
Young, N. 'Problems and Possibilities in the Study of Peace', Peace Studies Papers,
    no. 3, (Bradford University School of Peace, 1981)
Zimbalist, A. *Case Studies in the Labor Process* (Monthly Review Press, New
    York, 1979)

INDEX

abduction 19, 27
Abramson, L.Y. 228
abstraction 46-51, 279-80
Adam, G. 32
administration, school 193-200
Adorno, T.W. 56, 83-4, 176
agriculture 32, 34, 238
Albrow, M.C. 36-7
alienation 24
Alstyne, W. van 201
Althusser, L. 26, 125, 158
Amato, P.R. 228, 251
Amin, S. 26
Anderson, P. 26, 97, 125
Anderson, R.S. 174-6
Annenkov, P.V. 8, 17
Apple, M.W. 14, 94-6, 104, 183-4,
    189, 193-5
Archambault, R.D. 95
Archer, J. 235-6
Archer, M.S. 196
aristocracy 139-41
armed forces 159-64, 183
    and industry 32-3
Arnold, M. 42
Ashby, E. 67
atheism 28
attainment testing 122-5
Australia
    censorship 88, 90
    immigrants 141-2
    school curriculum 98-9
    schooling 211
    student organisations 199
    trade unions 259
Ausubel, D.P. 111-12
Avineri, S. 20, 27

Bacon, R. 144, 198
Bahro, R. 54
Bailey, R. 81, 147-8, 150
Bain, G.S. 144
Baker, W.J. 271, 275-6, 278
Balibar, E. 26
Balzer, R. 277
Baran, P.A. 11
Bardwick, J.M. 235

Barrett, M. 223, 225, 229, 251
Barrett Brown, M. 37
Baudelot, C. 103, 145, 192
Becker, E. 176
Beer, W. 148-9
Bell, D. 57
Bemis, E. 202
Benn, T. 153, 159
Bergmann, E. 239
Bernal, J.D. 50-1, 57, 61-4, 74, 217
Bernstein, B. 93-4, 190-1
Bessant, B. 199
Bhaskar, R. 27
Birks, R. 268
Blach, G.I. 111
Black Papers on education 99, 213,
    215, 220
Blackburn, R. 56, 198
Blasi, A. 114-15
Blaug, M. 29
Bloch, E. 53
Bloch, J. 9, 25
Bluestone, B. 32
Bock, H. 216-17
Boehm, W. 260, 269
Bourdieu, P. 78, 128, 191-2, 212
Bowles, S. 186-90, 193-4
Boyle Committee Report 147
Boyson, R. 99
Brace, D. 272
Brainerd, C.G. 111
Brake, M. 81, 147-8, 150
Branson, J. 144
Braverman, H. 35, 75-6, 194, 277
Brecht, B. 84
Brockway, F. 153
Broughton, J. 115
Brown, G. 113-14
Bruckner, P. 91, 203
Bunge, M. 14-15, 26
Bunn, R.F. 184
Bunyan, T. 87-8, 159
bureaucracy 36-7, 63-4, 86
    civil service 156-7
    schools 195-6
Burkhead, J. 123
Burns, A. 251

297